HANDBOOK OF SYSTEM SAFETY AND SECURITY

HANDBOOK OF SYSTEM SAFETY AND SECURITY

Cyber Risk and Risk Management, Cyber Security, Threat Analysis, Functional Safety, Software Systems, and Cyber Physical Systems

Edited by

EDWARD GRIFFOR

National Institute of Standards and Technology (NIST), Gaithersburg, MD, United States

ELSEVIER

AMSTERDAM • BOSTON • HEIDELBERG • LONDON • NEW YORK • OXFORD
PARIS • SAN DIEGO • SAN FRANCISCO • SINGAPORE • SYDNEY • TOKYO
Syngress is an imprint of Elsevier

SYNGRESS.

Syngress is an imprint of Elsevier
50 Hampshire Street, 5th Floor, Cambridge, MA 02139, United States

Notices
Knowledge and best practice in this field are constantly changing. As new research and experience broaden our
understanding, changes in research methods, professional practices, or medical treatment may become necessary.

Practitioners and researchers must always rely on their own experience and knowledge in evaluating and using any
information, methods, compounds, or experiments described herein. In using such information or methods they
should be mindful of their own safety and the safety of others, including parties for whom they have a professional
responsibility.

To the fullest extent of the law, neither the Publisher nor the authors, contributors, or editors, assume any liability
for any injury and/or damage to persons or property as a matter of products liability, negligence or otherwise, or
from any use or operation of any methods, products, instructions, or ideas contained in the material herein.

British Library Cataloguing-in-Publication Data
A catalogue record for this book is available from the British Library

Library of Congress Cataloging-in-Publication Data
A catalog record for this book is available from the Library of Congress

ISBN: 978-0-12-803773-7

For Information on all Syngress publications
visit our website at https://www.elsevier.com

Working together
to grow libraries in
developing countries

www.elsevier.com • www.bookaid.org

Publisher: Todd Green
Acquisition Editor: Chris Katsaropoulos
Editorial Project Manager: Anna Valutkevich
Production Project Manager: Punithavathy Govindaradjane
Cover Designer: Mark Rogers

Typeset by MPS Limited, Chennai, India

*I grew up in this town, my poetry was born between the hill
and the river, it took its voice from the rain,
and like the timber, it steeped itself in the forests.*

—Pablo Neruda

*If you have built castles in the air, your work need not be lost;
that is where they should be. Now put the foundations under them.*

—Henry David Thoreau

Dedication

For my wife, Mariela, who is a constant reminder that precision and righteousness
go hand and hand.

CONTENTS

About the Editor xi
About the Contributors xiii
Introduction xxiii

Part I SYSTEMS

Chapter 1 Editor's Preface 3
E. Griffor

1.1 The Need for a Broadly Targeted Handbook of System Safety
     and Security 4

Chapter 2 Composition and Compositionality in CPS 15
J. Sztipanovits, T. Bapty, Z. Lattmann, and S. Neema

2.1 Introduction 15
2.2 Horizontal Integration Platforms in the OpenMETA Tool Suite 18
2.3 AVM Component Model 21
2.4 Use Case for Semantic Integration 24
2.5 Component Interfaces and Composition Semantics
     for Dynamics 27
2.6 Formalization of the Semantic Interface for Modeling
     Languages 32
2.7 Conclusion 34
Acknowledgments 36
References 36

Chapter 3 Software Engineering for Model-Based Development
               by Domain Experts 39
M. Bialy, V. Pantelic, J. Jaskolka, A. Schaap, L. Patcas, M. Lawford, and A. Wassyng

3.1 Introduction and Motivation 39
3.2 Development Process: How Do You Engineer Software? 41

3.3 Requirements: What Should Your Software Do? 45

3.4 Design: How Will Your Software Do What It Does? 49

3.5 Implementation: Generating Code 56

3.6 Verification and Validation: How Do You Know Your Software Is Good? 58

3.7 Conclusion and Future Work 61

References 62

Part II PERSPECTIVES ON SAFETY AND SECURITY

Chapter 4 Evolving Security 67

A. Sonalker and E. Griffor

4.1 Need for Security in a Cyber-Physical System 67

4.2 New Adversary Modeling 73

4.3 "Connected" System Security Modeling 78

4.4 Directional Threat Assessment 80

4.5 Big Picture CPS Systems—IoT 81

4.6 Conclusion 81

References 82

Chapter 5 The Business of Safety 83

J.D. Miller

5.1 Introduction 83

5.2 Life Cycle of Safety 84

5.3 Management of Functional Safety 91

5.4 Conclusion 95

References 96

Chapter 6 Cybersecurity for Commercial Advantage 97

J.M. Kaplan

6.1 Turbulence Along the Value Chain 99

6.2 Resilience for Commercial Advantage 104

Chapter 7 Reasoning About Safety and Security: The Logic of Assurance 113

A. Piovesan and E. Griffor

7.1 Introduction 113
7.2 A Strategy for Safety Case Construction 114
7.3 Decomposing the Functions of a Safety Critical System 117
7.4 Formal Reasoning for Safety Properties 122
7.5 Assurance Case Logic 125
7.6 Future Challenges 127
7.7 Conclusion 128
References 128
Annex: Electronic Throttle Control (ETC) 129

Chapter 8 From Risk Management to Risk Engineering: Challenges in Future ICT Systems 131

M. Huth, C. Vishik, and R. Masucci

8.1 Introduction 131
8.2 Key Aspects of Future ICT Systems 132
8.3 Evolution of Risk Approaches and Models 140
8.4 Risk Engineering 142
8.5 Case Study: Block-Chain Technology 155
8.6 Model-Based and Language-Based Risk Engineering 165
8.7 Summary and Conclusions 169
Acknowledgments 170
References 171

Part III APPLICATIONS OF SYSTEM SAFETY AND SECURITY

Chapter 9 A Design Methodology for Developing Resilient Cloud Services 177

C. Tunc, S. Hariri, and A. Battou

9.1 Motivations 177
9.2 Resilient Cloud Services Design Methodology 179
9.3 RCS Architecture 180

9.4 Experimental Results and Evaluation 188
9.5 Conclusions and Future Work 194
Acknowledgments 195
References 195

Chapter 10 Cloud and Mobile Cloud Architecture, Security and Safety 199

C. Mahmoudi

10.1 Introduction to Cloud Computing 199
10.2 Architecture: From the Cloud to the Mobile Cloud................. 204
10.3 Safety Concerns 212
10.4 Cloud Security 216
References 222

Chapter 11 A Brief Introduction to Smart Grid Safety and Security 225

S. Khoussi and A. Mattas

11.1 Introduction to the Smart Grid... 225
11.2 Safety Analysis for the Grid 235
11.3 A Security Analysis for the Smart Grid System....................... 240
References 249
Appendix A: An example of the Hazard Analysis and
Risk Assessment Model Worksheet 252

Chapter 12 The Algebra of Systems and System Interactions with an Application to Smart Grid 253

C. Mahmoudi, H. Bilil, and E. Griffor

12.1 Design Behind Success of a Smart Grid 253
12.2 Trends in Renewable Energy Integration 254
12.3 Power Systems Laws 257
12.4 A Cyber-Physical System Algebra 257
12.5 Illustration 264
12.6 Conclusion 265
References 265

Index...267

ABOUT THE EDITOR

Dr. Edward Griffor is the Associate Director for Cyber-Physical Systems at the National Institute of Standards and Technology (NIST) in the US Department of Commerce. Prior to joining NIST in July of 2015, he was a Walter P. Chrysler Technical Fellow, one of the highest technical positions in the automotive industry and one that exists in multiple industry sectors, including transportation, aerospace, science, defense, energy, and medical. He served as Chairman of the Chrysler Technology Council until 2015 and continues to serve as Chairman of The MIT Alliance, a professional association of scientists, engineers, and business experts trained at the Massachusetts Institute of Technology.

He completed doctoral studies in Mathematics at MIT and was awarded Habilitation by the Mathematics and Engineering Faculty of the University of Oslo. He was named National Science Foundation/NATO Postdoctoral Fellow in Science and Engineering in 1980. He was on the faculty of Uppsala University in Uppsala, Sweden, from 1980 to 1997 and returned to the United States to lead advanced research in Electrical Engineering in the automotive industry.

He has been on the faculties of the University of Oslo in Norway, Uppsala University in Sweden, the Catholic University of Santiago in Chile as well as those of Harvard, MIT, and Tufts University in the United States. He is regarded as one of the world experts in the use of mathematical methods for the design and assurance of technologies used in developing advanced, adaptive cyber-physical systems, including those used to ensure the safety and security of autonomous systems. In addition to his work at Chrysler, he has led research in bio-system modeling and simulation. He is an Adjunct Professor at the Wayne State University School of Medicine in Detroit, MI, at the Center for Molecular Medicine and Genetics.

His work in the automotive industry provided advanced algorithms for Voice Recognition and Autonomous and Connected Vehicles. He has published three books previously, including *Handbook of Computability* by Elsevier, *Theory of Domains*, by Cambridge University Press, and *Logic's Lost Genius: The Life of Gerhard Gentzen*, by American Mathematical Society. He has published extensively in professional journals and has given invited presentations for the American Mathematical Society, Association for Symbolic Logic, North American Software Certification Consortium, Society of Automotive Engineers, the Federal Reserve Bank, and US government agencies, including NIST, DARPA, DOE, DOT, and NASA.

ABOUT THE CONTRIBUTORS

Ted Bapty is a Research Associate Professor and Senior Researcher at the Institute for Software Integrated Systems. He is interested in and leads research projects in Model-Integrated Systems as applied to: Cyber Physical System Design, Large-Scale & Distributed Real-Time Embedded Systems, C4ISR systems, Digital Signal Processing and Instrumentation Systems, and tools for Rapid System Prototyping and System Integration. Current and recent projects include DARPA AVM/META Cyber-Physical Design Tools and Model-Based tools for the Future Airborne Capabilities Environment (FACE) Standard. He holds a BSEE from the University of Pennsylvania and a PhD from Vanderbilt University, and has served as a Captain in the US Air Force. He is cofounder of Metamorph Software, a spin-off company formed to transition model-based engineering tools.

Abdella Battou is the Division Chief of the Advanced Network Technologies Division, within The Information Technology Lab at NIST. He also leads the Cloud Computing Program. Before joining NIST in 2012, he served as the Executive Director of The Mid-Atlantic Crossroads (MAX) GigaPop founded by The University of Maryland, The George Washington University, The Georgetown University, and The Virginia Polytechnic Institute. From 2000 to 2009, he was Chief Technology Officer, and Vice President of Research and Development for Lambda Optical Systems, where he was responsible for overseeing the company's system architectures, hardware design, and software development teams. Additionally, he served as senior research scientist for the Naval Research Laboratory's high-speed networking group, Center for Computational Sciences from 1992 to 2000. He holds a PhD and MSEE in Electrical Engineering from the Catholic University of America.

Monika Bialy is a PhD student in the Department of Computing and Software at McMaster University, Hamilton, ON, Canada. She received her master's degree in software engineering ("http://MASc" MASc) from McMaster University in 2014, and Honours Bachelor of Computer Science ("http://BCoSc" BCoSc) in 2012 from Laurentian University, Sudbury,

ON, Canada. Monika currently holds an NSERC Alexander Graham Bell Canada Graduate Scholarship-Doctoral (CGS D). Her main research interests include model-based development, safety-critical systems, and software engineering design principles.

Hasnae Bilil was born in Rabat, Morocco, in 1986. She received the Dipl.-Ing in 2010 and the PhD degree in 2014 in electrical engineering from Mohammadia School of Engineers, Rabat, Morocco. She is now a teaching assistant at Mohammadia School of Engineers, University Mohammed V in Rabat, Morocco. Since August 2015, she has been conducting research on "Smart grid" and "Information-centric networking" as guest researcher at National Institute of Standards and Technology. Her current research interests include renewable energy sources, power system, smart grid, and power management into a power system integrating renewable energy source.

Chris Greer is Senior Executive for Cyber Physical Systems, Director of the Smart Grid and Cyber-Physical Systems Program Office, and National Coordinator for Smart Grid Interoperability at the National Institute of Standards and Technology. Prior to joining NIST, he served as Assistant Director for Information Technology R&D in the White House Office of Science and Technology Policy (OSTP) and Cybersecurity Liaison to the National Security Staff. His responsibilities there included networking and information technology, research and development, cybersecurity, and digital scientific data access. He has also served as Director of the National Coordination Office for the Federal Networking and Information Technology Research and Development (NITRD) Program. This program coordinates IT R&D investments across the Federal government, including the cyber-physical systems research portfolio.

Salim Hariri is the Director of the NSF Center for Cloud and Autonomic Computing and Professor in the Electrical and Computer Engineering Department at the University of Arizona, 2004 to present. He holds PhD from the Computer Engineering Dept. in University of Southern California, Los Angeles, CA, and MSc from Electrical Engineering in The Ohio State University, Columbus, OH. His research areas include, but not limited to, autonomic computing, self-protection of networks and computers, high-performance distributed computing, cyber security, proactive network management, cloud computing, resilient system architecture, Internet of Things (IoT).

Michael Huth is Professor of Computer Science, Director of Research, and Head of the Security Research Group in the Department of Computer Science at Imperial College London. He is a Diplom-Mathematiker (TU Darmstadt, Germany), obtained his PhD in 1991 (Tulane University of Louisiana, USA), and completed several postdoctoral studies in the United States, Germany, and the United Kingdom on programming language semantics and design, formal verification, and probabilistic modeling. His present research focuses on cybersecurity, especially modeling and reasoning about the interplay of trust, security, risk, and economics. Currently funded projects of his include work on confidence building in arms verification and work on blockchain technology for centrally governed systems such as IoT. He is a member of the ACM and active as research and product advisor in the London Cybersecurity startup scene.

Jason Jaskolka is a US Department of Homeland Security Cybersecurity Postdoctoral Scholar at Stanford University within the Center for International Security and Cooperation (CISAC). He received his PhD in Software Engineering in 2015 from McMaster University, Hamilton, ON, Canada. His research interests include cybersecurity assurance, distributed multiagent systems, and algebraic approaches to software engineering.

James M. Kaplan is a partner with McKinsey & Company in New York. He leads McKinsey's global Cybersecurity Practices and server banks, manufacturers, and health institutions on a range of technology issues. In addition to publishing on enterprise technology topics in the *McKinsey Quarterly, McKinsey on Business Technology*, the *Wall Street Journal*, and the *Financial Times*, he is also the lead author of *Beyond Cybersecurity: Protecting Your Digital Business*.

Siham Khoussi graduated from the Mohammadia School of Engineers (EMI) as an Electrical Engineer majored in Automation and Industrial Computer Science. She has worked with the Research Institute for Solar Energy and New Energies (IRESEN). She is currently working at the National Institute of Standards and Technology (NIST). Her research of interests include smart grid and renewable energies, smart cities, Named Data networks (NDN), and Network verification.

Zsolt Lattmann is currently a Staff Engineer II at the Institute for Software Integrated Systems at Vanderbilt University. He has an undergraduate degree in Electrical Engineering from Budapest University of Technology and Economics in Hungary (2009), MSc and PhD degrees from Vanderbilt University in Nashville, TN, in 2010 and 2016, respectively. He was one of the lead developers on the META project of the Adaptive Vehicle Make program sponsored by DARPA between 2010 and 2014. He had joined this project in 2010 and had been researching, developing, and implementing solutions in a metamodel-based environment using various domain models and applications. He integrated an open-source optimization tool (OpenMDAO) to the OpenMETA tool chain to provide a higher level of abstraction for end users. He is currently the Principal Investigator of the WebGME project since 2015. WebGME is an open-source Web-based collaborative metamodeling environment. Domain-specific languages and tools can be developed using WebGME to improve engineer's productivity and reduce design time and cost. His primary interest includes electrical, mechanical, multibody, fluid, and thermal domains in modeling, simulation, and parametric and discrete design space studies. He has experience with the OpenMETA tool chain and WebGME, developing new domain-specific modeling languages, and implementing model transformation tools.

Mark Lawford is a Professor in McMaster University's Department of Computing and Software and the Associate Director of the McMaster Centre for Software Certification. He is a licensed Professional Engineer in the province of Ontario and a Senior Member of the IEEE. He received his PhD in 1997 from the Systems Control Group in Electrical and Computer Engineering at the University of Toronto and then worked at Ontario Hydro as a real-time software verification consultant on the Darlington Nuclear Generating Station Shutdown Systems Redesign project, receiving the Ontario Hydro New Technology Award for Automation of Systematic Design Verification of Safety Critical Software in 1999. He joined McMaster University's Department of Computing and Software in 1998 where he helped to develop the Software Engineering programs and Mechatronics Engineering programs. He served as the Section Chair for Computer Systems on the Computer Science Evaluation Group for the 2010 NSERC Discovery Grant Competition. From 2006 to 2007, he was a Senior Researcher in the Software Quality Research Lab at the University of Limerick, and in August 2010, he was a visiting researcher at the Center for Devices and Radiological Health, Office of Science and Engineering Laboratories of the US FDA. In 2014 he was a corecipient of the Chrysler Innovation Award for his work with Dr. Ali Emadi on the Automotive Partnership Canada (APC) project entitled "Next Generation Affordable Electrified Powertrains with Superior Energy Efficiency and Performance-Leadership in Automotive Powertrain (LEAP)." His research interests include software certification, application of formal methods to safety critical real-time systems, supervisory control of discrete event systems, and cyber physical systems.

Charif Mahmoudi received the MSc and PhD degrees in computer engineering from the University of Paris-EST (France) in 2009 and 2014, respectively. Since then, he has been a PostDoc at the National Institute of Standards and Technology. He participated as consultant then software architect to several successful telecommunication projects within France Telecom and Bouygues Telecom. His areas of research are on distributed systems, cloud-computing, mobile computing, and IoT.

Riccardo Masucci is a public policy professional. He currently works as Senior Manager at Intel Corporation and leads the activities related to data protection and cybersecurity policies in Europe, Middle East, and Africa. He previously served as policy advisor to Members of the Justice and Home Affairs Committee in the European Parliament. He studied in Italy and Austria and he holds a Master's Degree in International Relations.

Andreas Mattas is a member of the teaching stuff of the School of Economic Sciences of the Aristotle University of Thessaloniki. He holds a Diploma in Applied Mathematics of Aristotle University of Thessaloniki, Greece, and a Doctor's degree (PhD) in Information Security from the Aristotle University of Thessaloniki, Greece. His research interests include information security, information modeling and optimization.

Joseph D. Miller has served as the chairman of the United States Technical Advisory Group since 2005 which developed ISO 26262: Road Vehicles — Functional Safety. This was recognized by the SAE Technical Standards Board Outstanding Contribution Award. He provided the Technical Keynote at the Safety Critical Systems sessions of the 2011 SAE World Congress, teaches an SAE Webinar introduction to ISO 26262, and serves on the boards for the VDA safety conference in Berlin and the CTI safety conference in the United States. He is the Chief Engineer of Systems Safety at TRW Automotive responsible for the systems safety process. Prior to this, he has managed systems engineering, manufacturing planning, and program control for electric steering. He has also engineered communication, avionics, infrared, and radar systems, as well as and thick and thin film components. He has 20 US patents, a Master of Engineering (EE), and a Master of Business Administration.

Sandeep Neema is a Research Associate Professor of Electrical Engineering and Computer Science at Vanderbilt University, and a Senior Research Scientist at Institute for Software Integrated Systems. His research interests include Cyber Physical Systems, Model-based Systems Design and Integration, Mobile Computing, and Distributed Computing. He received his PhD from Vanderbilt University in 2001.

Vera Pantelic received the BEng in Electrical Engineering from the University of Belgrade, Belgrade, Serbia, in 2001, and MASc and PhD in Software Engineering from McMaster University, Hamilton, ON, Canada, in 2005 and 2011, respectively. She is working as a Principal Research Engineer with the McMaster Centre for Software Certification, and McMaster Institute for Automotive Research and Technology (MacAUTO), McMaster University. Her research interests include development and certification of safety-critical software systems, model-based design, and supervisory control of discrete event systems.

Lucian Patcas is a Postdoctoral Fellow in the Department of Computing and Software at McMaster University in Hamilton, ON, Canada, and also a Principal Research Engineer with the McMaster Centre for Software Certification (McSCert) and McMaster Institute for Automotive Research and Technology (MacAUTO). His main research interests lie in the area of formal methods for real-time and safety-critical software. Currently, he is involved in several research projects related to the safety of automotive software, simulation of CAN networks, and model-based development of automotive software. He received his PhD in Software Engineering from McMaster University in 2014, master's in Computer Science from University College Dublin, Ireland in 2007, and bachelor's in Software Engineering from Politehnica University of Timisoara, Romania in 2004.

Andrea Piovesan was born in Italy and received his Master of Science degree in Engineering Physics from the University of

Turin, Torino, Italy. He has started his professional career at Fiat Research Centre where he gained over 10 years' experience in safety and reliability of embedded electronic systems, for automotive and aeronautic industries. Always looking for new challenges in applying new processes and innovative technologies, Andrea is an R&D specialist focused on the development of complex, safety-critical systems. After a long experience spent on by-wire systems and innovative powertrain systems, he was assigned to the ISO Working Group 16 as a technical expert for the development of the automotive functional safety standard ISO 26262. Andrea is Functional Safety Expert at Metatronix S.r.l, a company of the Metatron Group, worldwide leader in research and development of Engine Control Systems dedicated to CNG, LNG, and LPG alternative fuels.

Alexander Schaap received his bachelor's degree in Computer Science in the Netherlands in 2013. After returning to Canada, he continued his studies, doing a master's degree in software engineering at McMaster University. He is currently a part of Leadership in Automotive Powertrain (LEAP) project. His research interests include not only the application of generative programming techniques and functional programming languages but also proper software engineering as a whole.

Dr. Anuja Sonalker, PhD, is founder of STEER auto cyber, where she leads development of cyber security for advanced and future vehicles. Prior to STEER she was Vice President of Engineering & Operations, North America, for TowerSec where she led engineering, operations, and market facing R&D for the North American market. She established the global engineering services division and led several new business contracts. She is an expert in cyber security for embedded and distributed networked systems. She brings together a broad set of technical skills, demonstrated leadership, and experience from working with government, academia, and industry leaders. She has led various efforts in the past 16 + years in automotive cyber security, intrusion detection, Internet infrastructure security, wireless systems security, sensor networks, security protocol design, and cryptography. She is currently the Vice Chair of the SAE Committee on Automotive Security Guidelines and Risk Development under Electrical Systems. Prior to TowerSec, she led innovation in automotive cyber security at Battelle. At Battelle she was co-inventor of the world's first and only Sigma Six accurate Intrusion Detection System for cars. She holds two patents in the area of automotive cyber security. She also executed field trials on decoupled projects with several automakers paving the way for carmakers to accept IDS as a necessity and issue requirements. She maintained industry outreach and was invited speaker to several technical and nontechnical venues across the world on automotive cyber security issues. She served as an advisory member of the Battelle Senior Technical Council. Prior to Battelle she worked as a PI/Branch Chief at Sparta, and was a Research Staff Member of security at IBM TJ Watson, and Fujitsu Labs. She had worked in various security domains during the time from Internet Infrastructure to wireless handhelds, and enterprise security. During this time, she was also a contributing author to several standardization activities including IEEE 802.11S, ANSI T11 cyber security, and IETF Secure Inter Domain Routing (SIDR). She completed her doctoral studies from the University of Maryland, College Park, in Electrical Engineering with her thesis in Wireless Distributed Systems Security. Her thesis was on securing collaborative services in wireless sensor networks in highly adversarial scenarios. In her spare time, she mentors high school kids toward STEM disciplines and women through the Scholarships for Women Studying Information Systems (SWSIS).

Dr. Janos Sztipanovits is currently the E. Bronson Ingram Distinguished Professor of Engineering at Vanderbilt University and founding director of the Vanderbilt Institute for Software Integrated Systems. Between 1999 and 2002, he worked as program manager and acting deputy director of DARPA Information Technology Office. He leads the CPS Virtual Organization and he is co-chair of the CPS Reference Architecture and Definition public working group established by NIST in 2014. In 2014/15 he served as academic member of the Steering Committee of the Industrial Internet Consortium. He was elected Fellow of the IEEE in 2000 and external member of the Hungarian Academy of Sciences in 2010.

Dr. Cihan Tunc is a Research Assistant Professor in the Electrical and Computer Engineering Department at the University of Arizona and associated with the Autonomic Computing Lab (ACL) in the University of Arizona. He holds PhD from the Electrical and Computer Engineering Department of the University of Arizona. His research areas include autonomic power, performance, and security management for the cloud computing systems, IoT, and cyber security.

Claire Vishik is Trust & Security Director at Intel Corporation. Her work focuses on hardware security, Trusted Computing, privacy enhancing technologies, and some aspects of encryption and related policy issues. She is a member of the Permanent Stakeholders Group of the European Network and Information Security Agency (ENISA). She holds leadership positions in standards development and is on the Board of Directors of the Trusted Computing Group (TCG) and a Council Member of the Information Security Forum. She is an active member of research organizations and initiatives; she is a Board member for Trust in Digital Life (TDL) and member of the Cybersecurity Steering Group for the UK Royal Society. She serves on advisory and review boards of a number of research initiatives in security and privacy in Europe and the United States. Prior to joining Intel, she worked at Schlumberger Laboratory for Computer Science and AT&T Laboratories. She is the author of a large number of peer-reviewed papers, as well as an inventor on 30 + pending and granted US patents. She received her PhD from the University of Texas at Austin.

Dr. Alan Wassyng is the Director of the McMaster Centre for Software Certification (McSCert). He has been working on safety-critical software-intensive systems for more than 25 years, and is licensed as a Professional Engineer in Ontario. After spending 14 years as an academic, he consulted independently on critical software development for more than 15 years. He helped Ontario Hydro (OH) develop methods for safety-critical systems, and was a key member of the team that designed the methodology and built the software for the shutdown systems for the Darlington Nuclear Station. In 1995 he was awarded an OH New Technology Award for "Development of Safety-Critical Software Engineering Technology." In 2002 he returned to academia. He publishes on software certification, and the development of safe and dependable software-intensive systems. He is a cofounder of the Software Certification Consortium (SCC), and has served as Chair of the SCC Steering Committee since its inception in 2007. He has consulted for the US Nuclear Regulatory Commission, and in July 2011, he was a visiting researcher in the Center for Devices and Radiological Health at the US Federal Drug Administration. In 2012 he was invited to give a keynote talk at Formal Methods (the premier conference in the field), and a keynote at FormaliSE 2013. In 2006 he was awarded the McMaster Students Union Award for Teaching Excellence in the Faculty of Engineering. He has served as a PI or co-PI on a number of funded projects at McMaster University.

INTRODUCTION

C. Greer

National Institute of Standards and Technology, Gaithersburg, MD, United States

With expectations for between 50 and 200 billion connected devices worldwide by 2020, the global Internet of Things market is predicted to expand at a compound annual growth rate of over 31%, exceeding $9T by the 2020 milestone.[1]

Internet of Things (IoT) concepts are expected to drive progress across nearly all sectors of the global economy. GE estimates of the Industrial Internet could add $10T to $15T to global GDP over the next 20 years. Gartner predicts that there will be 250 million connected vehicles on the road by 2020. Navigant predicts that the worldwide installed base of smart meters will grow from over 300 million today to more than 1 billion by 2022. IDC predicts that the wearable connected fitness device market will grow from 45 million units in 2015 to 126 million in 2019.

The impact of networking and information technology (NIT) is stunning. Virtually every human endeavor is affected as advances in NIT enable or improve domains such as scientific discovery, human health, education, the environment, national security, transportation, manufacturing, energy, governance, and entertainment.[2]

Realizing the full benefits of these emerging IoT concepts will require advances in science and engineering to meet the grand challenges posed by emerging IoT applications in terms of scale, connectivity, complexity, and interdependence. The numbers above speak to the issue of scale. The largest growth in connectivity is expected for devices not traditionally network-connected—devices like home thermostats, street lights,

---

[1]See, for example, http://www.intel.com/content/dam/www/public/us/en/images/iot/guide-to-iot-infographic.png; http://www.technavio.com/pressrelease/the-global-internet-of-things-market-is-expected-to-grow-at-a-cagr-of-3172-percent.
[2]President's Council of Advisors on Science and Technology, Designing a Digital Future: Federally Funded Research and Development in Networking and Information Technology, January 2013.

and automobiles—creating new markets for systems-of-systems designs. This connectivity is often multinodal—a connected vehicle may interact not just with the driver, but with other vehicles, road infrastructure, transportation management systems, public safety systems, and more—creating increased levels of complexity and new interdependencies.

These new connections and interdependencies create new safety and security concerns. Connectivity means that physical incidents in IoT systems may arise not only from physical means but from cybersources as well, increasing the attack vectors for important infrastructures with significant economic and life safety implications. And new interdependencies mean that a failure or an attack may not be limited to a single technology or sector.

> *Removing the cyber-physical barriers in an urban environment [smart city] presents a host of opportunities for increased efficiencies and greater convenience, but the greater connectivity also expands the potential attack surface for malicious actors. In addition to physical incidents creating physical consequences, exploited cyber vulnerabilities can result in physical consequences, as well.[3]*

These safety and security challenges are not limited to a single sector. Smart grid, intelligent vehicles, next-generation air traffic control, and smart cities are just a few examples of sectors where IoT concepts with new safety and security concerns are being developed and deployed.

> *The inherent level of automation and controllability of positive train control systems makes vulnerabilities particularly dangerous if a malicious actor can exploit them. After obtaining system-level access, an actor could execute a variety of commands, many of which could cause a chain of automated reactions with little or no human oversight.[4]*

Tackling these safety and security challenges requires an approach that embraces highly complex systems at scale and encompasses the full system life cycle from conceptualization

---

[3]Department of Homeland Security, The Future of Smart Cities: Cyber-Physical Infrastructure Risk. https://ics-cert.us-cert.gov/sites/default/files/documents/OCIA% 20-%20The%20Future%20of%20Smart%20Cities%20-%20Cyber-Physical% 20Infrastructure%20Risk.pdf, August 2015.

[4]Department of Homeland Security, The Future of Smart Cities: Cyber-Physical Infrastructure Risk, https://ics-cert.us-cert.gov/sites/default/files/documents/OCIA% 20-%20The%20Future%20of%20Smart%20Cities%20-%20Cyber-Physical% 20Infrastructure%20Risk.pdf.

to realization and assurance. This is the realm of advanced systems engineering and is the theme of this volume. Part I focuses on the fundamentals, describing how systems in an IoT world go beyond the ISO/IEC/IEEE 15288 definition of "a combination of interacting elements to achieve one or more stated purposes" to include those that are aware of, interact with, and shape the world around them. This Part also addresses compositionality—the fact that the properties of an IoT system emerge from the properties of its components and their interactions. For example, the properties of an intelligent transportation system emerge from those of connected vehicles interacting with each other and with intelligent intersections, which are in turn controlled by regional traffic management system, etc. Note that the interacting components at each level in this composition is an IoT application in its own right, a cyber-physical system that is a codesigned hybrid of information and operational technologies (IT and OT) that operates in real time. Analysis of cyber-physical systems—ranging from smart meters and smart phones to continental-scale electric grids and global communications networks—is also addressed in Part I.

Part II provides a series of perspectives on safety and security, starting with the importance of considering the perspective of an attacker in developing a safe and secure design for an IoT system. The perspective of those responsible for producing safe and secure systems is also addressed, with automobile manufacturers as a case study. Cybersecurity as a commercial advantage to a company is also discussed to provide a forward-looking business-model perspective to make up an intelligent transportation system. The assurance perspective—how one may know that a system will do safely and securely what it is designed to do and not do unsafe and insecure things—is also addressed. New perspectives in risk management—dubbed risk engineering—are described that embrace the intricate interdependencies within complex systems that render traditional approaches based on separation of concerns inadequate. Finally the role of standards in providing foundations for interoperability—effective interactions between systems and composability—the ability of systems to serve as components of safe and secure systems-of-systems—is described.

Part III describes application of the concepts in Parts I and II to real-world examples, with cloud computing and smart grid serving as the primary use cases. The first chapter describes combining an attack perspective with concepts from compositionality and risk engineering in designing cloud computing systems that are resilient through effectively managed redundancy, diversity, and reconfigurability. A systems-oriented approach and effective methods for designed-in cybersecurity for cloud computing systems are addressed in the next chapter. The third chapter describes the application of systems engineering and IoT concepts for a safe and secure smart grid. The final chapter describes the development of formal methods and languages for IoT applications, using smart grid as an example.

Collectively, the perspectives set out in this volume provide a foundation for considering the safety and security challenges posed by complex systems in the digital era. Only by meeting these challenges will IoT concepts emerge that can truly enable a world that is safer, more secure, sustainable, livable, and workable.

SYSTEMS

EDITOR'S PREFACE

E. Griffor

National Institute of Standards and Technology (NIST), Gaithersburg, MD, United States

A system is a set of interacting components that frequently form a complex whole. Each system has both spatial and temporal boundaries. Systems operate in, are influenced by and influence their environment. Systems can be described structurally, as a set of components and their interactions, or by reference to its purpose. Alternatively, a system can be referenced in terms of its functions and behaviors.

The notion of a system is ubiquitous. It is not simply a technical concept but it lies at the heart of how the mind deals with and conceives of and understands the surrounding world. It is the essence of how we design and build or make things and how we ultimately garner assurance about their behavior. Indeed, the phrase "what we make, makes us" captures a fundamental truth about the relationship between the act of altering our world and how it is we understand that world—we make the world over in the image of our thoughts. *Thought, through sensing and perception and abstraction or conception,* strives to bring order to our experience.

But what of the case where the products of significantly different ways of *thinking* begin to interact? Their interactions are not likely to meet the purposes of any of the designers. What about a world of systems that are allowed to interact, despite the fact that they were not engineered to do so, that they were not intended to do so? This is the world we live in where the Internet provides ubiquitous and unhindered connectivity, possibilities for interaction and composition. Some of the ways these systems interact were *intended* (or *by design*), but so many others were not intended or designed. Sometimes the results are beneficial, but sometimes they have the potential for harm, they are hazardous. The hazards associated with this type of *emergent system behaviors* may result in harm to person and property—this is the topic of system safety. Additionally a system may be vulnerable, may be subject to

Handbook of System Safety and Security. DOI: http://dx.doi.org/10.1016/B978-0-12-803773-7.00001-2

unauthorized access and modification—this is the topic of system security.

In this preface to the *Handbook of System Safety and Security*, we discuss the concept of a system, system safety and security and review the chapter topics.

1.1 The Need for a Broadly Targeted Handbook of System Safety and Security

The word *system* is *overloaded*, that is, has different meanings to different people. The effort to understand a particular system leads one to ask a few key questions:

- What are the componentor parts of the system?
- What are the interactions between the system's components?
- What are its spatial and temporal boundaries?
- What is its environment?
- What is its structure?
- What function or functions does the system perform?

The interactions between systems, due to the connectivity between systems and to their environment, including human operators, complicate the answers to questions about system safety and security. For example, our need to monitor, measure and control must take into account system connectivity. Hence there is a need to revisit traditional approaches to design for critical concerns such as safety and security. There are also new costs associated with this change in approach. Costs can range from additional component cost, to time delays, to process disruption until new mechanisms are streamlined in. In other words, revisiting these topics must be done from the perspective of all risks.

Though our understanding of systems, as they are rapidly being deployed in our communities and in our nations and across the sectors of the economy, is changing and our approaches to the topics of safety and security are correspondingly diverse, there is a need to begin a broader dialog in order to keep pace with these developments in technology, business, and government. For this reason, the chapters of this *Handbook* reflect the perspectives of experts in each of these sectors. The topics of the chapters are a selection, some technical and others business- and policy-related. It is the hope of the editor, and the contributors, that this volume will serve to inform and stimulate *cross-disciplinary* discussion, study and research on system safety and security.

Part I: Systems
Chapter 1: Editor's Preface and Introduction
Edward Griffor

Chapter 1 contains a preface and a brief introduction to the concept of a system (including a discussion of *cyber-physical systems* or CPS), more commonly known as the *Internet of Things* (IoT). CPS are systems that include both logical operations (such as control and feedback) and physical interactions, such as gathering information from the physical realm using sensors or taking an action or actuating that impacts the physical realm. CPS and IoT are the focus of current discussions due to the accelerating deployment of information systems to become the "smarts" of business, industry, government, as well as our cities and nation.

Finally we discuss the concepts of *system safety and security* that treated in this volume and how they relate to one another.

Chapter 2: Composition and Compositionality in CPS—Janos Sztipanovits, Ted Bapty, Zsolt Lattmann, and Sandeep Neema

Chapter 2 introduces composition and compositionality of systems, one of the key challenges to our understanding of systems and of their behaviors. These two notions raise the important questions about how to study and how to gain confidence about the composition of systems.

Cyber-physical systems (CPS) are engineered systems where functionalities and essential properties emerge through the interaction of physical and computational components. One of the key challenges in the engineering of CPS is the integration of heterogeneous concepts, tools, and languages. In order to address these challenges, the authors review a model-integrated development approach for CPS design that is characterized by the pervasive usage of modeling throughout the design process, including application models, platform models, physical system models, environment models, and models of interaction between these modeling aspects. The authors also discuss embedded systems where both the computational processes and the supporting architecture are modeled in a common modeling framework.

Chapter 3: Software Engineering for Model-Based Development by Domain Experts—Monika Bialy, Vera Pantelic, Jason Jaskolka, Alexander Schaap, Lucian Patcas, Mark Lawford, and Alan Wassyng

Chapter 3 discusses the model-based development (MBD) practices that have impacted the development of embedded software in many industries, especially in *safety-critical domains*. The models are typically described using *domain-specific languages and tools* that are readily accessible to domain experts. Domain experts, despite not having formal software engineering training, find themselves creating models from which embedded code is generated and therefore contributing to the design and coding activities of software development. This new role of the domain experts can create new and different dynamics in the interactions with software engineers, and in the development process. In this chapter, the authors describe their experiences as software engineers in multiyear collaborations with domain experts from the automotive industry, who are developing embedded software using the MBD approach. The authors aim to provide guidelines meant to strengthen the collaboration between domain experts and software engineers, in order to improve the quality of embedded software systems, including the safety and security of their systems.

Part II: Perspectives on Safety and Security
Chapter 4: Evolving Security—Anuja Sonalker and Edward Griffor

The topic of system security, and in particular that of cybersecurity differs in a critical way from the other concerns we have about systems. Though concerns like safety and resilience do have challenges associated with design, realization, and validation to an ever changing operating environment, security faces an ever evolving adversary. When faced with constantly changing conditions under which a system must continue to deliver its function, designers attempt to model those conditions and test their design against that model. Modeling also becomes important from a measurement standpoint. In order to assess systems and determine their overall risk, their overall security posture, design countermeasures, and then re-assess systems to determine the effectiveness of countermeasures in a provable, reproducible, repeatable quantitative manner, we must be able to model the security, vulnerability, and risk of these systems.

In this chapter the authors introduce new modes of modeling for security adversaries and discuss some basic foundations for adversary modeling. They also discuss how connectivity of systems increases the complexity of system interactions. These complexities also need to be identified and modeled to understand the derivative effect on the overall security posture.

Chapter 5: The Business of Safety—Joseph D. Miller

Chapter 5 discusses system safety from the perspective of system producers. The author illustrates the practice of product or system safety, using the example of system safety in the automobile industry.

Automobiles are some of the most widely deployed, complex systems in our society. While their drivers have a minimal amount of preparation or training to operate them, these systems are growing more complex by the day. Current aspirations are to deploy connected, autonomous vehicles. All involved will face challenges. The title of this chapter "The Business of Safety" is intended to address and discuss several questions, like: What is system safety about? What is it made up of? What do people in this "business" do? What are their fundamental activities and concerns? What do they need to carry on their business? What do they actually produce and how does that relate to the other activities necessary for producing the whole product, other activities necessary for producing the product and addressing other relevant concerns?

Chapter 6: Cybersecurity for Commercial Advantage—James M. Kaplan

Many elements of the work required for a business's offerings are viewed as *noncommercial*, such as cybersecurity. They are regarded by business managers simply as an additional cost that cannot be passed on to customer and that therefore are not recoverable. Many of these elements, and in particular cybersecurity, differ in a critical way from the other concerns that business has. Uneven adoption, including adoption by current or potential business partners, can be a cause of delays in achieving cross-business agreements and can make it much more difficult and costly to achieve and follow your own business's policies regarding those concerns.

In this chapter the author discusses the business of cybersecurity and describes how cybersecurity policies and implementation can be turned into a commercial advantage.

Chapter 7: Reasoning About Safety and Security: The Logic of Assurance—Andrea Piovesean and Edward Griffor

An approach to system safety that emphasizes the work products of the design, verification, and validation activities forces us, in the system's evaluation, to reconstruct the argument and even then there is no standard against which to assess the types of reasoning used. Some constraints on the argumentation are captured in standards that describe how these activities should be performed but only implicitly in the dictates of the standards and not through explicit constraints on the argument itself.

In this chapter we introduce a framework for developing a safety case that clearly distinguishes the part of this reasoning that is common to the analysis of any system and the patterns of acceptable reasoning, identified in standards for specific classes of *cyber-physical systems*. Examples of these prescribed patterns of reasoning can be found in ISO 26262, a standard for automotive software safety and in its predecessors in similar standards in other domains. This framework provides guidance both for the construction of argumentation in a case for system safety and also for assessing the soundness of that s*afety case.*

Chapter 8: From Risk Management to Risk Engineering: Challenges in Future ICT Systems—Michael Huth, Claire Vishik, and Riccardo Masucci

Information and communications technology (ICT) is an umbrella term that includes any communication device or application, as well as the various services and applications associated with them. Conventional approaches to the design, implementation, and validation of ICT systems deal with one core system concern or two system concerns at a time, for example, the functional correctness or reliability of a system. Additional aspects are often addressed by a separate engineering activity. This *separation of concerns* has led to system engineering practices that are not designed to reflect, detect, or manage the interdependencies of such aspects. For example, the interplay between security and safety in modern car electronics, or between security, privacy, and reliability in connected medical devices.

Current trends and innovation suggest a convergence of disciplines and risk domains in order to deal effectively and predictively with such interdependencies. However, identification and mitigation of composite risks in systems remains a challenge due to the inherent complexity of such interdependencies and the dynamic nature of operating environments.

This environment requires risk management and mitigation be a central and integral part of engineering methods for future systems. In order to address the requirements of the modern computing environment, the authors argue that one needs a new approach to risk, where risk modeling is included in design as its integral part. In this chapter the authors identify some of the key challenges and issues that a vision of risk engineering brings to current engineering practice; notably, issues of risk composition, the multidisciplinary nature of risk, the design, development, and use of risk metrics, and the need for an extensible risk language. This chapter provides an initial view on the foundational mechanisms needed in order to support the vision of risk engineering: risk ontology, risk modeling and composition, and risk language.

Part III: Applications of System Safety and Security
Chapter 9: A Design Methodology for Developing Resilient Cloud Services—Cihan Tunc, Salim Hariri, and Abdella Battou

Cloud Computing is emerging as a new paradigm that aims to deliver computing as a utility. For the cloud computing paradigm to be fully adopted and effectively used, the authors argue that it is critical that the security mechanisms are robust and resilient to malicious faults and attacks. Security in cloud computing is of major concern and a challenging research problem since it involves many interdependent tasks, including application layer firewalls, configuration management, alert monitoring and analysis, source code analysis, and user identity management. It is widely accepted that one cannot build software and computing systems that are free from vulnerabilities and cannot be penetrated or attacked. Therefore it is widely accepted that cyber resilient techniques are the most promising solutions to mitigate cyberattacks and to change the game to the advantage of the defender over the attacker.

Moving Target Defense (MTD) has been proposed as a mechanism to make it extremely difficult for an attacker to exploit existing vulnerabilities by varying the attack surface of the execution environment. By continuously changing the environment (e.g., software versions, programming language, operating system, connectivity, etc.), we can shift the attack surface and, consequently, evade attacks.

In this chapter the authors present a methodology for designing resilient cloud services that is based on *redundancy, diversity, shuffling*, and *autonomic management*. Redundancy is used to tolerate attacks if any redundant version or resource is compromised. Diversity is used to avoid the *software monoculture problem* where one attack vector can successfully attack many instances of the same software module. Shuffling is needed to randomly change the execution environment and is achieved by "hot" shuffling of multiple functionally equivalent, behaviorally different software versions at runtime. The authors also present their experimental results and evaluation of the RCS design methodology. Their experimental results show that their proposed environment is resilient against attacks with less than 7% in overhead time.

Chapter 10: Cloud and Mobile Cloud Architecture, Security and Safety—Charif Mahmoudi

In Chapter 10 the author reviews the notions of *cloud computing* or, more simply, *cloud architecture*. He discusses security and safety as it relates to cloud implementation of systems. This chapter aims to provide guidance about the cloud and the mobile cloud, needed to analyze and make choices, regarding cloud implementation, that are optimal with respect to security and safety constraints. The guidance provided by this chapter can help the software architect to understand the cloud architecture in a manner that will assist in integrating security and safety aspects in an organization's information technology architecture. This chapter targets also technologists, researchers, and scientists; this chapter provides a survey of state-of-the-art techniques, recommendations, and approaches used to make the cloud platform-based systems secure and safe.

In short, the author provides guidance on *cloud architecture for security and safety.* Small and medium businesses, researchers, and government agencies that are planning to implement solutions based on the cloud may find this guidance useful in developing cloud architectures that are suitably adapted to their businesses. The guidance provided will contribute to the success of their cloud implementation even if it is an implementation of a private, hybrid cloud, or an implementation of software components as services in the cloud. Moreover this guidance will assist in ensuring the security and the safety of their implementation.

Chapter 11: A Brief Introduction to Smart Grid Safety and Security—Siham Khoussi and Andreas Mattas

Chapter 11 is intended as a brief introduction to the concepts of the Smart Grid and notions of safety and security for the Smart Grid. It can serve as a guidance for those working within multiple domains related to smart grid and smart grid systems and even for readers interested in understanding what the Smart Grid is, what its basic elements are, and how it differs from the conventional electric power grid. The intended audience includes those working in government, industry, as well as academia in areas related to electric power generation and the environmental aspects of electric power generation.

The authors provide the reader with an overview of the grid and the smart grid architectures, including their component elements and general operation. Based on safety and security paradigms in other domains, the authors highlight some concepts for safety and security of the Smart Grid. Finally the authors provide examples of harm, to both individuals and system assets, that can be caused by not provisioning specific efforts toward understanding system vulnerabilities or hazards. They also give examples of some vulnerabilities and hazards and how they can be addressed in design and operation of the smart grid.

Chapter 12: The Algebra of Systems and System Interactions With an Application to Smart Grid—Charif Mahmoudi, Hasnae Bilil, and Edward Griffor

The existing electric power grid has components for generation, for transmission, and finally for distribution of electric power to large and small users. Power flows from generation components over transmission components to distribution components, servicing large commercial and public facilities, as well as our homes. Growth in demand is responded to by augmenting the grid with additional generation, transmission, and distribution capacity. This enhanced capacity is costly and takes years to provision. Failure to accurately predict growth in demand or inaccurate estimates of grid performance can lead to excessive and unnecessary cost or inadequate capacity. Some have concerns about the impact of less than optimal operation of the power grid and about the impact of continued use of fossil fuels for generation that have increased.

As a result, societal leadership and the public are increasingly aware of alternative approaches to meeting the demand for electric power. As a result, there are current discussions about how one might reshape the electric power "grid" as a "Smart Grid." The proposed changes pose challenges to traditional approaches to grid infrastructure and organization. The "smartness" of the Smart Grid consists in two distinct innovations. The first involves our integrating new technologies into the power grid and the second involves our radically changing the ways that grid elements relate to one another. A Smart Grid manages distributed generation and bidirectional power flow. In the Smart Grid, each new component could potentially affect adversely the performance of other elements of the grid and so one must have a means of expressing and evaluating these proposed grid innovations.

In this chapter the authors propose a language, for expressing the elements of a Smart Grid, and a *composition operator* for composing grid elements. The authors show how this representation of grid elements forms an algebra, under this composition operator, that can facilitate the assessment of architectures for smart grid. They argue that this approach can assist planners and engineers design the Smart Grids of the future and that it can enable planners and engineers to design, and ultimately simulate the composition and the integration of future grid system. This "smart grid algebra" is based on a formal language that offers the expressive power needed to capture the observable behavior and interactions of smart grid components, enables the study of existing smart grid systems, and supports a methodology for the study of critical concerns about the grid such as safety and security.

COMPOSITION AND COMPOSITIONALITY IN CPS

J. Sztipanovits, T. Bapty, Z. Lattmann, and S. Neema
Vanderbilt University, Nashville, TN, United States

2.1 Introduction

Cyber-physical systems (CPS) are engineered systems where functionalities and essential properties emerge from the networked interaction of physical and computational components. One of the key challenges in the engineering of CPS is the integration of heterogeneous concepts, tools, and languages [1]. In order to address these challenges, a model-integrated development approach for CPS design was advocated by Karsai and Sztipanovits [2], which is characterized by the pervasive use of models throughout the design process, such as application models, platform models, physical system models, environment models, and the interaction models between these modeling aspects. For embedded systems, a similar approach is discussed in Ref. [3], in which both the computational processes as well as the supporting architecture (hardware platform, physical architecture, and operating environment) are modeled within a common modeling framework.

The primary challenge in model-based CPS design flows is improving predictability of system properties "as manufactured" at the end of the design process. A typical characteristic of the current systems' engineering practice is that limited predictability forces the development process to iterate over lengthy design → build/manufacture → integrate → test → redesign cycles until all essential requirements are achieved. There are three fundamental contributors to radically shortening systems development time:

- selecting the *level and scope of abstractions* in the design flow,
- reusing design knowledge captured in component model (CM) libraries and using compositional design methods, and

Handbook of System Safety and Security. DOI: http://dx.doi.org/10.1016/B978-0-12-803773-7.00002-4

- introducing extensive automation in the design flow for executing rapid requirements evaluation and design trade-offs.

The most notable example for highly automated model- and component-based design processes is VLSI design supported by electronic design automation tools. While there are arguments that this experience is not portable for a broader category of engineering systems [4], our experience showed that significant improvements can be achieved with the development of horizontal integration platforms for heterogeneous modeling, tool chains, and tool execution [5,6].

The need for establishing horizontal integration platforms for CPS design flows is the consequence of the traditional engineering approach to dealing with heterogeneity and complexity by adopting the "separation of concerns" principle. Sources of heterogeneity in the CPS design space are structured along three dimensions in Fig. 2.1:

- Hierarchical component abstractions that represent CPS designs on different levels of details and fidelity.
- Modeling abstractions that span a wide range of mathematical models such as static models, discrete event models, lumped parameter dynamic models represented as ordinary differential equations, hybrid dynamics, geometry and partial differential equations.
- Physical phenomena including mechanical, electrical, thermal, hydraulic, and other.

Heterogeneous domains &
abstractions: **model integration**

Heterogeneous tools & asset
libraries: **tool integration**

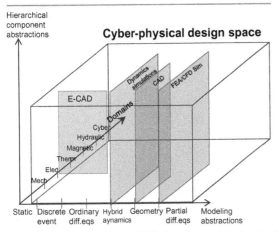

Integrated engineering tools

Figure 2.1 Heterogeneity of CPS domains and design tools.

While CPS design requires the exploration of the integrated design space, the separation of concerns principle establishes "slices" in this complex space such as physical dynamics domain, computer-aided design (CAD) domain, electronic CAD (E-CAD) domain, or finite element analysis (FEA) domain. These individual design domains are relatively isolated, linked to different engineering disciplines, and supported by domain-specific tool suites (right side of Fig. 2.1). Since the existing tool suites represent enormous value in terms of design knowledge, established modeling languages, and model libraries, the only reasonable approach to providing support for CPS design flows is to reuse existing assets. This approach works well if the design concerns are independent—but in most cases this is not the case—unless the system is specifically architected for decoupling selected design concerns [1]. Neglecting interdependences across design concerns is one of the primary sources of anomalies and unexpected behaviors detected during system integration. In conclusion, finding solution for the model integration and tool integration challenges are the only practical approach for creating CPS design tool suites.

Heterogeneity of CPS has a significant impact on the central issue of all model- and component-based design methods and on the establishment of a semantically precise composition framework that enable the construction of system models from the models of components. The general requirement for any composition framework is the establishment of composability and compositionality [7]. Composability means that the components preserve their properties in a composed system. Compositionality is achieved if selected essential properties of a system can be computed from the properties of its component. Different engineering disciplines usually have their domain-specific composition frameworks that are synergistic with the modeling abstractions, modeling domains, and properties to be composed. The challenge is to understand how the integration platforms interfere with domain-specific composition and how compositionality can be provided for different properties simultaneously.

In this chapter we discuss some issues of heterogeneous composition for CPS design. The example we use is based on our experience with the development of a model- and component-based design automation tool suite, OpenMETA as part of DARPA's AVM program [8]. The goal of our project was the design, integration, and validation of an end-to-end tool suite for vehicle design. The OpenMETA tool suite [5] gave us opportunity for experimenting with design automation approaches for CPS and for assessing their effectiveness in a sequence of CPS design challenges.

We focus on two issues that are central to model- and component-based design of CPS: model composition and tool composition. First, we show an example of a CPS component model that comprises a suite of domain models with heterogeneous interfaces. The interfaces are designed for supporting domain-specific composition operators and cross-domain interactions. Second, we show that tool integration platforms also bring about composition challenges that interact with model composition. We restrict our discussion to model and tool integration methods for lumped parameter dynamics, which is in itself a complex multifaceted problem.

2.2 Horizontal Integration Platforms in the OpenMETA Tool Suite

Model- and component-based CPS design flows implement a design space exploration process that proceeds from early conceptual design toward detailed design using models and virtual prototyping. This progressive *refinement process* starts with the composition of abstract system models from CMs that capture essential aspects of the system behavior. The system models are evaluated against requirements using simulation and verification tools. The promising designs are refined using higher fidelity CMs and more detailed modeling abstractions. The design process is completed by optimizing relatively few high-fidelity models. The automation of this design process has been a fundamental goal of the OpenMETA tool suite [9−12].

To facilitate the seamless integration of heterogeneous models and tools, OpenMETA complemented the traditional, vertically structured, and isolated model-based tool suites with horizontal integration platforms [13] for models, tools, and executions as shown in Fig. 2.2 [14]. The function of the integration platforms are summarized below.

The modeling functions of the OpenMETA design flow are built on the introduction of the following model types:

1. Component Models (CMs) that include a range of domain models representing various aspects of component properties and behaviors, a set of standard interfaces through which the components can interact and the mapping between the component interfaces and the domain models.
2. Design Models (DMs) that describe system architectures using components and their interconnections.
3. Design Space Models (DSM) that define architectural and parametric variabilities of DMs.

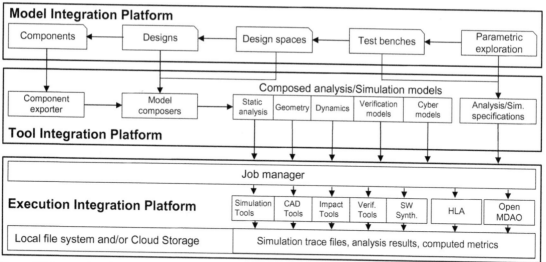

Figure 2.2 Integration platforms.

4. Test Bench Models (TBM) that specify analysis models and analyzes flows for computing key performance parameters linked to specific requirements.
5. Parametric Exploration Models (PEM) that specify regions in the design space to be used for optimizing key performance parameters.

The first three model types focus on the designed system, while the last two represent models of evaluation/optimization processes implemented by test benches. Each test bench contains a link to a system design (the "system under test" object). The system design can be a crude system mock-up composed of low-fidelity CMs at the early stages of the design process, with placeholders for certain subsystems and components whose implementation is not yet clear. Hierarchical DMs define the architecture of a system with its subsystems. Individual designs can be extended to form a design space by adding alternative components and subsystems [15]. The root of a design space has the same interfaces for all design points. Accordingly, even if the number of architectural variants is very large, all associated test benches will remain functional and can be used to evaluate the associated requirements across all point designs generated from the design space. Thus by defining test benches early and executing them periodically, the design space will continually evolve toward containing only satisfying designs.

The fundamental model-integration challenge for OpenMETA is the integration of the five model types described above with the different domain models encapsulated by the components. For example, mobility requirements for a power train, such as "Maximum Speed Hill Climb Sand," are evaluated by a test bench that utilizes lumped parameter dynamic simulation of the power train model with appropriate terrain data. For a given power train architecture, the OpenMETA model composer for lumped parameter dynamics accesses the dynamics models of the individual components in the architecture and composes them into a system model that can be simulated by the Modelica [16] simulation engine. The CMs and the composition mechanism must be flexible enough to enable the use of CMs of different levels of fidelity, even represented in different modeling languages (e.g., Modelica models, Simulink/Stateflow models, Functional Mockup Unit (FMUs), or Bond Graph models) [9]. The TBM links the environment model and the integrated system model to the simulator and creates an executable specification for the evaluation of the "Maximum Speed Hill Climb Sand" performance parameter. Since all design points in the overall design space have the same interface, the TBM can be linked to a design space with many alternative, parameterized architectures. Using the Open MDAO (Multidisciplinary Design Analysis and Optimization) optimization tool, a multiobjective parametric optimization can be performed if the exploration process requires it.

Lumped parameter dynamics and simulation-based evaluation of system designs against mobility requirements is just one example for the many different kinds of test benches required for evaluating alternative powertrain designs. However the general pattern in the overall integration architecture can be clearly seen:

1. *Model Integration Platform*: Heterogeneous models represented in different domain-specific modeling languages are encapsulated in CM libraries. To facilitate model integration, heterogeneous CMs are established with precise composition interfaces and composition operators.
2. *Tool Integration Platform*: Model composers automatically synthesize DMs for test benches by extracting the appropriate CMs from the CM libraries and composing them according to the specification of a candidate architecture. Using models of test benches and parameter exploration processes, analysis flows are integrated for execution on the high-level architecture (HLA) [17] or on Open MDAO.[1]

---

[1]http://openmdao.org/.

3. *Execution Integration Platform*: Executable TBMs are associated with resources and scheduled for execution on cloud platforms.

Composition of models deposited in the CM libraries, composition of analysis flows inside test benches using simulation and verification tools, and composition of executable analysis images on cloud platforms are in the center of the OpenMETA horizontal integration platforms. In this chapter we restrict our discussion to the selected heterogeneous CM (named AVM component model after the overall program name) and to the composition approach for lumped parameter dynamics.

2.3 AVM Component Model

In a component- and model-based design flow, system models are composed of CMs guided by architecture specifications. To achieve correct-by-construction design, the system models are expected to be heterogeneous multiphysics, multiabstraction, and multifidelity models that also capture cross-domain interactions. Accordingly, the CMs, in order to be useful, need to satisfy the following generic requirements:

1. Elaborating and adopting established, mathematically sound principles for compositionality. Composition frameworks are strongly different in physical dynamics, structure, and computing, which need to precisely defined and integrated.
2. Inclusion of a suite of domain models (e.g., structural, multiphysics lumped parameter dynamics, distributed parameter dynamics, and manufacturability) on an established number of fidelity levels with explicitly represented cross-domain interactions.
3. Precisely defined component interfaces required for heterogeneous composition. The interfaces need to be decoupled from the modeling languages used for capturing domain models. This decoupling ensures independence from the modeling tools selected by the CM developers.
4. Established bounds for composability expressed in terms of operating regimes where the CM remains valid.

These requirements are accepted, but not necessarily practiced in engineering design where component-based approaches are used. A common misconception in physical system modeling is that useful models need to be handcrafted for specific phenomena. One explanation for this is the quite common use of modeling approaches that do not support

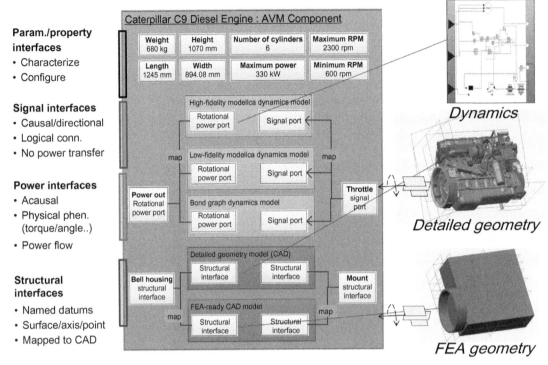

Figure 2.3 Conceptualization of the AVM component model.

compositionality. The AVM component model (Fig. 2.3) placed strong emphasis on compositional semantics that can resolve this problem [18].

A CPS component model must be defined according to the needs of the design process that determines (1) the type of structural and behavioral modeling views required, (2) the type of component interactions to be accounted for, and (3) the type of abstractions that must be utilized during design analytics. We believe that it does not make sense to strive for a "generic" CPS component model, rather, CMs need to be structured to be the simplest that is still sufficient for the goal of "correct-by-construction" design in the given context.

The AVM component model was designed to integrate multi-domain, multiabstraction, and multilanguage structural, behavioral and manufacturing models, and to provide the composition interfaces for the OpenMETA model composers consistently with the needs of power train and hull design [11]. In Fig. 2.3 we illustrate the overall structure of the AVM component model. The main elements of the CM are the followings:

1. The model is a *container of a range of domain models* expressed using domain-specific languages. The actual domain models are referenced from the CMs but stored in separate repositories.

2. Components are characterized by a range of static, physical properties, and labels defined in established ontologies. These static properties are extended with a set of parameters that are changeable during the design process. Fig. 2.3 shows examples for the properties characterizing a Caterpillar C9 Diesel Engine. The static properties and mutable parameters are used in the *early design-space exploration* process [19,20].

3. Lumped parameter physical dynamics plays an essential role in evaluating dynamic behaviors such as mobility properties of designs. Since compositional modeling has been a fundamental goal for us, we chose the *acausal modeling approach* for representing multiphysics dynamics [21]. In this approach dynamics models are represented as continuous time Differential Algebraic Equations (DAE) or hybrid DAEs. Since model libraries may come from different sources, CMs are potentially expressed in different modeling languages such as Bond Graphs (although we dominantly used Modelica-based representations). The multifidelity models are important in assuring scalability in virtual prototyping of systems with a large number of complex components.

4. Models of dynamics implemented computationally inside CPS components are represented using *causal modeling approaches* using modeling languages such as Simulink/ Stateflow, ESMoL [22], Functional Mock-up Units [23], or the Modelica Synchronous Library [24].

5. Geometric structure is a fundamental aspect of CPS design. Component geometry expressed as course or detailed CAD models are the basis for deriving geometric features of larger assemblies and performing detailed FEA for a range of physical behaviors (thermal, fluid, hydraulics, vibration, electromagnetic, and others).

6. Modeling and managing cross-domain interactions are in the center of CPS correct-by-construction CPS design. The component modeling language of OpenMETA (described later) includes constructs to define parametric interactions across domain models using formulas.

In constructing an AVM component model from a suite of domain models (such as from Modelica models representing lumped parameter dynamics of physical or computational behaviors, CAD models, models of properties and parameters, and cross-domain interactions) and the mapping of domain modeling elements to component interfaces are time-consuming and error prone. In order to improve productivity, the OpenMETA tools include a full tool suite for importing domain models (such as Modelica dynamic models), integrating them with standard AVM component model interfaces, automatically checking compliance with the standard, and automatically checking model properties, such as restrictions on the types of domain models, well-formedness rules, executability, and others. Based on our direct experience, the automated model curation process resulted in orders-of-magnitude reduction in required user effort for building AVM component model libraries.

In summary, CPS component models are containers of a selected set of domain models capturing those aspects of component structure and behavior that are essential for the design process. While the selected modeling domains are dependent on CPS system categories and design goals, the overall integration platform can still be generic and customizable to a wide range of CPS.

The remaining issue in defining a CPS component model is the specification of component interfaces and the related composition operators.

2.4   Use Case for Semantic Integration

In a heterogeneous multimodeling component approach, component interfaces play a crucial role in making the Model Integration Platform and model composition infrastructure independent from the individual domain-specific modeling languages. This is particularly important, because the different modeling languages (such as Modelica, Simulink, Bond Graphs, CAD, and others) offer internal component and composition concepts that are incompatible with each other and do not match the composition use cases needed in CPS design flows. The design of domain model independent CM interfaces and composition operators must reflect the needs of use cases in the planned design flows.

Due to the complexity and richness of the OpenMETA design flows, we discuss briefly only key elements of the lumped parameter dynamics use cases summarized in Fig. 2.4 [25]. The list of modeling languages used for representing lumped parameter dynamics are shown in the second row in the figure. (TrueTime[2] is a Matlab/Simulink-based simulator for real-time

---

[2]http://www.control.lth.se/truetime/.

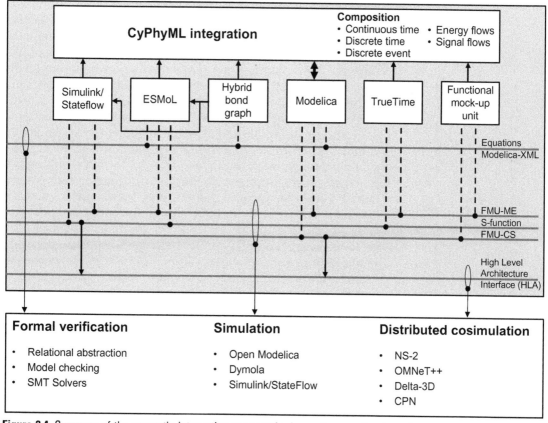

Figure 2.4 Summary of the semantic integration concept for lumped parameter dynamics.

control systems. It enables simulation of controller task execution in real-time kernels, network transmissions in conjunction with continuous plant dynamics.) The modeling languages cover causal (Simulink/StateFlow, ESMoL, TrueTime, and Functional Mock-up Unit) and acausal (Modelica and Hybrid Bond Graph) approaches, continuous, discrete time and discrete event semantics, and facilities for defining physical interactions and signal flows. The connection between the Hybrid Bond Graph language and Simulink/StateFlow and ESMoL represents existing transformation tools from bond graphs to the other languages.

The horizontal bars (Equations, FMU-ME/S-function/FMU-CS, and HLA) represent the target integration domains required by the design flow. Equation-based representations are required by various formal verification tools. The FMU-ME/S-function/FMU-CS bars represent models in the form of input–output computation blocks that can be integrated in simulators. Simulation tools used in OpenMETA include OpenModelica, Dymola, and Simulink/StateFlow. The HLA[3] bar represents the integration domain for distributed cosimulations. OpenMETA uses the HLA standard as distributed simulation integration platform. Cosimulation is effective when single-threaded simulation execution is extremely slow due to the large dynamic range in heterogeneous CPS [17]. Distributed cosimulation is used for virtual prototyping where the simulated system is integrated into and interacts with a complex environment that is simulated by network simulators (OMNeT++ and NS-2), physical environment simulator (Delta-3D), or discrete process simulator (CPN). The vertical dashed lines between the modeling languages and the integration domains represent their relevance for the individual domains. For example, Modelica models (if specified carefully) may contain specification of dynamics in the form of equations that can be exported in Modelica-XML format. In the same time Modelica environments (such as OpenModelica or Dymola) can export models as compiled input—output computation blocks using FMU-ME wrapper or as cosimulation blocks integrated with a solver [23].

The lumped parameter dynamic models encapsulated in AVM components are composed with each other using component interfaces and composition operators. The abstractions describing component interfaces and composition operators are collected in the CyPhyML Model Integration Language (see Fig. 2.4). As the figure suggests CyPhyML is constructed such that the domain-specific languages used for representing component dynamics export a subset of their modeling constructs via a semantic interface. This semantic interface is specified as mapping between the dynamics interface in the AVM component model and abstractions in the different modeling languages. There are two important consequences of introducing the model integration language concept as the cornerstone of semantic integration.

1. Model integration languages (such as CyPhyML) are designed for modeling interactions across domain models. Their semantics is determined by the selected component interfaces and composition operators and not by the domain-specific modeling languages used for specifying embedded CMs (such as Modelica). Accordingly, model integration languages are designed for simplicity. They need to be rich enough for representing cross-domain

[3]https://standards.ieee.org/findstds/standard/1516-2010.html.

interactions, but they can be significantly simpler than the various modeling languages they integrate.

2. Model integration languages evolve as needed. If changing needs of design flows extend to new modeling concepts, new cross-domain interactions, they need to be modified. The most important consequence of the evolving nature of model integration languages is that their semantics need to be formally and explicitly specified to maintain the overall semantic integrity of the multidomain model composition process. This need led to the design and implementation of a Semantic Backplane [10].

The OpenMETA Semantic Backplane [26,27] is at the center of our semantic integration concept. The key idea is to define the structural [28] and behavioral semantics [26,29] of the CyPhyML model integration language using formal metamodeling, and use a tool-supported formal framework for updating the CyPhy metamodels and verifying its overall consistency and completeness as the modeling languages are evolving. The selected tool for formal metamodeling is FORMULA from Microsoft Research [30]. FORMULA's algebraic data types (ADTs) and constraint logic programming (CLP)-based semantics is rich enough for defining mathematically modeling domains, transformations across domains, as well as constraints over domains and transformations.

In Section 2.5 we discuss about component interfaces and composition semantics in OpenMETA, but restrict of the discussion to physical dynamics.

2.5   Component Interfaces and Composition Semantics for Dynamics

As shown in Fig. 2.3, the AVM component model includes four types of interfaces:
1. Parameter/property interface
2. Power interface for physical interactions
3. Signal interface for information flows
4. Structural interface for geometric constraints

Regarding physical interactions, we follow the acausal modeling approach [21]: interactions are nondirectional and there are no input and output ports. Instead, interactions establish simultaneous constraints on the behavior of the connected components by means of variable sharing. For instance, a resistor can be modeled as a two port element, where each port represents a voltage and a current, and the behavior of the resistor is defined by the equations $U1 - U2 = R^*I1$ and $I1 = I2$. In addition to acausal modeling, we adopted the Port-Hamiltonian approach, where physical systems are modeled as network of power-conserving elements like transformers, kinematic pairs, and ideal constraints, together with energy dissipating elements. In this approach, physical components interacting via power ports. These interconnections usually give rise to algebraic constraints between the state space variables of the subsystems leading to a system model which is a mixed set of differential and algebraic equations. The explanation, why such a pair of power variables (effort and flow) is used for describing physical connections, is out of scope in this chapter, but the interested reader can find a great introduction to the topic in Refs. [31,32].

Specification of the CM requires three steps:

1. Specification of the interfaces as typed power ports (electrical power ports, mechanical power ports, hydraulic power ports, and thermal power ports).
2. Specification of the static semantics of the composition by defining constraints over the connection of power ports.
3. Specification of the semantics of connections.

Physical interactions are interpreted over continuous time-domain. (We note here again, that by restricting our discussion to composition of physical interactions, we omit many interesting details regarding the specification of other interactions types and their relationships to each other (e.g., composing causal and acausal models, establishing the link between continuous time and discrete time representations, etc.). For interested readers, these issues are discussed in other papers, such as Refs. [24,26,33−35].

Formally, a component model M from the point of view of dynamic interactions is a tuple M≡{C, A, P, contain, portOf, EP, ES} with the following interpretation:

- C is a set of components,
- A is a set of component assemblies,
- $D = C \cup A$ is the set of design elements,
- P is the union of the following sets of ports: $P_{rotMech}$ is a set of rotational mechanical power ports, $P_{transMech}$ is a set of translational mechanical power ports, $P_{multibody}$ is a set of multi-body power ports, $P_{hydraulic}$ is a set of hydraulic power ports, $P_{thermal}$ is a set of thermal power ports, $P_{electrical}$ is a set of electrical power ports, P_{in} is a set of continuous-time input signal ports, P_{out} is a set of continuous-time output

signal ports. Furthermore, P_P is the union of all the power ports, and P_S is the union of all the signal ports,

- contain : $D \rightarrow A^*$ is a containment function, whose range is $A^* = A \cup \{root\}$, the set of design elements extended with a special root element root,
- portOf : $P \rightarrow D$ is a port containment function, which uniquely determines the container of any port,
- $E_P \subseteq P_P \times P_P$ is the set of power flow connections between power ports,
- $E_S \subseteq P_S \times P_S$ is the set of information flow connections between signal ports.

The specification of the dynamics interface (including both power and signal ports) of the AVM component model using FORMULA ADTs is the following:

```
// Components, component assemblies and design elements
Component :: = new (name: String, id: Integer).
ComponentAssembly :: = new (name: String, id: Integer).
DesignElement :: = Component + ComponentAssembly.
// Components of a component assembly
ComponentAssemblyToCompositionContainment :: =

   (src:ComponentAssembly, dst:DesignElement).

// Power ports
TranslationalPowerPort :: = new (id:Integer).
RotationalPowerPort :: = new (id:Integer).
ThermalPowerPort :: = new (id:Integer).
HydraulicPowerPort :: = new (id:Integer).
ElectricalPowerPort :: = new (id:Integer).
// Signal ports
InputSignalPort :: = new (id:Integer).
OutputSignalPort :: = new (id:Integer).
// Ports of a design element
DesignElementToPortContainment :: = new (src:DesignElement,
dst:Port).
// Union types for ports
Port :: = PowerPortType + SignalPortType.
MechanicalPowerPortType :: = TranslationalPowerPort

               + RotationalPowerPort.

PowerPortType :: = MechanicalPowerPortType +
ThermalPowerPort

           + HydraulicPowerPort
           + ElectricalPowerPort.

SignalPortType :: = InputSignalPort + OutputSignalPort.
// Connections of power and signal ports
```

```
PowerFlow :: =

    new (name:String,src:PowerPortType,dst:PowerPortType,...).

InformationFlow :: =

    new (name:String,src:SignalPortType,dst:SignalPortType,...).
```

The structural semantics for interconnecting dynamics ports are represented as constraints over the connections expressing that the model may not contain any dangling ports, distant connections, or invalid port connections:

```
conforms
no dangling(_),
no distant(_),
no invalidPowerFlow(_),
no invalidInformationFlow(_).
```

For this, we need to define a set of auxiliary rules. Dangling ports are ports that are not connected to any other ports:

```
dangling :: = (Port).
dangling(X) :- X is PowerPortType,
no { P | P is PowerFlow, P.src = X },
no { P | P is PowerFlow, P.dst = X }.
dangling(X) :- X is SignalPortType,
no { I | I is InformationFlow, I.src = X },
no { I | I is InformationFlow, I.dst = X }.
```

A distant connection connects two ports belonging to different components, such that the components have different parents, and neither component is parent of the other one:

```
distant :: = (PowerFlow + InformationFlow).
distant(E) :-E is PowerFlow + InformationFlow,
DesignElementToPortContainment(PX,E.src),
DesignElementToPortContainment(PY,E.dst),
PX ! = PY,
ComponentAssemblyToCompositionContainment(PX,PPX),
ComponentAssemblyToCompositionContainment(PY,PPY),
PPX ! = PPY, PPX ! = PY, PX ! = PPY.
```

A power flow is valid if it connects power ports of same types:

```
validPowerFlow :: = (PowerFlow).
validPowerFlow(E) :- E is PowerFlow,
X = E.src, X:TranslationalPowerPort,
Y = E.dst, Y:TranslationalPowerPort.
validPowerFlow(E) :- E is PowerFlow,
X = E.src, X:RotationalPowerPort,
Y = E.dst, Y:RotationalPowerPort.
```

```
validPowerFlow(E) :- E is PowerFlow,
X = E.src, X:ThermalPowerPort,
Y = E.dst, Y:ThermalPowerPort.
validPowerFlow(E) :- E is PowerFlow,
X = E.src, X:HydraulicPowerPort,
Y = E.dst, Y:HydraulicPowerPort.
validPowerFlow(E) :- E is PowerFlow,
X = E.src, X:ElectricalPowerPort,
Y = E.dst, Y:ElectricalPowerPort.
```

If a power flow is not valid, it is invalid:

```
invalidPowerFlow ::= (PowerFlow).
invalidPowerFlow(E) :- E is PowerFlow, no validPowerFlow(E).
```

An information flow is invalid if a signal port receives signals from multiple sources, or an input port is the source of an output port:

```
invalidInformationFlow ::= (InformationFlow).
invalidInformationFlow(X) :-X is InformationFlow,
Y is InformationFlow,
X.dst = Y.dst, X.src != Y.src.
invalidInformationFlow(E) :-E is InformationFlow,
X = E.src, X:InputSignalPort,
Y = E.dst, Y:OutputSignalPort.
```

After defining the port types and the structural semantics of the connections, the remaining step in the specification is the semantics of the composition operators (connections). for power flows is represented denotationally through their transitive closure. Using fixed-point logic, we can easily express the transitive closure of connections as the least fixed-point solution for ConnectedPower. Informally, ConnectedPower(x,y) expresses that power ports x and y are interconnected through one or more power port connections:

```
ConnectedPower ::= (src:CyPhyPowerPort, dst:
CyPhyPowerPort).
ConnectedPower(x,y) :-PowerFlow(_,x,y,_,_), x:
CyPhyPowerPort,
y:CyPhyPowerPort;
PowerFlow(_,y,x,_,_), x:CyPhyPowerPort, y:CyPhyPowerPort;
ConnectedPower(x,z), PowerFlow(_,z,y,_,_), y:
CyPhyPowerPort;
ConnectedPower(x,z), PowerFlow(_,y,z,_,_), y:
CyPhyPowerPort.
```

More precisely, $Px = \{y \mid ConnectedPower(x, y)\}$ is the set of power ports reachable from power port x. The behavioral semantics of power port connections is defined by a pair of equations generalizing the Kirchoff equations. Their form is the following:

$$\forall x \in CyPhyPowerPort \cdot \left(\sum_{y \in \{y | ConnectedPower \ (x,y)\}} e_y = 0 \right)$$

$$\forall x, y (ConnectedPower(x, y) \rightarrow e_x = e_y)$$

We can formalize this FORMULA in the following way:

```
P : ConnectedPower → eq + addend.
P [[ConnectedPower]] =

    eq(sum("CyPhyML_powerflow",flow1.id), 0)
    addend(sum("CyPhyML_powerflow",flow1.id), flow1)
    addend(sum("CyPhyML_powerflow",flow1.id), flow2)
    eq(effort1, effort2)
```
where
```
    x = ConnectedPower.src, y = ConnectedPower.dst, x != y,
    DesignElementToPortContainment(cx,x), cx:Component,
    DesignElementToPortContainment(cy,y), cy:Component,
    PP [[x]] = (effort1,flow1),
    PP [[y]] = (effort2,flow2).
```

The specifications above are only short illustrations of the nature and scope of the full formal specification of the AVM component model and the CyPhyML Model Integration Language. Together with the specification of the model composers, the size of the Semantic Backplane is nearly 20K line of FORMULA code. It is our experience that development and consistent application of the specification frameworks was key in keeping the OpenMETA model and tool integration components consistent.

2.6 Formalization of the Semantic Interface for Modeling Languages

So far, we formally defined the semantics of the compositional elements of CyPhyML but we have not specified the semantic interface between the domain-specific modeling languages such as Modelica, Simulink/StateFlow, Bond Graph Language, ESMoL, and CyPhyML. Note that we can easily add other languages to the list following the same steps as presented here. We show the specification of semantic interface only for Modelica.

Modelica is an equation-based object-oriented language used for systems modeling and simulation. Modelica supports component-based development through its model and connector concepts. Models are components with internal behavior and a set of ports called connectors. Models are interconnected by connecting their connector interfaces. A Modelica connector is a set of variables (input, output, acausal flow or potential, etc.) and the connection of different connectors define relations over their variables. In the following we discuss the integration of a restricted set of Modelica models in CyPhyML: we consider models that contain connectors that consist of either exactly one input/output variable, or a pair of effort and flow variables.

The semantics of Modelica power ports are explained by mapping to pairs of continuous time variables:

```
MPP : ModelicaPowerPort → cvar,cvar.
MPP [[ModelicaPowerPort]] =

    (cvar("Modelica_potential",ModelicaPowerPort.id),
     cvar("Modelica_flow",ModelicaPowerPort.id)).
```

The semantics of Modelica signal ports is explained by mapping to continuous time variables:

```
MSP : ModelicaSignalPort → cvar.
MSP [[ModelicaSignalPort]] =
cvar("Modelica_signal",ModelicaSignalPort.id).
```

The semantics of Modelica and CyPhyML power port mappings is equality of the power variables. Formally,

```
MP : ModelicaPowerPortMap → eq.
MP [[ModelicaPowerPortMap]] =

    eq(cyphyEffort, modelicaEffort)
    eq(cyphyFlow, modelicaFlow)

where

    modelicaPort = ModelicaPowerPortMap.src,
    cyphyPort = ModelicaPowerPortMap.dst,
    PP [[cyphyPort]] = (cyphyEffort, cyphyFlow),
    MPP [[modelicaPort]] = (modelicaEffort, modelicaFlow).
```

The semantics of Modelica and CyPhyML signal port mappings is equality of the signal variables.

```
MS : ModelicaSignalPortMap → eq.
MS [[ModelicaSignalPortMap]] = eq(MSP

    [[ModelicaSignalPortMap.src]],
    SP [[ModelicaSignalPortMap.dst]]).
```

An interesting aspect of the specification of semantic interface between CyPhyML and the domain-specific modeling languages is the assignments of physical units for power ports. Each PortUnit assigns two units to each power port: one to its effort variable and one to its flow variable:

```
PortUnit ::= [port:PowerPort ⇒ effort:Units, flow:Units].
PortUnit(x,"V","A") :- x is ElectricalPowerPort;

    x is ElectricalPin;
    x is ElectricalPort.

PortUnit(x,"m","N") :- x is TranslationalPowerPort;

    x is TranslationalFlange.

PortUnit(x,"N","m/s") :- x is MechanicalDPort.
PortUnit(x,"rad","N.m") :- x is RotationalPowerPort;

    x is RotationalFlange.

PortUnit(x,"N.m","rad/s") :- x is MechanicalRPort.
PortUnit(x,"kg/s","Pa") :- x is HydraulicPowerPort;

    x is FluidPort;
    x is HydraulicPort.

PortUnit(x,"K","W") :- x is ThermalPowerPort;

    x is HeatPort;
    x is ThermalPort.

PortUnit(x,"NA","NA") :- x is MultibodyFramePowerPort.
PortUnit(x,"Pa,J/kg","kg/s,W") :- x is FlowPort.
```

2.7 Conclusion

We have presented an example for establishing aspects of composition and compositionality in a CPS design flow. After deciding the goal of the composition, the required steps are generic: we need to establish a CM, define interfaces, define composition operators, and make a mapping between the modeling describing the component behavior and the modeling language representing the composed system. Although we did not cover many aspects and details of composition we developed in the AVM project, the example is sufficient for illustrating some general conclusions:

1. We believe that CPS design problems require different kinds of CMs and composition methods. Components are containers of relevant and reusable design knowledge represented in domain-specific languages. The selection of model types

need to be matched with the CPS category and the type of analyses required during the design process. It is not the particular combination of domain models are generalizable, but the fact that the formation of CPS component models require cross-domain modeling and model integration. This insight led us to construct a reusable Model Integration Platform that includes methods, tools, and libraries for creating model integration languages, specifying their formal semantics, and structuring those in a Semantic Backplane that provides foundation for CPS composition frameworks in highly different application domains. The OpenMETA Semantic Backplane is at the center of our semantic integration concept. The key idea is to define the semantics of the CyPhyML model integration language using formal metamodeling, and to use a tool-supported formal framework for updating the CyPhyML metamodels and verifying its overall consistency and completeness as the modeling languages are evolving. The selected tool for formal metamodeling is FORMULA [36] from Microsoft Research. FORMULA's ADTs and CLP-based semantics are effective at mathematically defining modeling domains, transformations [37] across domains, as well as constraints over domains and transformations. At the conclusion of the AVM project, the OpenMETA Semantic Backplane included the formal specification of CyPhyML, the semantic interfaces to all constituent modeling languages, and all model transformations used in the tool integration framework. (The size of the specifications is 19,696 lines out of which 11,560 are autogenerated and 8136 are manually written.)

2. Composition occurs in several semantic domains in CPS design flows even inside a single analysis thread. For example, the system level Modelica model for a power train using the composition semantics described above yields a large number of equations for which the simulation with a single Modelica simulator may be extremely slow. In this case we may take the composed system level model and decompose it again, but not along the component/subsystem boundaries but along physical phenomena (mechanical processes and thermal process) so that we can separate the fast and slow dynamics [17]. This decompositions leads to two models that can be cosimulated using the HLA cosimulation platform (see Fig. 2.4), so the recomposition of the system level model occurs in a different semantic domain.

3. In a naïve view, model and tool integration is considered to be an interoperability issue between multiple models that

can be managed with appropriate syntactic standards and conversions. In complex design problems, these approaches inevitably fail due to the rapid loss of control over the semantic integrity of the diverse set of models involved in real-design flows. The "cost" of introducing a dynamic, evolvable model integration language is that mathematically precise formal semantics for model integration had to be developed under OpenMETA.

4. The dominant challenge in developing OpenMETA was integration: models, tools, and executions. The OpenMETA integration platforms included $\sim 1.5M$ lines of code that is reusable in many CPS design context. In the AVM project, OpenMETA integrated 29 open source and 8 commercial tools representing a code base which is estimated 2 orders of magnitude larger than OpenMETA [6]. The conclusion is that integration does matter. It is scientifically challenging and yields major benefits. This is particularly true in design automation for CPS, where integrated design flows are still not reality.

Acknowledgments

The reported results are conclusions of research partly supported by the Defense Advanced Research Project Agency (DARPA) under award #HR0011-12-C-0008 and #N66001-15-C-4033, the National Science Foundation under award #CNS-1035655 and #CNS-1238959, and NIST Award #NIST 70-NANB15H312.

References

[1] J. Sztipanovits, X. Koutsoukos, G. Karsai, N. Kottenstette, P. Antsaklis, V. Gupta, et al., Toward a science of cyber-physical system integration, Proc. IEEE 100 (1) (2012) 29–44. <http://ieeexplore.ieee.org/lpdocs/epic03/wrapper.htm?arnumber=6008519>.

[2] G. Karsai, J. Sztipanovits, Model-integrated development of cyber-physical systems, Software Technologies for Embedded and Ubiquitous Systems, Springer, 2008, pp. 46–54. <http://link.springer.com/chapter/10.1007/978-3-540-87785-1_5>.

[3] G. Karsai, J. Sztipanovits, A. Ledeczi, T. Bapty, Model-integrated development of embedded software, Proc. IEEE 91 (1) (2003) 145–164. <http://ieeexplore.ieee.org/xpls/abs_all.jsp?arnumber=1173205>.

[4] D.E. Whitney, Physical limits of modularity, MIT Working Paper Series ESD-WP-2003-01.03-ESD Internal Symposium, 2003.

[5] J. Sztipanovits, T. Bapty, S. Neema, X. Koutsoukos, E. Jackson, Design tool chain for cyber physical systems: lessons learned, in: Proceedings of DAC'15, DAC'15, 07–11 June 2015, San Francisco, CA, USA.

[6] J. Sztipanovits, T. Bapty, S. Neema, X. Koutsoukos, J. Scott, The METa Toolchain: Accomplishments and Open Challenges, No. ISIS-15-102, 2015 (Google Scholar Download: The META Toolchain_Accomplishments and Open Challenges.pdf).

[7] G. Gossler, J. Sifakis, Composition for component-based modeling, Sci. Comput. Program. 55 (1−3) (2005).

[8] P. Eremenko, Philosophical Underpinnings of Adaptive Vehicle Make, DARPA-BAA-12-15. Appendix 1, December 5, 2011.

[9] Zs. Lattmann, A. Nagel, J. Scott, K. Smyth, C. van Buskirk, J. Porter, et al., Towards automated evaluation of vehicle dynamics in system-level design, in: Proceedings of the ASME 2012 International Design Engineering Technical Conferences & Computers and Information in Engineering Conference IDETC/CIE 2012, 12−15 August 2012, Chicago, IL.

[10] G. Simko, T. Levendovszky, S. Neema, E. Jackson, T. Bapty, J. Porter, J. Sztipanovits, Foundation for model integration: semantic backplane, in: Proceedings of the ASME 2012 International Design Engineering Technical Conferences & Computers and Information in Engineering Conference IDETC/CIE 2012, 12−15 August 2012, Chicago, IL.

[11] R. Wrenn, A. Nagel, R. Owens, D. Yao, H. Neema, F. Shi, K. Smyth, Towards automated exploration and assembly of vehicle design models, in: Proceedings of the ASME 2012 International Design Engineering Technical Conferences & Computers and Information in Engineering Conference IDETC/CIE 2012, 12−15 August 2012, Chicago, IL.

[12] O.L. de Weck, Feasibility of a 5× speedup in system development due to meta design, in: 32nd ASME Computers and Information in Engineering Conference, August 2012, pp. 1105−1110.

[13] J. Sztipanovits, T. Bapty, S. Neema, L. Howard, E. Jackson, OpenMETA: a model and component-based design tool chain for cyber-physical systems, in: S. Bensalem, Y. Lakhneck, A. Legay (Eds.), From Programs to Systems—The Systems Perspective in Computing, LNCS, vol. 8415, Springer-Verlag, Berlin Heidelberg, 2014, pp. 235−249.

[14] J. Sztipanovits, Model integrated design tool suite for CPS, Invited Talk at University of Hawaii, Honolulu, 9 April 2015 (Figure 2).

[15] H. Neema, S. Neema, T. Bapty, Architecture Exploration in the META Tool Chain, ISIS-15-105, Technical Report, ISIS/Vanderbilt University, 2015.

[16] Modelica Association, Modelica—A Unified Object-Oriented Language for Physical Systems Modeling. Language Specification, Version 3.2. <www.modelica.org/documentas/ModelicaSpec32.pdf>, March 24, 2010.

[17] H. Neema, J. Gohl, Z. Lattmann, J. Sztipanovits, G. Karsai, S. Neema, et al. Model-based integration platform for FMI co-simulation and heterogeneous simulations of cyber-physical systems, in: Proceedings of the 10th International Modelica Conference, Lund, Sweden, 10−12 March 2014, pp. 235−245.

[18] T. Bapty, OpenMETA Project Overview, Project Briefing, March 2012 (Figure 3).

[19] H. Neema, Z. Lattmann, P. Meijer, J. Klingler, S. Neema, T. Bapty, et al., Design space exploration and manipulation for cyber physical systems, in: IFIP First International Workshop on Design Space Exploration of Cyber-Physical Systems (IDEAL' 2014), Springer-Verlag Berlin Heidelberg, 2014.

[20] E. Jackson, G. Simko, J. Sztipanovits, Diversely enumerating system-level architectures, in: Proceedings of EMSOFT 2013, Embedded Systems Week, September 29−October 4, 2013, Montreal, CA.

[21] J.C. Willems, The behavioral approach to open and interconnected systems, IEEE Control Systems Magazine, December 2007, pp. 46–99.

[22] J. Porter, G. Hemingway, H. Nine, C. van Buskirk, N. Kottenstette, G. Karsai, J. Sztipanovits, The ESMoL language and tools for high-confidence distributed control systems design. Part 1: Design Language, Modeling Framework, and Analysis. Tech. Report ISIS-10-109, ISIS, Vanderbilt Univ., Nashville, TN, 2010.

[23] Functional Mock-up Interface. <www.fmi-standard.org>.

[24] Modelica Association, Modelica Language Specification Version 3.3. Revision 1. <https://www.modelica.org/documents/ModelicaSpec33Revision1.pdf>, 11July 2014.

[25] J. Sztipanovits, Model Integration Challenge in Cyber Physical Systems, Tutorial, NIST, 19 January 2012 (Figure 4).

[26] G. Simko, J. Sztipanovits, Model integration challenges in CPS, in: R. Rajkumar (Ed.), Cyber Physical Systems, Addison-Wesley, 2015.

[27] G. Simko, T. Levendovszky, M. Maroti, J. Sztipanovits, Towards a theory for cyber-physical systems modeling, in: Proc. 3rd Workshop on Design, Modeling and Evaluation of Cyber Physical Systems (CyPhy'13), 08–11 April 2013, Philadelphia, PA, USA, pp. 1–6.

[28] E. Jackson, J. Sztipanovits, Formalizing the structural semantics of domain-specific modeling languages, J. Softw. Syst. Model. (September 2009) 451–478.

[29] K. Chen, J. Sztipanovits, S. Neema, Compositional specification of behavioral semantics, in: R. Lauwereins, J. Madsen (Eds.), Design, Automation, and Test in Europe: The Most Influential Papers of 10 Years DATE, Springer, 2008.

[30] E.K. Jackson, T. Levendovszky, D. Balasubramanian, Reasoning about metamodeling with formal specifications and automatic proofs, in: J. Whittle, T. Clark, T. Kühne (Eds.), Model Driven Engineering Languages and Systems, vol. 6981, Springer Berlin Heidelberg, Berlin, Heidelberg, 2011, pp. 653–667.

[31] A. van der Schaft, D. Jeltsema, Port-Hamiltonian systems theory: an introductory overview, Found. Trends Syst. Control 1 (2–3) (2014) 173–378. Available from: http://dx.doi.org/10.1561/2600000002.

[32] D. Karnopp, D.L. Margolis, R.C. Rosenberg, System Dynamics Modeling, Simulation, and Control of Mechatronic Systems, John Wiley & Sons, Hoboken, NJ, 2012.

[33] G. Simko, D. Lindecker, T. Levendovszky, E.K. Jackson, S. Neema, J. Sztipanovits, A framework for unambiguous and extensible specification of dsmls for cyber-physical systems, in: Engineering of Computer Based Systems (ECBS), 20th IEEE International Conference and Workshops on the, IEEE, 2013, pp. 30–39.

[34] D. Lindecker, G. Simko, I. Madari, T. Levendovszky, J. Sztipanovits, Multi-way semantic specification of domain-specific modeling languages, in: Engineering of Computer Based Systems (ECBS), 2013 20th IEEE International Conference and Workshops on the, IEEE, April 2013, pp. 20–29.

[35] G. Simko, D. Lindecker, T. Levendovszky, S. Neema, J. Sztipanovits, Specification of cyber-physical components with formal semantics—integration and composition, in: Model-Driven Engineering Languages and Systems, MODELS'2013, Springer Berlin Heidelberg, 2013, pp. 471–487.

[36] <http://research.microsoft.com/formula>.

[37] D. Lindecker, G. Simko, T. Levendovszky, I. Madari, J. Sztipanovits, Validating transformations for semantic anchoring, J. Object Technol. 14 (3) (August 2015), pp. 2:1-25, <http://dx.doi.org/10.5381/jot.2015.14.3.a2>.

SOFTWARE ENGINEERING FOR MODEL-BASED DEVELOPMENT BY DOMAIN EXPERTS

M. Bialy[1], V. Pantelic[1], J. Jaskolka[2], A. Schaap[1], L. Patcas[1], M. Lawford[1], and A. Wassyng[1]

[1]McMaster University, Hamilton, ON, Canada [2]Stanford University, Stanford, CA, United States

3.1 Introduction and Motivation

Early in the computer age, it was recognized that an ad hoc programming approach was not suitable for developing nontrivial software systems. In the words of a famous computer scientist, Edsger Dijkstra: "To put it quite bluntly: as long as there were no machines, programming was no problem at all; when we had a few weak computers, programming became a mild problem, and now we have gigantic computers, programming has become an equally gigantic problem." Therefore, a systematic engineering approach including planning, problem understanding, requirements gathering and specification, design, programming, and verification became necessary. This is how *software engineering* was born. According to ISO/IEC/ IEEE Standard 24765 [1], software engineering is defined as, "The application of a systematic, disciplined, quantifiable approach to the development, operation, and maintenance of software, that is, the application of engineering to software."

Unfortunately, decades later, software development and maintenance is still not practiced with the same discipline exercised in other engineering fields. Developing software is often deemed trivial by nonpractitioners. This perception is mostly due to software's *malleability*. Since software itself is not physical, a modification to software is considered "merely a code change." This perception, however, is wrong. Experience teaches us that software should be modified with the same rigor as any other engineering product, e.g., an engine, power inverter, or airplane

Handbook of System Safety and Security. DOI: http://dx.doi.org/10.1016/B978-0-12-803773-7.00003-6

brakes. The effect of a change should be evaluated on a design first, and then thoroughly verified. This is an approach especially necessary in modern systems, which increasingly rely on software. Software accounts for 80% of military aircraft functions [2] and 80% of innovations in vehicles [3]. Software has also grown to be a significant source of accidents and product recalls [4]. Moreover, numerous examples of software-related accidents span the safety-critical domains of aerospace [5], medical [6], and automotive [7], with many more examples listed in [8,9]. For such safety-critical systems, errors can potentially result in loss of life, environmental damage, and/or major financial loss. Therefore, practicing software engineering with the same rigor and discipline recognized in other areas of engineering is crucial to the successful development and safe operation of modern software-intensive systems.

Model-Based Development (MBD) has become a predominant paradigm in the development of embedded systems across industries, including aerospace, automotive, and nuclear. This is mostly due to its appeal of automatic code generation from models, early verification and validation, and rapid prototyping. Furthermore, domain-specific modeling languages used in MBD are easily learned and used by domain experts (experts in the field of the application), allowing them to design, generate code, and verify their own algorithms, using familiar terminology and abstractions. Therefore, the MBD paradigm assigns domain experts a different role than the one they typically have in a traditional software development process. However, domain experts have backgrounds in mechanical engineering, electrical engineering, or other related fields, but typically have no formal education in software engineering. For example, many leading Japanese software specialists believe the majority of Japanese software developers have not been formally educated in software engineering [10].

Our work builds on experience drawn from collaborations between our team of software engineers and domain experts in the automotive industry. While working on multiyear projects with automotive Original Equipment Manufacturers (OEMs), we have interfaced with a number of domain experts from both academia and industry.

First, we have witnessed a large difference in terminology used by software engineers and automotive domain experts[1]. We (partially) address this communication gap between the two communities by explaining the terminology originating in

---

[1]In fact, the term *domain experts* is widely known and used within the software engineering community, while domain experts themselves are largely unaware of the term.

software engineering that is commonly used in development of embedded systems.

Second, domain experts use and/or help develop various software artefacts, often without a clear picture of their intent and their ultimate effect on the quality of software.

This chapter clarifies the role of some of the most commonly used (and those that are not, but should be) software engineering principles, practices, and artefacts by viewing them from a software engineering perspective, and presenting how they affect software correctness, safety, and other software qualities. Therefore, this chapter aims at strengthening the collaboration between software engineers and domain experts, by offering domain experts a high-level understanding of software engineering practices and artefacts, enabling their more effective use. In the process, a number of MBD misconceptions and limitations are addressed. Further, we discuss issues in the industrial practice of MBD, and suggest solutions whenever possible, or point to avenues for research to address issues for which a solution currently does not exist. The chapter is focused on the development of embedded software using Matlab Simulink, the de facto standard in model-based design of embedded systems. Ironically, Simulink itself neglects some major software engineering principles, and this issue is also discussed in this chapter. While the focus of this chapter is on the MBD of embedded systems using Matlab Simulink, many of the discussions are applicable to software engineering in general. Therefore, we view this chapter as a useful tutorial primarily for domain experts involved in the development of software intensive systems, but also for software practitioners in general, managers in related fields, and any staff involved in software and/or software development.

The remainder of this chapter is organized as follows. Section 3.2 describes the overall MBD software engineering process and serves as a prelude to the subsequent sections. The subsequent sections, Sections 3.3, 3.4, 3.5, and 3.6, then provide insight into commonly encountered questions and misconceptions in industry regarding requirements, design, implementation, and verification and validation, respectively. Finally, Section 3.7 presents conclusions and directions for future work.

3.2 Development Process: How Do You Engineer Software?

Software is not only code, and developing software is not just programming. Software includes requirements, design, test

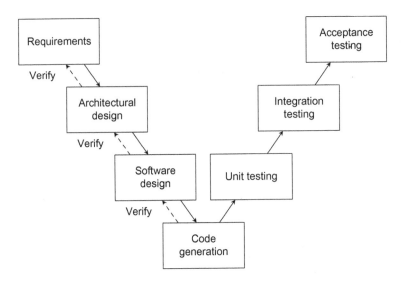

Figure 3.1 V-Model development process for model-based development (MBD).

reports, and other documentation which are artefacts resulting from the different phases in the engineering process. As with all engineering disciplines, well-defined processes must be followed in order to construct quality systems which operate safely. The most common description of the software engineering process within the MBD of embedded software is known as the V-model, shown in Fig. 3.1. Although many process models exist for software systems, the V-model is the most widely accepted model for embedded safety-critical systems because of its focus on testing at different levels. Moreover, standards such as the automotive standard ISO 26262 [11] prescribe its use. In this section, we provide a summary of the phases of the V-model which are further elaborated in the sections that follow.

3.2.1   What Are the Phases of the Engineering Process? How Are Domain Experts Involved?

The development process begins with the gathering and specification of requirements. In this phase, a high-level description of *what* the system should do is determined, without providing any details as to *how* it is done. As a result of the requirements phase, a software requirements specification (SRS) is produced and agreed upon in order to act as a contract between stakeholders and developers, that is, a mutual agreement of the expectations from the system. This phase typically involves close collaboration between software engineers, analysts, managers, with domain experts providing technical breadth and depth within their respective domains. For example, our experience is that a separate team of safety experts plays an integral role in contributing to the development and analysis of safety requirements for automotive systems.

Once a working set of requirements for the system has been established, a high-level architectural design is planned. The architectural design should strive to integrate principles of software engineering (e.g., *modularity* and *encapsulation*), that will be further explained in Section 3.4, in order to minimize complexity and facilitate component reusability. Again, managers, software engineers, and domain experts are primarily involved at this stage, with third-party suppliers also participating where necessary. Architectural design is then verified by way of reviews, simulations (if the corresponding executable specification exists), etc. Next, a software solution that satisfies the requirements and conforms to the architectural design is developed. In MBD, this is largely done by constructing models in accordance with language guidelines and standards. This phase includes defining the necessary component modules, algorithms, data structures, and other detailed design elements necessary for the implementation (or in the case of MBD, code generation). In practice, one or more components or modules are assigned to an individual to "own," that is, to develop and maintain. In current MBD practice, we have found that domain experts design software and rapidly prototype designs, which are later transferred to other engineers to prepare for production as well as maintain. Ideally, these software development activities should be performed by software engineers. They will be well-versed in implementing software using accepted engineering best practices and principles. Close collaboration with a domain expert, knowledgeable about the domain-specific context, will provide guidance toward a solution.

A major benefit of the MBD approach is the ability to automatically generate the implementation code from design models. This significantly reduces implementation errors and development time when compared to traditional programming [12], and also enables domain experts' deep involvement in the development process. The same component "owners" responsible for designing the software will generate its corresponding code. If needed, another separate team of engineers may be responsible for code generation rule customization, which typically comes from the recommendations and suggestions of domain experts. After generating an implementation of the software system, verification takes place to ensure that the system that is implemented is the one that was designed and expected. MBD offers the ability to perform tests early in the development cycle, at different levels, before the software even makes it onto the hardware. There are various stages of testing which occur throughout the development process. For example, *unit testing* verifies each software component individually and independently from the rest of the system, whereas *integration testing* combines software components to verify the system as a whole, and *acceptance testing* verifies that the system satisfies its requirements and performs as expected. In general, the embedded system under development is modeled as a controller, which aims to control some physical system using supervisory logic. The physical system is described in a plant model, which provides the controller with inputs. Depending on the development stage of the controller and the platform upon which the plant is simulated, different testing strategies can be utilized throughout the MBD process:

Model-in-the-Loop (MiL): The controller and plant models are simulated in their development environment (e.g., Simulink).

Software-in-the-Loop (SiL): The controller embedded code, generated from the model into hardware-dependent code, is simulated with the plant model, both on the same machine, typically on PC hardware.

Processor-in-the-Loop (PiL): The controller embedded code is loaded onto the embedded processor (hardware), and is simulated with the plant model in real time.

Hardware-in-the-Loop (HiL): The controller embedded code is run on the final hardware, an electronic control unit (ECU), with a simulated plant model in real time.

The phase following software release is *maintenance* (not depicted in Fig. 3.1), where either defects are fixed or software is modified to satisfy new requirements. In fact, ease of maintenance (maintainability) is one of the very important qualities of software, that, although often not explicitly required, motivates many of the activities in the development process from Fig. 3.1. Software is maintained through collaborative efforts between domain experts and software engineers. For example, in some companies, a software engineer will be in charge of maintaining a software feature (Simulink model). The software will be modified in collaboration with a domain expert, typically in charge of several similar features (Simulink models).

3.2.2 How Important Are the Tools?

Appropriate tool support in each phase of the process by way of a comprehensive tool-chain that facilitates different activities, including change management, build management, bug tracking, etc., is crucial for the success of a development process [13]. Engineering a system often requires many iterations of the development process and its phases. For example, as the software design is developed, requirements can change, making it necessary to go back and repeat the requirements phase. In fast-paced industries such as automotive, performing such iterations quickly is greatly facilitated through the use of tool-chains which span the entire process, and can fully- or semiautomate designing and implementing changes.

3.2.3 An Illustrative Example: Transmission Control Software

For the purpose of illustrating and highlighting the software engineering process for MBD described in the remainder of this chapter, we will consider a small automotive example that was provided by one of our industrial partners, as presented in [14]. Suppose that we need to design and develop the embedded software to control the automatic transmission system of a hybrid-electric vehicle based on requests made by the driver to change gears between park (P), reverse (R), neutral (N), and drive (D) via a "PRND" shifter, typically in the form of a lever or knob within the vehicle console. When using the vehicle, a driver makes requests to change the transmission gear via the shifter (e.g., switch from park to drive), at which point the embedded software needs to decide whether or not to grant the driver's request based on a number of system conditions, such as faults and the availability of certain components. In the subsequent sections of this chapter, we will use this simple illustrative example to demonstrate how to specify software requirements, to translate those requirements into suitable model-based designs, and to verify and validate that the implemented design exhibits the expected system behavior.

3.3 Requirements: What Should Your Software Do?

3.3.1 How Important Are Good Requirements?

Contrary to common belief, software rarely fails. More often than not, the software behaved *exactly* as it was required to, but it was the requirements that were flawed [15]. Some sources assert that over 90% of software issues result from deficient requirements, leaving merely 10% of issues to be caused by design and coding problems [16]. Therefore, experience teaches us that getting requirements right as well as precisely specifying them is essential for the establishment of safe and effective systems [17]. The terms "requirements" and "requirements specification" are taken from software engineering, and are not a part of domain experts' jargon. Our experience shows that domain experts would rather refer to it as "specification" or "spec" only.

3.3.2 What Is the Purpose of a Requirements Specification? Who Uses It?

Before building a safe and usable system, an understanding of what it is meant to accomplish and what qualities it should possess is required. Requirements specify *what* the system should do, and a SRS is an artefact in which software requirements are documented and maintained. A requirements specification acts as a contract between users and software developers. It is also used by verifiers to show that the software satisfies its requirements and by managers to estimate and plan for resources. In our experience, the requirements specification is essential for helping mitigate the impact of developer turnover, especially within the automotive industry which experiences frequent movement of personnel.

3.3.3 Simulink Models Are NOT Requirements

Requirements should state *what* the system should do, whereas design and code state *how*. In practice, however, while the line between the two is not always clear, even in traditional development approaches, it is significantly blurred in MBD. For example, a Simulink model is often considered both the requirements specification and the detailed design specification. Graphical models are often used to help understand requirements. They may also provide a convenient means for facilitating communication between domain experts and software developers. However, Simulink models are *not* requirements. Simulink models contain too many design (implementation) details, making it difficult to see the black-box behavior of a system. Furthermore, a Simulink model lacks a means for specifying nonfunctional requirements and properties of the system (e.g., confidentiality).

3.3.4 What Is Wrong With Requirements Specifications Today?

Many organizations using MBD recognize the importance of separating requirements specification from design. However, the requirements are often written using natural language, and are therefore bound to be ambiguous. Furthermore, the requirements are often incomplete, that is, they specify the required functionality of the system for particular combinations of inputs, but often fail to specify the functionality for all the combinations.

We have also often seen inconsistent requirements specifications, that is, those containing contradictory statements. Using a language with precise syntax and semantics (meaning) helps alleviate these issues. Consider, for example, the requirement captured in the tabular expression [18] shown as Table 3.1. Tabular expressions are one of many ways to specify requirements. However, they offer precise and concise semantics, and are used in the nuclear and aerospace industries due to their understandability. They can be interpreted straightforwardly as if-then-else statements. Consider writing a requirement for driver request arbitration from the Park position in the illustrative example described in Section 3.2.3 that states: "If there is no fault and the component is unlocked, grant the driver's request; otherwise, stay in the current gear." This requirement can be compactly specified as a tabular expression for the Park position as shown in Table 3.1, where each row represents a subexpression of the function such that if a Condition is evaluated to be true, the corresponding Result cell value is the returned output.

Given the requirement specified in Table 3.1, it is straightforward through the use of tool support [19] to verify that

Table 3.1 Requirement for Driver Request Arbitration From Park

fArbRequestFromPark(eDrvrRequest:enum, bUnlocked, bFaulty:bool): enum =

Condition		Result
		eArbRequest
bFaulty		*cPark*
¬bFaulty	*bUnlocked*	*eDrvrRequest*
	¬bUnlocked	*cPark*

the requirement is complete (requiring consideration of all possible inputs) and consistent (ensuring determinism through nonoverlapping input cases), both of which are integral to safety-critical systems, as they raise the confidence in correct system performance in all conditions, and also aid in detecting gaps for the input cases considered.

3.3.5 Who Writes the Requirements Specification?

Ideally, domain experts would write the requirements specification themselves, without the help of software engineers. However, this is seldom the case, with software engineers producing the requirements specification based on communication with domain experts. The knowledge of the domain experts is instrumental to the specification of requirements, but the developer possesses the knowledge of how to specify the requirement precisely and succinctly. While getting requirements right necessitates continual interaction between domain experts and software engineers, there is commonly a disconnect, as they often do not "speak the same language." Specifying requirements such that they are understandable to domain experts, and the use of notations like the aforementioned tabular expressions are integral to the development of a quality requirements specification. MBD notations like Simulink/Stateflow have proven to be useful in this regard, given that they are readable by both domain experts and software engineers.

3.3.6 What Information Should an SRS Contain?

The structure and content of a SRS have been thoroughly investigated, with several standards and templates available [20]. At minimum, an SRS typically consists of the following elements:

Purpose: A clear statement of the system's fundamental reason for existence. This is meant to provide a rudimentary understanding of the system and why it is needed.

Scope: Includes a brief overview of the system to be developed and should indicate the goals and benefits of building the system. It also specifies the boundaries within which these goals are met. An accurate scope definition is important since it is often used by project managers to determine timing and budget estimates.

Functional Requirements: A *functional requirement* specifies an action or feature that needs to be included in the software system in order for the system to be fit for purpose. Table 3.1 is an example of a functional requirement.

Nonfunctional Requirements: A *nonfunctional requirement* specifies a property or quality that the software system shall possess in order to judge its operation. Nonfunctional requirements often specify the performance, security, and usability requirements of the software system, among others.

An SRS should also contain specifications of the tolerances on *accuracies* of outputs, *rationale* justifying the reason for the existence of requirements (with alternatives considered, if any), specifications of *interfaces* documenting how the software communicates with its environment, and documentation of *anticipated changes* to existing requirements so that they may be better accommodated by the eventual design.

Once a preliminary set of requirements can be agreed upon by the domain experts and other stakeholders, and there is a general understanding of *what* the system must do, thought can start being put into *how* the system is going to do what it does. It should be noted that requirements specification is an iterative process that continues in subsequent phases.

3.4 Design: How Will Your Software Do What It Does?

Designing software is similar to design activities in other engineering fields. It is the process of determining how a system will perform its intended functions. The software design process is regularly comprised of two stages: *architectural design* and *detailed software design*. The design starts with determining the software architecture, which is the description of the high-level decomposition of the system into its main components, their interfaces, and interactions between the components. Software architecture is then gradually refined into a detailed design of modules and algorithms. In MBD, the software design refers to the modeling of the software in a language such as Simulink/Stateflow, with the models effectively serving as blueprints for the software implementation, done via automatic code generation.

3.4.1 How Is Design Different From Requirements?

Design is directly driven by the requirements gathered in the previous phase. Models are created and continually modified until a design has been achieved that meets all the requirements. Although closely tied together, it is important to emphasize again that requirements are *not* the same as design models. As previously mentioned, this is one of the most prevalent misconceptions when it comes to MBD, with MathWorks also perpetuating this idea in the recent past [21]. Requirements and design must be viewed as separate entities, and we can illustrate exactly why using the automotive example given in Section 3.2.3.

Table 3.1 specifies a requirement, while Tables 3.2 and 3.3 provide two detailed Stateflow designs which both satisfy this requirement. These Stateflow truth table designs are structured in two sections, where the top subtable defines conditions to check. Should the conditions be evaluated to the values given in the columns, (T, F, or -, representing true, false, or "don't care," respectively), the corresponding action for the column is executed. Actions are defined in the bottom subtable. It is apparent that pinpointing the requirement within these designs is difficult due to the additional design details also included. Moreover, this example demonstrates that multiple, yet distinct, designs can implement the same requirement in different ways. For these reasons, it is imperative to document requirements separately from design. Just as in engineering in general, the motivation for choosing one design over another will lie in the

Table 3.2 First Design Stateflow Truth Table

fArbRequestFromPark(eDrvrRequest:enum, bUnlocked, bFaulty:bool): enum =

#	Condition	1	2	3	4	5	6	7	8	9	10	11
1	*eDrvrRequest == cPark*	T	F	F	F	F	F	F	F	F	F	-
2	*eDrvrRequest == cReverse*	F	T	F	F	T	F	F	T	F	F	-
3	*eDrvrRequest == cNeutral*	F	F	T	F	F	T	F	F	T	F	-
4	*eDrvrRequest == cDrive*	F	F	F	T	F	F	T	F	F	T	-
5	*bUnlocked*	-	T	T	T	-	-	-	-	-	-	-
6	*bFaulty*	-	F	F	F	T	T	T	-	-	-	-
	Actions	1	2	3	4	1	1	1	1	1	1	1

#	Action
1	*eArbRequest = cPark*
2	*eArbRequest = cReverse*
3	*eArbRequest = cNeutral*
4	*eArbRequest = cDrive*

Table 3.3 Second Design Stateflow Truth Table

fArbRequestFromPark(eDrvrRequest:enum, bUnlocked, bFaulty:bool): enum =

#	Condition	1	2	3
1	*bFaulty*	T	F	F
2	*bUnlocked*	-	T	F
	Actions	1	2	1

#	Action
1	*eArbRequest = cPark*
2	*eArbRequest = eDrvrRequest*

added need to satisfy other requirements or accommodate constraints. For example, if the component containing design implementing the requirement from Table 3.1 has a tight timing requirement, the second design may be used due to its more efficient condition checking. However, if maintainability over different, but similar, software versions containing this component, is the bigger concern, the first design will more likely be used, as will be explained later in this section.

3.4.2 What Are Important Principles of Software Design?

It is well known in software engineering that good designs lead to high-quality software systems. For systems other than trivial examples, it is necessary to *decompose*, or break up, the system into manageable modules in order to improve its reusability, overcome complexity, and to divide labor. There are typically several ways of decomposing a system. The criteria used in the decomposition of a system plays a significant role in determining the quality of a design. One of the most important principles in software design is *design for change* [22] which prescribes that a developer needs to be able to anticipate changes that the system might undergo, and design software capable of accommodating those changes. For example, when designing powertrain software, engineers need to *anticipate* powertrain configurations that might have to be supported in the future, and design software so that, if the change is made, the effect of the change will be localized as much as possible. Closely related to the *design for change* and *anticipation of change* principles is the concept of a *software product line*. A product line necessitates a core architecture of common functionality across the various configurations, but will also provide the ability to include variations in order to create different products within the line. For example, a large part of electrified powertrain software can be reused throughout different powertrain configurations. All of the software versions corresponding to different powertrain configurations will constitute products within a software product line. As another example, the model shown in Table 3.2 was developed to satisfy the requirement from Table 3.1, but was also devised with the product line approach in mind, because the logic it implements varies only slightly with different vehicle variants. More precisely, while the conditions listed in the columns of the first table of Table 3.2 remain the same for each product in the product line, the set of actions on these conditions is the only part of the design that varies throughout the different products within the product line. Roughly speaking, the actions are encoded as calibrations, so that they are easy to change, and maintain. Calibrations, in fact, are often used to implement variability in software across products within a software product line.

The mechanism crucial in implementing *design for change* in software engineering is *information hiding* [22]. Information hiding seeks to decompose a system such that modules each "hide" a requirement or design decision that is likely to change, that is, the interface of the module does not reveal its inner workings. Typically, design decisions creep into the interfaces of the modules, making them context-dependent, and not easily modifiable or reusable. Design decisions typically correspond to hardware, behavior, and software design decisions which are likely to change in the future, and hiding their details within a module will make future changes easier to accommodate. Continuing with the aforementioned electrified powertrain software example, a module that will "hide" the powertrain architecture from the rest of powertrain software represents a *hardware hiding module*. However, while the principle of information hiding has fared well in traditional software development paradigms, it might not be as useful and widely applicable in MBD. We are currently undertaking research into the role of information hiding in MBD.

3.4.3 How Does Simulink Support the Application of Software Engineering Principles?

For MBD, Simulink enables the introduction of various levels of hierarchy in order to decompose a system into various levels of abstraction. Unfortunately, a challenge in Simulink is understanding how to employ information hiding, how designs will benefit from it, as well as how to decompose a system into reusable modules. The *subsystem* is the accepted Simulink equivalent of a module, however, they are neither reusable, nor do they effectively encapsulate their internal design. Degrees of reusability can be achieved with other mechanisms such as libraries, model references, function-call subsystems, code reuse subsystems, and Simulink functions, however, they all fail to encapsulate their internals with respect to hidden data flow [23]. For example, Data Store Memory blocks are able to bypass the typical inport/outport interface of a subsystem, and read/write data directly from/in the subsystem. Adding explicit interfaces which include Data Store Memory blocks such as those described in [23] can alleviate this problem. However, a new block mechanism within the Simulink language is needed; one which restricts hidden data flow to effectively encapsulate data, as well as be easily reused in multiple locations of a model. Such a mechanism is not currently available and presents itself as a challenge when employing information hiding in Simulink designs. Research into the development of such mechanisms is needed.

Furthermore, Simulink lacks self-documenting capabilities of imperative programing languages. For instance, an analog of a module interface in C, as defined in C header files, does not exist in Simulink [23].

3.4.4 How Can Guidelines Help?

When it comes to achieving a good design, as with most languages, there are conventions and guidelines available which give best practices that should be adhered to. Likewise, for Simulink/Stateflow, standards such as [24,25] have been developed with the aim of facilitating desirable model qualities, mostly readability. Making models readable with appropriate block colors and positions is comparable to including white spaces and new lines in textual languages, and makes a difference when it comes to achieving qualities such as modifiability and maintainability.

Nevertheless, in working with industrial-sized models from OEMs and the currently available guidelines, we have noticed shortcomings in the guidelines in addressing actual design principles, such as modularity. For example, using global variables in traditional programming languages is strongly regarded as bad practice because global variables hinder encapsulation, reuse, and understandability. However, modeling guidelines for Simulink typically do not recommend against the use of analogous constructs such as Data Store Memory blocks at the top-level of models (which would be analogous to them being declared as global variables), or above their needed scope. Such a recommendation can easily be formulated and automated, as done in Ref. [26] with the *Data Store Push-Down Tool*. In general, more guidelines and supporting tools are needed, which aim to increase the use of other important software engineering principles.

3.4.5 What Information Should a Software Design Document Contain?

As with other traditional development approaches, designs in MBD must be properly documented. A software design description (SDD) is an artefact documenting the design of the software system and describing how the system will be structured in order to satisfy its requirements. An SDD effectively translates the requirements from the SRS into a representation using software components, interfaces, and data. Commonly used templates which outline the content and format of compiling an SDD exist [27]. At minimum, an SDD typically consists of the following elements:

Purpose: A clear statement describing what the system is ultimately meant to accomplish. It is meant to reinforce the understanding of why the system needs to be developed.

Rationale: Provides justification for the chosen design. This often includes a description and justification of the design decisions that were made in the development of a module, and a list of the alternatives that were considered, along with reasons why they were rejected.

Interface Design: Describes the intended behavior of a module from an external viewpoint, such that other entities can interact with the module without knowing its internal design. This should include the any imported modules, inputs, outputs, and their types, ranges, etc.

Internal Design: Describes the internal structure of a module, including subsystems, algorithms, internal variables/data, and constants.

Anticipated Changes: A list of the ways in which a module is expected to change in the future. This offers insight into the future direction of the development of a module. In this way, one can *design for change* so that when requirements of the system change, the design can accommodate those changes with only moderate modifications, rather than with complete overhauls.

Although the need for documenting Simulink models has been recognized in industry, to the best of our knowledge, there has not been any research on how this is to be done. Our own efforts show that the principles and content of an SDD from traditional software engineering equally apply to documentation of Simulink models, and we have been working to develop a template for an SDD for Simulink models.

3.4.6 Are Models Documentation?

In MBD, we are often met with the "models are documentation" fallacy that we believe has further perpetuated the lack of proper documentation across industries using MBD. However, any engineer responsible for maintaining real-world industrial-size Simulink models understands that a Simulink model is notoriously hard to reverse engineer or maintain without additional information about the model that can be documented in an SDD. For example, Simulink lacks facilities to explicitly represent the interface inputs/outputs of a model/subsystem. This issue was discussed and suggestions were made in [23]. Also, a model does not contain rationale for design decisions. However, experience teaches us that documenting rationale is crucial for proper software development and maintenance.

We illustrate the importance of having a good SDD by an anecdotal story from our collaboration with one of our industrial partners. Their newly hired engineer was tasked with maintaining a Simulink model implementing algorithms within his expertise area. There was no documentation associated with the model. Although the engineer was very familiar with the model's algorithms and their application, comprehending the model took approximately 2 months due to the fact that no requirements specification, and particularly, design documentation, existed for this model. As a result, every part of the model had to be manually examined and understood. After reverse engineering the model, the engineer asked for our help with documenting the model to significantly ease the maintenance efforts in the future. This is not the only instance of such setbacks we saw, and it clearly illustrates that even a domain expert, with all of the relevant background knowledge, is still hampered significantly by a lack of documentation. Again, this is a clear example that the Simulink model is *not* the requirements, nor effective documentation in and of itself.

3.4.7 What Is Wrong With Software Design Documentation Today?

In general, it is a common attitude that SDDs are ultimately nonessential to the deployment of embedded software. The companies that develop and maintain large and complex embedded software in Simulink, also develop and maintain a large number of SDDs documenting the designs. For example, a company we worked with documents every software feature (i.e., a large Simulink model) with an SDD. To improve the documentation, the company developed a template defining the format and content of SDDs and then distributed it to developers in charge of models' maintenance. However, the template very loosely defined the content of SDDs, partly due to the use of undefined terminology. This resulted in developers subjectively interpreting the template, leading to inconsistent documentation throughout different features of the same software. The SDDs are also consequently ambiguous and incomplete. Under-defined content of documentation is a general (not only SDD) software documentation problem, ultimately rendering the resulting documentation meaningless. Instead, the template for documentation should define the structure of the documentation, using well-defined terminology that includes explanation of all relevant terms, as well as the instructions for the developers on the required content. Improving documentation is not a short-term project—consequently, the managers consider it a burden on the development/maintenance process already under tight resource constraints. We feel, however, that the benefits of producing and maintaining proper documentation would by far outweigh its costs.

Additionally, a challenge we have encountered in industry, especially those with fast development cycles, is that SDDs are not always kept up-to-date. We contend that every model change should also necessitate a change in the associated SDD. Ideally, the change management should be built into software development environments with revision control, with rules requiring that changes to models are not allowed without an updated SDD.

3.5 Implementation: Generating Code

3.5.1 Why Is Code Generation Crucial to the Success of MBD?

Automatic code generation in an MBD process is vital to the cost effectiveness of development. It eliminates the manual effort in coding from design, therefore, accelerating the process while decreasing the chance of errors when compared to manual coding from requirements or models. For example, GM has attributed the success of the Chevrolet Volt's development to automatic code generation [28]. Since code is automatically generated from design, traceability links are also automatically generated. Tools exist that automatically generate code from Simulink models and have been widely used in the industry (e.g., MathWorks Embedded Coder, dSPACE TargetLink). Any manual modification of the code after code generation is strongly not recommended, given the high chance of introducing errors, and maintainability issues—the manual modifications will be overwritten upon code regeneration.

While verification that the code implements the Simulink design is still needed (performed by, e.g., *back-to-back testing*[2] that is well supported by current tools), verification efforts can typically be reduced by using the "proven in use" argument behind commercial code generation tools—the fact that those tools have extensively been successfully used in different applications for a reasonable amount of time. Some industries go further by certifying code generators, additionally reducing the effort needed for verification of code against design.

Automatic code generation enables a variety of applications including SiL, PiL, HiL, and rapid prototyping. It allows for quick generation of code from Simulink controller implementations for deployment code on a desktop machine, instruction set simulators, or target (the microprocessor). Further more, for HiL, e.g., the plant model can also be coded into C (whether from Simulink or another physical modeling tool more appropriate for plant modeling) and used in real time. The embedded code generated for ECUs should also run in real time, satisfy efficiency requirements (speed, memory usage), integration with legacy code requirements, etc.

3.5.2 What Are the Limitations of Code Generation?

Not all of the Matlab language and Simulink constructs are supported by code generation tools. Furthermore, while efficiency of model-generated code is comparable to hand code[3], the efficiency of code can typically be increased by hand coding

---

[2]Back-to-back testing checks whether the outputs of the model and code are the same for the same inputs.
[3]In fact, model-generated code can outperform handwritten code [29].

when the code is manually developed by a skilled embedded developer that is knowledgeable about the importance of using proper data types, memory alignment, etc. Consequently, if the size of code, or RAM usage, or speed of execution, is a major concern, developers may decide to hand code the critical parts of system. The integration of hand code with other legacy or generated code is supported by existing tools. However, our experiences confirm that, whenever possible, automatic code generation is strongly preferred given its cost effectiveness.

3.6 Verification and Validation: How Do You Know Your Software Is Good?

Although the terms *verification* and *validation* are often used interchangeably, the difference between the two is significant. While verification answers the question, "Are we building the system right?", validation answers, "Are we building the right system?" Typically, verification and validation (V&V) activities are classified into two large groups: testing and analysis, where testing is dynamic, and analysis is static.

Domain experts are typically involved in a number of V&V activities. For instance, they are involved in the validation of requirements by either e.g., manual inspection of requirements specifications and/or by simulation of requirements, if their specification is executable. They might also be further involved in developing test cases at different software levels. However, domain experts might lack the understanding of automatic generation of tests and its impact on the quality of software. Furthermore, they may not have a clear picture of the V&V activities throughout the development process as a whole. In this section, we strive to present a brief overview of V&V techniques used in traditional software engineering, and, in particular, how they map to and impact MBD practices.

In the remainder of this section, we will not distinguish between the terms verification and validation.

3.6.1 Why Is Early Verification Important? Does MBD Help?

The cost of fixing software bugs increases dramatically with respect to how late they are found during the development of the system. A bug discovered postrelease can cost 100 times more to find and correct than if it were found and corrected at the requirements or early design phase [30]. The cost effectiveness is precisely one of the main reasons for the widespread adoption of MBD in practice. MBD enables a significant part of the V&V activities to be moved from after the code phase to the design phase, leading to a significant reduction of development costs. For example, because a model in Simulink representing a design is an executable specification, testing can be performed at the model level (MiL testing) before testing at the code level. In fact, as will be discussed in this section, MBD was able to leverage some of the most promising verification techniques that came out of computer science research but previously found only limited application in traditional software development.

3.6.2   Is Testing Software Different Than Testing Other Engineering Products?

Testing software is very different from testing systems in other engineering products. This is due to the lack of the *continuity property* of software functions: if the inputs of a function change slightly, the outputs might change drastically [31]. This also means that exhaustive testing is not possible for any non-trivial software system, because it is infeasible to test a system for all the possible combinations of inputs and sequences of inputs. Therefore, testing can never show the absence of bugs, only their presence.

3.6.3   How Do You Choose Tests? When Do You Stop Testing?

Unfortunately, the question of when to stop testing is still one of the most significant open problems in software engineering. However, strategies exist to help cleverly choose test inputs, so as to increase confidence that an adequate set of representative behaviors of the system has been exercised. Both domain experts and software engineers determine appropriate test cases[4], given their complimentary skills and roles in the development. While domain experts typically manually develop cases based on their intimate knowledge of the application, software engineers are accustomed to using tools to automatically generate test cases based on requirements and/or models/code. The tools use software testing measures as criteria to maximize the probability that representative behaviors of the system have

[4]A test case includes a test sequence of inputs and corresponding outputs.

been covered. The notion of coverage criteria was first used for testing programs in traditional programming languages, and then adapted to Simulink/Stateflow, allowing early verification at the design level, before the testing at the code level as in traditional development paradigms.

For example, decision coverage for Simulink/Stateflow targets all decision points in a Simulink/Stateflow model (e.g., Switch, If, While blocks, Triggered/Enabled subsystems, as well as Stateflow transitions) such that each decision has been exercised, i.e., every decision evaluates to true and false. For the design given in Table 3.2, that means test cases corresponding to each of the 11 columns evaluated to true and false will be generated.

A number of good commercial tools exist to automatically generate tests for both Simulink models and the C-code generated from it. For example, Reactis by Reactive Systems tests Simulink designs by trying to maximize the coverage of both the requirements and the design in a number of coverage metrics, while requirements, also specified in Simulink, are used as a *testing oracle*—a means of defining expected outputs for each test case. This emphasizes the importance of having formalized requirements—requirements specified using notations with well-defined meaning and syntax, such that they can be checked by a computer.

Testing tools too have limitations when it comes to supporting all the various design constructs of Simulink. For example, for the Stateflow truth tables shown in Tables 3.2 and 3.3, Reactis will not aim to exercise the decision behavior of the tables, but will merely seek to execute the table at least once.

3.6.4 What Other Verification Techniques Are Used in MBD?

As in any traditional engineering, MBD relies on manual inspection of relevant artefacts (requirements, design specifications, etc.) by experts. For example, the requirements specification is typically written by software engineers, and then reviewed by domain experts. For this reason, it is very important to choose a notation readable by domain experts, as previously noted. A specification can also be reviewed for completeness and consistency. For example, simple manual inspection of the requirements specification from Table 3.1 reveals that the specification is complete and consistent. Given that the notation from Table 3.1 is formal—has a precisely defined meaning and syntax—the check for completeness and consistency can be automated. In fact, a Simulink toolbox exists that allows the tabular expressions to be used within Simulink designs, where tables can be checked for completeness and consistency with the push-of-a-button [19].

MBD leverages a number of tools that examine models/code in much the same manner that a human reviewer would. For example, automatic static checks can be run on models and code to check for conformance to rules defined in modeling style guidelines and coding guidelines, respectively, as discussed in Section 3.4. Furthermore, MBD uses a number of tools that discover run-time errors, such as division by zero, overflow, out-of-bound array index, etc., at both the model and the code levels. Formal verification uses mathematics to verify software. For example, Simulink Design Verifier (SDV) by MathWorks can be used to discover run-time errors at the model level. Also, MathWorks' PolySpace can be used to find run-time errors at the code level. These tools leverage *formal verification*.

A formal verification technique called *model checking* has been successfully used by e.g., MathWorks' SDV to *prove* that Simulink designs meet their requirements, where the requirements are also specified in Simulink.[5] The significant difference between verifying Simulink designs with respect to their requirements in Reactis (based on testing), and verifying with SDV is that SDV *exhaustively* verifies the system using mathematical techniques. However, model checking suffers from scalability issues, and is often infeasible for very large systems. Nevertheless, it can still be used on industrial models, particularly for the safety-critical parts of designs. We also note that we have found the term "model checking" to be quite misused in MBD to mean either checking models for compliance to modeling guidelines, or for testing models against their requirements. A question that naturally arises next is whether testing is needed at all if models have been previously exhaustively verified. The answer is in the positive, because formal verification is performed on a *model* of the system, not on the *actual system*.

3.7 Conclusion and Future Work

With the advent of MBD, we have seen a shift in the role of domain experts in the embedded software engineering process. Despite not having formal software engineering training, domain experts often find themselves creating models from

---

[5]SDV also supports an alternative, C-like notation, for specifying requirements.

which code is generated, thus significantly contributing to the design and coding activities of software development. At the moment, MBD does not completely relieve the software developer from having to know software principles that help us develop safe and dependable systems. The adoption of sound software engineering practices by domain experts is thus very important for the safety of those systems.

In this chapter, we addressed common misconceptions that domain experts encounter when adopting software engineering practices in MBD. We also aimed to clarify some of the most widely used software engineering principles, and their links with well-known concepts from MBD. Nevertheless, in some cases it is not clear how specific well-established software engineering principles translate to MBD. For example, research is needed to better understand the effectiveness of the information hiding principle in MBD.

We expect that the guidelines we provided will increase the effectiveness of the interaction between software engineers and domain experts, which is crucial for the successful development and operation of software-intensive, safety-critical, embedded systems. Although the examples and discussions in this chapter center around the development of safety-critical automotive embedded software in Simulink, the guidelines are applicable to the MBD of embedded software in general.

References

[1] International Organization for Standardization (IST/15), ISO/IEC/IEEE 24765:2010, 2010.
[2] D.L. Dvorak, NASA study on flight software complexity, American Institute of Aeronautics and Astronautics, Reston, VA, 2009.
[3] M. Broy, I.H. Kruger, A. Pretschner, C. Salzmann, Engineering automotive software, Proc. IEEE 95 (2) (2007) 356–373.
[4] P. Koopman, A case study of Toyota unintended acceleration and software safety, <https://users.ece.cmu.edu/~koopman/pubs/koopman14_toyota_ua_slides.pdf> in: Presentation, 2014 (accessed April 2016).
[5] N.G. Leveson, Role of software in spacecraft accidents, J. Spacecr. Rockets 41 (4) (2004) 564–575.
[6] N.G. Leveson, C.S. Turner, An investigation of the Therac-25 accidents, Computer 26 (7) (1993) 18–41.
[7] R.N. Charette, This car runs on code. <http://spectrum.ieee.org/transportation/systems/this-car-runs-on-code> 2009 (accessed February 2016).
[8] P.G. Neumann, Computer-Related Risks, Addison-Wesley, Boston, MA, 1995.
[9] W.E. Wong, V. Debroy, A. Restrepo, The role of software in recent catastrophic accidents, IEEE Reliability Society 2009 Annual Technology Report 59 (3) (2009).

[10] R.E. Cole, Killing innovation softly: Japanese software challenges, Manufacturing Management Research Center (MMRC) Discussion Paper Series, 2013.

[11] International Organization for Standardization/Technical Committee 22 (ISO/TC 22), ISO 26262-6:2011, Geneva, Switzerland, 2011.

[12] M. Broy, S. Kirstan, H. Krcmar, B. Schätz, J. Zimmermann, What is the benefit of a model-based design of embedded software systems in the car industry? Software Design and Development: Concepts, Methodologies, Tools, and Applications, IGI Global, Hershey, PA, USA, 2014 (Chapter 17), pp. 310−334.

[13] A. Hunt, D. Thomas, Ubiquitous automation, IEEE Software 19 (1) (2002) 11.

[14] M. Bialy, M. Lawford, V. Pantelic, A. Wassyng, A Methodology for the Simplification of Tabular Designs in Model-Based Development, in: 3rd FME Workshop on Formal Methods in Software Engineering (FormaliSE), IEEE Press, 2015, pp. 47−53.

[15] N.G. Leveson, Software safety: why, what, and how, ACM Computing Surveys (CSUR) 18 (2) (1986) 125−163.

[16] D. Jackson, Why is software so hard? And what can we do about it? Slides of a talk given at Accenture's India Delivery Center, November 29, Bangalore, India, 2007. <https://people.csail.mit.edu/dnj/talks/accenture07/accenture-india-07.pdf> (accessed April 2016).

[17] A. Murugesan, M.P. Heimdahl, M.W. Whalen, S. Rayadurgam, J. Komp, L. Duan, et al., From requirements to code: model based development of a medical cyber physical system, in: Proceedings of the 4th International Symposium on Foundations of Health Information Engineering and Systems (FHIES) and the 6th International Workshop on Software Engineering in Healthcare (SEHC), Washington, DC, USA, 2014.

[18] Y. Jin, D.L. Parnas, Defining the meaning of tabular mathematical expressions, Sci. Comp. Program. 75 (11) (2010) 980−1000.

[19] C. Eles, M. Lawford, A tabular expression toolbox for Matlab/Simulink, in: M. Bobaru, K. Havelund, G.J. Holzmann, R. Joshi (Eds.), Proceedings of the 3rd NASA Formal Methods Symposium, vol. 6617 of LNCS, pp. 494−499. Springer, Berlin/Heidelberg, 2011.

[20] IEEE, Systems and software engineering—life cycle processes—requirements engineering, in: ISO/IEC/IEEE 29148:2011(E), 2011, pp. 1−94.

[21] P.A. Barnard, Software development principles applied to graphical model development, AIAA Modeling and Simulation Technologies Conference and Exhibit, American Institute of Aeronautics and Astronautics, San Francisco, CA, USA, 2005.

[22] D.L. Parnas, On the criteria to be used in decomposing systems into modules, Commun ACM 15 (12) (1972) 1053−1058.

[23] M. Bender, K. Laurin, M. Lawford, V. Pantelic, A. Korobkine, J. Ong, et al., Signature required: Making Simulink data flow and interfaces explicit, Sci. Comp. Program. 113 (Part 1) (2015) 29−50. Model Driven Development (Selected & extended papers from MODELSWARD 2014).

[24] Orion Crew Exploration Vehicle Flight Dynamics Team, Orion Guidance, Navigation, and Control MATLAB and Simulink Standards, fifteenth ed., 2011.

[25] The MathWorks, MathWorks Automotive Advisory Board (MAAB): Control Algorithm Modeling Guidelines Using MATLAB, Simulink, and Stateflow, Version 3.0, 2012.

[26] V. Pantelic, S. Postma, M. Lawford, A. Korobkine, B. Mackenzie, J. Ong, et al., A toolset for Simulink: improving software engineering practices in development with Simulink, in: 3rd International Conference on Model-Driven Engineering and Software Development (MODELSWARD). IEEE, 2015, pp. 50–61.

[27] IEEE, Standard for information technology—systems design—software design descriptions, in: IEEE STD 1016-2009, 2009, pp. 1–35.

[28] T. Liang, Automatic code generation for embedded control systems, Slides of a talk given at MathWorks' MATLAB Conference 2015, May 19–June 3, Australia and New Zealand. <https://www.mathworks.com/company/events/conferences/matlab-conference-australia/2015/proceedings/automatic-code-generation-for-embedded-control-systems.pdf> 2015 (accessed April 2016).

[29] S. Ginsburg, Model-based design for embedded systems. Slides of a talk given at the Embedded Computing Conference, September 2, Winterthur, Switzerland. <http://www.embeddedcomputingconference.ch/download_sec/3B-Ginsburg.pdf> 2008 (accessed April 2016).

[30] B.W. Boehm, Software Engineering Economics, vol. 197, Prentice-Hall, Englewood Cliffs, NJ, 1981.

[31] C. Ghezzi, M. Jazayeri, D. Mandrioli, Fundamentals of Software Engineering, second ed, Prentice-Hall, 2002.

PERSPECTIVES ON SAFETY AND SECURITY

4

EVOLVING SECURITY

A. Sonalker[1] and E. Griffor[2]

[1]STEER Tech, Columbia, MD, United States [2]National Institute of Standards and Technology (NIST), Gaithersburg, MD, United States

4.1 Need for Security in a Cyber-Physical System

The need for security began with four simple questions:
- *Is the claimant who they claim to be?*
- *Is the claimant allowed to do what they intend to do?*
- *Did the data change in transit?*
- *Can the data be kept secret to all except the intended party?*

These four tenets are commonly referred to as authentication, authorization, integrity, and confidentiality, respectively, and are an excellent starting point in laying the ground work for "secure" design. With cyber-physical systems (CPS) the problem begins at this same initial point, except the two end parties could be machine-to-human, human-to-machine, or machine-to-machine and that there exist some nondigital elements of the system (mechanical, hydraulic, pneumatic, nuclear, electrical, etc.). An important aspect of CPS systems, availability, was introduced much later by Needham and Price [1] and comes from reliability engineering. Availability has much to do with fault tolerance and robustness to failure. Any good distributed system is designed to be highly available in the presence of faults [2,3] or fall back to a fail-safe state if it cannot remain available, with or without security in the picture. The chunk of availability attributable to security then is of intrusion tolerance and flow control (predominantly seen in Denial of Service attacks).

CPSs were originally intended to be physical systems with varying levels of automated controls enabled by computation. Control was direct, or remote via a controller network. With the advent of the cyber component and broad connectivity across the Internet of Things (IoT), remote truly became *long-range remote* (off-site). While this transition became a major enabler

Handbook of System Safety and Security. DOI: http://dx.doi.org/10.1016/B978-0-12-803773-7.00004-8

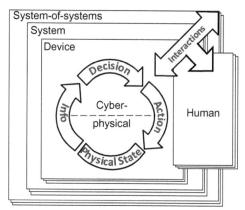

Figure 4.1 Cyber-physical systems.

in making CPSs more efficient, lower cost, as well as easily accessible and controllable, this transition clearly impacted security needs. The questions posed earlier become even more critical, and need to be reassessed, even readdressed. Besides end-point security and credential verification and integrity of the control data, there is a need to ensure that there is *no insertion, fabrication, or replay of legitimate commands*. This aspect is not covered by the four questions, as it happens to be part of the normal and correct functioning of the system. However lack of such a check can result in compromise of control over the assets that comprise many CPSs (Fig. 4.1).

The likelihood of a security breach is a probability determination of *threat capability and vulnerabilities* in the system. Threat capability is a function of accessibility to more sophisticated open source and custom tools, more powerful hardware at lower prices, more knowledge of systems due to the use of more open source software. While there potentially are a few more factors that influence threat capability, our opinion is that the three factors listed above have the highest directly proportional effect on hacker capability, and therefore on the likelihood of breach. Vulnerabilities are directly related to the complexity of the system [4]. The number of lines of code (thousands), i.e., KLOC is a good measure of project size, and therefore software system complexity. A modern automobile, e.g., contains approximately 80–100 million lines of code [5]. Most CPSs today are being driven toward software defined-x, whether it is software-defined networking, software-defined radio, x-by-wire, and more. This is intended for cost reduction, mechanical failure reduction, ease of maintenance compared to hardware maintenance, and even lightweighting (cost and fuel efficiency benefit). As more and more electromechanical systems are replaced by software, these systems become incrementally complex. Legacy software is often not removed, code is incrementally updated in modules without testing the entire system or understanding interactions with other modules, and testing becomes highly complex and expensive. Defect density (defects per thousand lines of software code), a measurement for software quality, for known systems like Microsoft Windows 10, e.g., is 5 bugs/KLOC, NASA Goddard Flight Systems, which performs very rigorous (very expensive) software testing, has a defect ratio of 0.1 bugs/KLOC [6]. Defects are mainly caused by either design or implementation and can be reduced by rigorous testing. Often times, in a rush to deliver releases, software is not tested as rigorously as needed. While defenders need to find and address most defects, a competent adversary often leverages a single one of these defects (vulnerabilities) to launch an attack and penetrate the system.

4.1.1 Hacker Capability and System Complexity

In Fig. 4.2, *hacker capability* and *system complexity* are graphed for the past, present, and future to convey the changes in trends. As discussed earlier, both system complexity and hacker capability have independently increased over time.

System complexity has increased due to (1) capability enhancement, (2) system expansions, (3) security enhancements, (4) replacing mechanical and hardware functions with software equivalents, (5) incremental development and software complexity associated with leaving legacy codes, and often following suboptimal software engineering practices. As seen above system complexity is directly related to the number of vulnerabilities that can only be mitigated through rigorous testing.

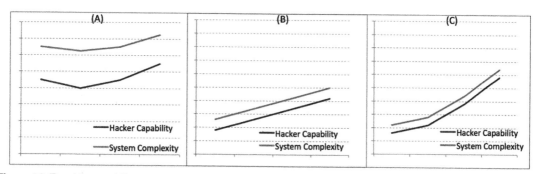

Figure 4.2 Trend in capability versus system complexity as a defense mechanism (A) Past, (B) Present, and (C) Future. STEER Tech.

4.1.2 Security Enhancements to Systems

Take the case of a defense-in-depth model for a CPS. In most cases that I have examined in the automotive domain, system vulnerabilities went from linear to exponential because of the complexity of implementation, as measured by the increased number of lines of software code. While each vulnerability may not directly result in a system breach (access to a core critical function), there are now more vulnerabilities overall. The only reason why each vulnerability does not result in a system breach is because the "gaps" in each layer of the depth model were not directly aligned. Some vulnerabilities are deep within a layer and do not have external exposure, but if an adversary was to penetrate each layer and gain access and control of system resources in each layer, and can then move around in the system, it can find the next vulnerability, expose it and continue to breach deeper into the system. To reiterate, this result has a lot to do with capabilities of the adversary, access to sophisticated tools, and the biggest advantage—increased knowledge of the system. For example, consider what happens when the adversary gets shell access and control and realizes that it is an open source system the adversary is already familiar with. From these graphs, we conclude that the aim of secure system design, in a nutshell, should be to ensure that system defense is always ahead of hacker capability.

4.1.3 Risk Versus Asset Balance

As CPSs become more and more connected, including connectivity for purposes of measurement, control, and transactional purposes, there is a need to revisit traditional security thinking and mechanisms. Obviously, there is a new cost associated with this *change*. This cost can range from additional component costs, to time delays, to process disruption until new mechanisms are streamlined in. Even with new mechanisms there is again a new testing and validation phase. At the very least it will incur additional time, money, and operational delays or, alternately, time-to-market delays in case of production of CPS systems. Therefore to minimize disruption and incremental process cost, we must prioritize. The reassessment of security must be done from a *risks versus assets perspective* keeping this new connectivity and subsystem interplay in mind. Without the latter, the revaluation and reevolution is ineffective. From a risk perspective the questions to ask would be:

- *What are the assets that must be protected at all times?*
- *What kind of "protection" do they need (authentication, authorization, integrity, confidentiality)?*

A threat assessment that begins with identifying the true assets and their protection needs, the six questions, the four initial questions plus these additional two, must be conducted. Once we understand this, then we have to assess what the practical risk factor is given all this new connectivity and the *reach-in* to the assets that were not typically present before. This new reach-in, typically called a *vector* is a particular strategic direction, taken using a particular approach, using a unique path that may either be directly coming in from the outside, or through other subsystems and components.

The point of entry of a vector is called an *entry point*. The set of all exploitable entry points along a logical or physical surface is called an *attack surface*. We will revisit this definition more concretely in the following sections. For example, consider an automobile as our example of a CPS. An external attack surface would be the outer perimeter of the vehicle with all its vulnerable communication entry points. A second attack surface would be an in-cab attack surface, which is still external to the automotive CPSs, but physically inside the car. A third attack surface, now internal to the CPSs, could be the level where noncritical systems meet critical systems, at a *gateway*, for example, that enables communication between subsystems of the CPSs.

A further *security evolution* is that the adversary model needs to be revaluated for a variety of reasons. Systems have evolved beyond single standalone systems; remote monitoring, command and control, and increasing productivity being the chief reasons for increasing the level of automation and connectivity between multiple systems. Traditional adversary models do not take these complex interactions into account. For example, traditional models include:
- byzantine (arbitrary failures),
- natural failures,
- human error,
- economic espionage (economically motivated cybercriminal).

All of these models are meant for nonadaptive interaction between the adversary and the system. They are also not intended for modeling cascading failures due to an external trigger. Most byzantine failures are countered by letting the systems fall back into a fail-safe mode. Fail-safe modes are created for each individual subsystem but rarely for the entire system overall. An *air-gap* is presumed: the notion is that by design, a system in fail-safe mode will do no harm to an adjacent system. Today, we find this assumption to be grossly inadequate. Therefore today systems must be designed to respond to failure, intrusion, or any type of anomaly while keeping transactions, interactions, and system responses "in mind." An intelligent adversary can leverage these transactions to bootstrap into a more powerful and undetectable attack. In essence, the system functionality, by design, can be leveraged to attack the system itself. Today, the adversary we face is far more motivated; an adversary whose intent is to subvert the system to the point of critical failure and cause cascading failures of other reliant systems. Today, the most intelligent adversaries aim to exploit systems in a manner that is *consistent with the design and function of the system* but has a disruptive intention. We have seen several examples of this today ranging from cybercriminals to rookie hackers to cyberterrorists and nation states exploiting built-in features used in a manner not intended by the designers of the system, yet fully consistent with the functioning of the system. Power shell control, access through open ports, and gaining root are some of the ways these adversaries initially enter the system. Replaying legitimate messages to increment system state to the point of failure, for example, is another way of exploiting legitimate functions for malicious use. All these are possible because the system designers did not ask the right questions at the time of design, or because the security model was not reevaluated when the system was incrementally updated with new connectivity entry points.

It should be sufficiently clear now why the adversary model used in designing and evaluating cybersecurity in these CPSs must be remodeled, that is, reconsidered and modeled again. While this is true universally for all electronic systems including financial networks and their systems, it is especially important for CPSs due to the intermix of digital electronics with electrical, mechanical, pneumatic, hydraulic, and systems with kinetic components. Traditionally air-gapped systems also need to be revisited because the air gaps may be in one dimension (mechanical, digital, or pneumatic) but may still be penetrable in a different dimension.

In the rest of the chapter, we will revisit adversary strategies and model them. Then we will model attack surfaces from a risk probability perspective, and assign probabilistic risk values to the attack vector paths resulting in a composite risk value for each attack vector. Then we will determine the overall risk posture for a connected system by weighing that risk value against the asset. Finally, we will subject the most critically risky assets in the connected system to "secure design." By this point the design that will emerge will be flexible. The design framework will be flexible and easy to reevaluate when additional system capabilities (and connectivity points) are added over time. We have now created an *evolving security model!*

4.2   New Adversary Modeling

Most CPSs are built with significant fault tolerance via closed loop control systems and/or redundancy. This makes it hard for a single message adversary to be successful. Most successful strategies we have seen involve multiple messages built on top of each other, or involving contextual information that allows the attack to penetrate through the system's defenses.

To model this type of adversary, we make the following assumption:

(AO) The Adversary is adaptive, and "Online."

Before we delve deeper into adversary strategies, it is essential to review the classes of adversaries we have considered.

The oblivious adversary, or the stateless adversary. This is the weakest form of adversary model. This type of adversary can simply send messages (attack packets) to the system but does not know how the system will respond. Each message is in isolation from the next one and does not form a sequence. In that sense, this adversary has the weakest advantage.

The adaptive online adversary. This adversary has an understanding of the system, and its response. It can craft a series of messages, or a comprehensive attack strategy consisting of multiple messages that are contextually relevant and can mimic real messages in pattern and time. This adversary is assumed to be "online" in the sense that it must be real-time in its decision making, and its strategy decisions are made *before* the system response. The next decision, however, can be made based on the previous decision or the response of the system. In this sense, this adversary has medium advantage. (Greater than the oblivious adversary, but lesser than the adaptive offline adversary.)

The adaptive offline adversary. This adversary not only has the ability to build and launch sophisticated multimessage attacks like the previous adversary, but it can also build all its strategies offline. The implied assumption here is that in order to do so, it has access to the data dictionary of the system, any and all relevant cryptographic primitive generators, and all timing/pattern information. In that sense this is an extremely powerful adversary. Most insider attackers and nation state attackers would fall into this category.

An adaptive offline adversary is less likely to be our main and most probable adversary. Similarly the oblivious adversary is also very less likely to be one we need to spend considerable resources to defend. The medium adversary, that is, the adaptive online adversary is the most commonly encountered, and most likely threat to connected CPS systems.

For the rest of the chapter, we will base our work on the adaptive online adversary. However, we will also show how modifications can be made to model the adaptive offline adversary for the most critical scenarios that do face nation state threats (e.g., Electric Grid).

If M_1 is the first message sequence in the *adaptive online adversary strategy* S_1, and R_1 is the first system response sequence to that first adversary message sequence, then we can describe the strategy and *causal chain* in a clear way. A general interaction between the adversary and the system has the form:

Interaction: I: $M_1 R_1 M_2 R_2 \ldots$.

Thus the general form of an *adversarial interaction* is a sequence of messages sent by the adversary, followed by a sequence of system responses, followed by a sequence of adversary messages and then a sequence of system responses, and so on.

For example, $M_1 = m_1.m_2.m_3\ldots m_n$

that is, M_1 consists of all messages $m_1:m_n$ that are sent before the system response R_1.

Similarly, R_1 can be a single message response r_1, or a series of response messages $r_1: r_n$.

Note that because M_2 is dependent on R_1 therefore, R_1 becomes a part of adversary strategy S_1, hence the *online dependency*.

Adversaries can create multiple strategies that involve getting the system to respond (R) and use that response as the adversary's next step in the attack strategy. Each of the attack messages and their responses will have a probabilistic risk value associated with it in our model. These are used to "add up" the risk probability associated with an attack strategy and is ultimately used to model an appropriate protection strategy.

4.2.1 Attack Surfaces

For each *threat*, there exist several attack surfaces with multiple entry points per attack surface. Each type of entry being an attack vector. It would be exhaustive to model each and every one of them. However, we can generalize and create *rules of thumb* that would be useful for understanding how systems can be impacted by attack vectors. Further, this can facilitate evaluation of the risk associated with a given entry point, and demonstrate how interactions between interconnected systems, modules, or software routines can increase/decrease risk. Finally, we can use it to model how connectivity impacts risk.

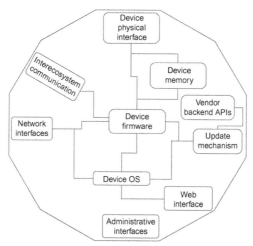

Figure 4.3 Attack surface, and typical entry points.

4.2.2 Weighting the Attack Surfaces

In the colloquial sense the phrase *exterior attack surface* refers to the exterior, penetrable boundary of a CPS system in its entirety; a boundary that an adversary can connect directly with. Components controlling critical functions may not necessarily have an obvious connection to the exterior surface. However there is risk associated with the malfunction or arbitrary failure of a component that can lead to catastrophic loss. Most risk assessment exercises capture this component of risk well. However a thought must be lent here to the fact that these critical components are connected to, and interact with other components. Therefore, there must be some risk associated with interactions with another component that could lead to failures. This, in other words, becomes the "attack surface" of the internal component! Extrapolating this further, we see that one is likely to find a path from the exterior attack surface to the interior attack surface of a critical component sometimes by sheer perseverance, but often by stacking known vulnerabilities and exploits *from the outside in*. Often there may be multiple paths from the exterior surface to the interior through different components.

Therefore a true risk assessment must be able to capture and calculate the risk arising from an exterior attack surface for a component that is buried deep within the system. This risk assessment should capture the different paths that one may take to get to the interior systems and their "penetrability."

4.2.3   Attack Entry Points

For each attack surface, and a given threat vector, we enumerate each entry point. For a CPS, it begins at each point with which an adversary can interact, irrespective of access control. On a software level this translates to an entry point that can be accessed through global identifiers, handlers, input strings, and public methods to name a few. On a network level, open ports, socket identifiers, other communication handles are the main entry points to that module. These entry points will allow an adversary to gain access commensurate with its access privileges.

Formally, we enumerate the attack entry points associated with an attack surface as a sequence $e_1{:}e_n$ where each lower case e is an element of E, the set of all attack entry points.

4.2.4   Role-Based Access

Most systems today have varying degrees of access control. Access control for multiuser systems is used to limit the ability of users from accessing all parts of the system. Users, as defined earlier, for CPS systems can be humans, machines, interprocess communication routines, and more. Role-based access control reduces the breadth of entry points, but increases the depth of each entry point for an interconnected system. Therefore role (access control) is an important parameter in the risk assessment equation. Similarly, resources that can be accessed via entry points (subject to role-based access) are a third important parameter in risk assessment.

If any entry point e_1 is limited by access control (role-based only), then we assign a weight w_1 to it. This weight has a probabilistic component to it that is determined by examining the underlying system. For systems that are greater than one-hop away from the exterior surface weight w is calculated for each entry point, and combined with the probabilistic risk factor of the upstream component/system. These calculations can be done on a per-system down to a per-component basis based on need and relevance.

Vector for entry point $e_1 = e_{1j} \cdot w_{1j}$.

If there exist multiple ways of entering the same entry point (e.g., as in the case with Bluetooth stacks, or OBD-II in case of a vehicle) then

$$\textit{Entry point risk } \mathscr{R}_i = \sum e_{ij} w_{ij}$$

where the second index j represents the subsystem from where the vector originates. A two index entry point therefore

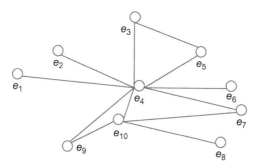

Figure 4.4 Connected subsystem graph.

denotes an entry point internal to the CPS but outside the sub-system. As discussed earlier, an internal entry point (often a critical system) can be reached by multiple entry points. That is, there exist multiple vectors to reach an internal entry point e_k (where k belongs to all n subsystems). Then, e_k is the sum of all vectors leading into it. This can now be represented by a graph. Taking the example of Fig. 4.3 further, we represent it as a graph in Fig. 4.4.

Then, *risk for* $e_{10} = e_4 w_4 + e_7 w_7 + e_8 w_8 + e_9 w_9$
While $e_4 = e_{1:3} w_{1:3} + e_{5:7} w_{5:7}$, and so on.

Cyclic graphs will need to be resolved, and directionality will need to be weighted separately (if there exists any). This topic can take a whole course of its own, and if readers are interested there are several graph theoretical concepts that can be applied to reduce risk for e_4 and e_{10} (and any system under consideration in general). Readers are encouraged to pursue independently as this depth would be outside the scope of this chapter.

4.2.5 Resource Access

The resources that can be accessed by an adversary from each entry point must be identified. For a CPS, resources can be data, databases, cryptosystems, access control libraries, meta-data, services, computation power, memory, network channels, user privileged information, credentials, and more. All resources must be attributed a priority value that reflects the damage that results from the loss of control over the resource. A loss of control of a resource is a *gain* for the adversary. The adversary may use resources gained to further penetrate the system and cause more damage. Clearly, for an interconnected system, resource risk multiplies as the attacker penetrates the system further. Similarly, connectivity increases the resource risks *if* there exists a path to the resource from the exterior surface that is a combination of penetrating internal attack surfaces, *adaptive* access control, and *adaptive* resource capture.

Formally resources are represented as $g_1:g_n$ where G is the overall system (as a resource). The goal of an adversary is to gain access to a coveted resource. The goal of a systems security professional is to protect coveted resources. Coveted resources have higher risk. Both systems and resources can be captured. However captured resources can be leveraged to reduce penetration effort in subsequent system captures (Adaptive Strategy).

Therefore the overall game of the adversary becomes—how to strategize to maximize overall gain of system resources while minimizing effort (optimal RoI). Part of the strategy is to pick the right entry points with the shortest/fastest vector to get to a node with gainful assets. To realize this attack strategy once potential entry points have been selected and the attacker establishes a best guesstimate of the vector path, the attacker will construct appropriate messages, factor in responses and build the attack strategy S.

This is how we would connect all the concepts we have laid out so far.

The role of the cybersecurity practitioner and system designers is to make entry point access harder (increase adversary effort to lower RoI), decrease the likelihood of penetration of each system, lengthen the attack vector path to increase adversary cost (e.g., by increasing partitioning between systems), and maximize protection strategies around gainful assets. This can be done using a combination of hardware and software security techniques and primitives. Mixing hardware (and even physically derived primitives) can be a very high return countermeasure as an adversary now has to find a way to bridge the gap between digital and physical systems (or between digital cyber and digital secure hardware).

4.3 "Connected" System Security Modeling

Now that we can specify system components, entry points, and the likelihood of penetration through an entry point, we can begin modeling connected systems.

We have seen two examples of connected systems thus far. Fig. 4.5 illustrates digitally interconnected subcomponents that pass data and control through them. Fig. 4.6 illustrates interconnected components that are potentially air gapped over one physical medium but may be connected via another. We will use the earlier figure for the purpose of modeling connected systems security.

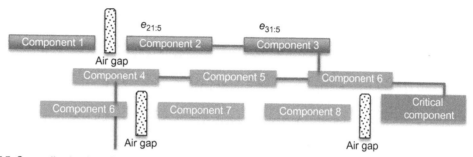

Figure 4.5 Generalized cyber-physical system from an interconnected composable perspective.

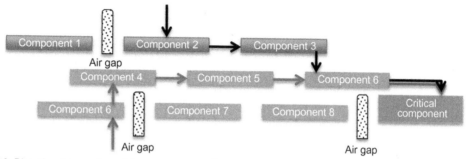

Figure 4.6 Directional impact on risk assessment and countermeasure design.

The best place to start would be at nodes that have no upstream, only downstream connections into the system under consideration. Typically, these are external facing points, and one can easily see that these will be potential attack entry points. Referring back to our example Figure 4.1, e_1, e_2, e_3, e_7, e_8, e_9, are external facing interfaces (Fig. 4.6).

We calculate the likelihood of penetration of each entry point. This is a security analytic operation in itself. We will find that the likelihood follows a Pareto distribution. Let us assign a symbolic notation w to each of them.

Therefore, risk at e_4

$$\mathscr{R}e_4 = e_1 w_1 + e_2 w_2 + e_3 w_3 + e_5 w_5 + e_6 w_6 + e_7 w_7,$$

Now, e_4 happens to have resources. If penetrated and e_4 is captured, then the adversary will have access to all the resources that e_4 has. The collective shared resources and private resources at e_4 is g_4. For example, here e_4 shares memory resources with e_5 and e_{10}, so part of g_4 comes from e_5 and e_{10}'s resources.

The aim of the adversary is to maximize gain g_4 while minimizing its effort leading into e_4. In other words the adversary needs to find the shortest, least resistance path to e_4 among e_1 to e_9.

Now, while the penetration itself has a likelihood of being successful, the adversary's choice of which entry point and what technique is not. It is a carefully crafted decision after assessment. Therefore, we use Wald's min max model [7] to pick decisions and create strategies that the adversary will use to play off the system. Note that we are using the adaptive online adversary which implies that the adversary builds its strategy by choosing messages, then letting the system respond and building on top of the response. The Wald's min max model suits this adaptive online adversary model very well because it is a nonprobabilistic, robust decision-making model in which the optimal decision (which is the overall intention for an optimal RoI) is one whose worst outcome is at least as good as the worst outcome in any other scenario.

Mathematically,

$$f^* = \max_{s \in \mathcal{S}} \min_{M \in \rho(S)} f(s, M)$$

where $\mathcal{S}$ is a set of alternate decisions, actions or strategies, $\rho(S)$ is the set of states associated with actionable message M, and $f(s, M)$ is the return of a strategy that takes place in the state of s.

In this manner a strategy S is selected and executed by an adversary that comprises of actionable messages M.

At the next node the adversary's advantage is evident as

$$f^* = \max_{s \in \mathcal{S}} g_{n=4} \cdot \min_{M \in \rho(S)} f(s, M)$$

In other words, for interconnected systems, the likelihood of success for an adversary, as the play develops increases since the adversary collects more resources (gains) as he proceeds.

4.4   Directional Threat Assessment

So far we have focused on external attack surfaces and the probability of an attacker penetrating the external surface to make their way *in* to a critical system (or component). Most often times, system designers miss the fact that attackers can exist on the inside of a system and work their way out. They either get in via a *physical* security lapse or, are *insiders* to begin with. This has been the predominant modus operandi in a vast majority of the successful high-profile attacks on CPSs we have seen recently [8–11]. Even if systems are built with more resistance to outside threat, they are built with almost no resistance going from inside out. As a result, the threat vector is asymmetric in one direction; there is significantly less work to be done to penetrate from the inside out.

Threat assessment ultimately should be *directionally oriented* because of this asymmetry.

Since we are holistically dealing with security evolution, measuring cybersecurity risk in CPSs with the intention of being able to prioritize, assign resources, and design countermeasures commensurate with risk, we must consider this type of attack as well. Additionally, insider attacks and IoT attacks fall into this category. Both types of attacks are the most common and most destructive types of attacks known today. And rightly so, most systems lack defenses against insider threats and IoT threats.

4.5 Big Picture CPS Systems—IoT

The approach presented in this chapter to new age online adversary modeling, modeling systems as a graph of interconnected nodes complete with individual resources and capabilities that can be conquered and leveraged, can with some expertise be applied at several different levels of abstraction. In this chapter we presented it for a single CPS system, say for example an automobile or a scada system. We modeled interactions, entry points, probabilities of being subverted, and sequential strategies at a single CPS level. By changing the level of abstraction from a single system point of view to larger systems point of view, we can model highly diverse systems of systems like those typical of the *IoT ecosystem*. Everything in the IoT is a CPS system. Therefore, by abstracting a given system as a larger IoT system, and then decomposing it into its individual CPS systems, one can model IoT security using the approach shown in this chapter. One can model an IoT adversary's strategies and moves, and upon successful automation of adversarial strategies, one can even create automated defenses for IoT.

4.6 Conclusion

In the course of this chapter, we began an honest discussion from the fundamental tenets of security and how they evolved from those for closed systems to those appropriate for connected cyberphysical systems. The right questions that were asked to visualize system behavior at system boundaries and model them as discrete interactions allowed us to formally specify these highly complex systems at their various attack surfaces. Correctly realizing an evolved adversary, at its full capabilities and intelligence more powerful than the typical offline adversary, enabled us to formally model and analyze the full extent of the damage an evolved adversary is capable of exerting. With a clear understanding of a system's capabilities, vulnerabilities, and available resources, we could then realize the full extent of protective measures needed and understand where they need to be localized for maximum protection and ROI. The novel use of the combination of graph theory to model a system, subsystem connections, and resources that can be leveraged, as they are owned and acquired along with powerful adaptive game theory to model adversary and defense strategies, allows us to automate the defense process. As the *game* develops further, our defense now has the intelligence to calculate what resources are now lost to adversarial control and the best strategic moves to be made, under ever changing circumstances, in order to mount a defense. In other words, we can create *autonomous defense systems* fully capable of detecting advanced persistent threats and making their best attempt to automatically respond and recover from them, i.e., the evolution of security from static authentication systems and cryptosystems to fully autonomous computing systems capable of automated defense. The future will simply be more automated and more autonomous intelligent system security.

References

[1] Geraint Price, The interaction between fault tolerance and security, Technical Report Number 479, UCAM-CL-TR-479, ISSN 1476-2986 Cambridge, UK, 1999.

[2] T. Anderson, P.A. Lee, Fault Tolerance: Principles and Practice, Prentice-Hall International, Englewood Cliffs, NJ, 1981.

[3] T. Anderson, P.A. Lee, S.K. Shrivastava, A model of recoverability in multi-level systems, IEEE Trans. Softw. Eng SE-4 (6) (1978) 486–494.

[4] V. Mishra, H. Dion, Y. Bar-Yam, Vulnerability analysis of high dimensional complex systems, in: S. Dolev, J. Cobb, M. Fischer, M. Yung (Eds.), Stabilization, Safety, and Security of Distributed Systems, Springer-Verlag, Berlin, 2010.

[5] Battelle, NEM–Automotive Intrusion detection system, Columbus, OH. < http://www.battelle.org/newsroom/press-releases/new-system-detects-and-alerts-to-automobile-cyber-attacks >, 2014.

[6] R. Stephens, Testing, Beginning Software Engineering (Chapter 8), John Wiley and Sons Publishing, 2015, p. 174.

[7] A. Wald, Statistical Decision Functions, Wiley, New York, NY, 1950.

[8] T. Maiziere, The IT Security in Germany in 2014 Publication, in: *Die Lage der IT-Sicherheit in Deutschland*, December 2014.

[9] R. Lee M. Assante, T. Conway, German Steel Mills Attack, in: SANS ICS Defense Control Use Case, Case Study 2, December 2014.

[10] D. Kushner, The real story of Stuxnet, IEEE Spectrum 50 (3) (2013) 48–53.

[11] A. Greenberg, Hackers remotely kill a Jeep Cherokee on the highway—with me in it, Wired Magazine (Online edition) (July 2015).

THE BUSINESS OF SAFETY

J.D. Miller

ZF TRW, Farmington Hills, MI, United States

5.1 Introduction

This chapter discusses safety of a system from the perspective of system producers. We illustrate the practice of product or system safety through the example of system safety in the automobile industry. Automobiles are some of the most widely deployed, complex systems in our society. While their drivers have a minimal amount of preparation or training to operate them, these systems are growing more complex by the day. Current plans to deploy connected, autonomous vehicles will only increase the challenge both to drivers and to those responsible for the safety of the system.

The title of this chapter "The Business of Safety" is intended to address several questions that will be discussed here, like: What is system safety about? What is it made up of? What do people in this "business" do? What are their fundamental activities and concerns? What do they need to carry on their business? What do they actually produce and how does that relate to the other activities necessary for producing the whole product?

This chapter considers each link in the entire supply chain for automotive as producers. Each has a role in ensuring the safety of the vehicle produced for the general public. This chapter discusses safety from the perspective of those who are responsible for producing a safe product. This is a different perspective than those who are purchasing the vehicle. This is a different perspective than those who are regulating it. This is different from those who consult and advise about it. Nevertheless, it is important that each of these understands the viewpoint of the producer. This perspective determines product safety.

Having said this, the producers need to satisfy the expectations of their customers, including the end user. Continuous improvement is expected by all customers in all areas, including safety.

Handbook of System Safety and Security. DOI: http://dx.doi.org/10.1016/B978-0-12-803773-7.00005-X

The business drives both differentiations of product, as well as assurance that the commonly understood state of the art is respected concerning safety. This is partially supported by regulation. However, regulation must, by its nature, lag the state of art and science. The vehicle manufacturers and Tier 1 suppliers drive inclusion of state-of-the-art technology while still ensuring that the regulations are met. Thus safety is driven by producers.

Clearly, there is demand for safety. This demand results in the consumption of products differentiated by safety and that are trusted. This trust is built on history, experience, regulation, and image. Safe, trustworthy products are demanded. The producers compete to supply this demand. They manage resources to supply it. It is a business.

5.2 Life Cycle of Safety

5.2.1 Definition of Safety

The word "safety" is used with different connotations in different domains, and even in the domain of automotive producers. Sometimes safety has been discussed as absolutely no harm to people or even no accidents whether there is harm to people or not. This definition can lead to useful analysis and results [1]. Since there are accidents, the products today would not be described as safe using this definition. Despite the efforts of producers, the driver can still cause an accident. Producers strive to prevent this.

Another approach is to define safety as freedom from unacceptable risk [2]. In this definition safety is not absolute. The concept of risk is introduced. Risk may be subjective, but for purposes of determining safety, the level of risk is assessed with rules or efforts to quantify the risk. The severity of the mishap is quantified, usually based on the extent of the potential loss. This loss may be restricted to harm to people. Then the frequency of the event that may cause the mishap is considered. To be safe the risk must be tolerable. This depends on the norms of society. Context is taken into account.

A now common definition will be used in this chapter. It is to define safety as the absence of unreasonable risk [3]. This definition also introduces the concept of risk and is similar to the previous definition from which it was derived. The probability of some level of harm resulting from a mishap, the ability to avoid that harm, and the exposure to situations that may result in the mishap are all taken into account. A judgment about acceptability is left to others. That the risk involved is reasonable may be determined by the measures taken to prevent the mishap. Many of these measures are discussed in Ref. [3]. Other measures may be taken. This results in "no unreasonable risk" and safety, in the above sense of the word, is achieved.

5.2.2   Safety Life Cycle of the Product

Every product has a life cycle, a beginning and an end. However the safety life cycle of products varies from product to product. Consider a utility plant as a product. Safety may be achieved by the plant in the end, but the plant matures over time to become safe. First the plant is designed and built. Then safety mechanisms are added to mitigate risks and ensure safety. The plant then starts operation.

Automotive products have a different safety life cycle. The business activity itself requires differentiation, to distinguish its product and attract buyers, so different concepts are developed. The product must be safe in concept. After an initial product concept is achieved, the design activity is performed. This design also must take into account safety measures. The product must be safe in design. The design is then manufactured and must be safe in manufacture. How the consumer will use the product is taken into account. The product must be safe in use. All automotive products are exposed to the possible need for maintenance. The product must be safe in maintenance. Finally the product's life comes to an end. It must be safe in disposal.

5.2.3   Evaluating Risk

To determine safety, the risk must be determined. The risk being considered here is the risk of harm to people. The authority of the product is considered when determining the role the product may have in causing harm to people. If the product is a system, this determination can start by analyzing what actuation of any of the product's functions, included in the system as a whole, can do. Frequently guidewords are used to systematically determine what harm actuation of system function can bring with it when it exhibits what is called *malfunctioning behavior*. For example, we consider whether harm can result for each of the functions if it has the following potential malfunctions:
1. Too much
2. Too little
3. Wrong timing
4. In error
5. None

This malfunction, of the given system function, is then cascaded up to the vehicle level to determine if harm may result. To illustrate this, consider a steering actuator in an automobile. If the steering actuator provides steering assistance in error (guideword **4**), when not requested by the driver or inappropriately in the case of automated steering function, such as steering in the "wrong direction," this may cause the vehicle itself to turn in the wrong direction and lead to the vehicle departing from its lane of travel. A lane departure could result in a wide variety of types of accident, such as sideswiping a neighboring vehicle, a head-on collision, or a rear-end collision. This has potential for serious harm. This reasoning is then repeated for each of the guidewords in the list.

To further determine risk, system communications are also considered, including communications between the subsystems of the vehicle as well as between vehicle and driver and, in future connected vehicles, between the vehicle system and other vehicles or infrastructure. This includes messages sent and received. Again these are systematically analyzed. For example, consider if harm can result for each of the following communication malfunctions:

1. No communication
2. Communication error
3. Communicates with the wrong timing
   a. Late
   b. Early
   c. Frequency

Again this is cascaded up to the vehicle level. To illustrate, again consider a steering system providing a *steering angle signal* that may be used by a stability control system. Depending on the diagnostic capability of the receiving system, the ability to assess the "health" of the sending system for error or fault, this could lead to an intervention by the stability control system that could lead to a lane departure at the vehicle level. The same evaluation as above for this actuation may result. This again has potential for harm. As in the previous example, this reasoning is then repeated for each of the *communication malfunctions* guidewords.

5.2.4 Exposure to Risk

The potential for harm is evaluated in different driving situations. Such situations include highway driving, country road driving, parking, and other situations. These situations and other considerations are described in Ref. [4]. The quantification of this potential for harm may be determined using traffic statistics from various sources. Both Refs. [3,4] refer to this. This helps quantify risk by relating it to the likelihood of being exposed to it.

Not all risks are discussed in Refs. [3,4]. It is also important to consider harm that may result from fire, smoke, and toxicity. Often toxicity is considered in the choice of materials for the product. Fire and smoke are considered for the case when the vehicle is occupied and also for the case when the vehicle is not occupied. In the case when it is occupied, the ability to control the vehicle is considered. This will vary if the system is in or out of the passenger compartment. When the vehicle is not occupied, the potential for harm due to fire and smoke is controlled by the ability of the system to be supplied with energy. External switching may reduce this probability to a reasonable level without further consideration within the system. Otherwise further consideration may be warranted. The harm could be catastrophic.

In determining risk, we also consider the duration or frequency of exposure to the situations that provide an opportunity for harm caused by the product. For example, if each exposure may be a trigger for harm due to a latent product malfunction, then frequency is important. Otherwise duration, such as driving in rain, is considered. This is further discussed in Ref. [4]. Then the risks can be prioritized. This can be done for malfunctions, for example, using the automotive safety integrity level (ASIL) of a system function found in Ref. [3]. For other cases that are out of scope of Ref. [3], a similar prioritization can be done. It should be done systematically. The same principles apply.

5.2.5   Reducing the Risk

To reduce the risk to an acceptable level, the safety requirements for each life cycle phase are determined. For example, to have safety of the concept, the requirements for the concept to be safe are determined. This is repeated for each phase. The requirements are then verified.

5.2.6   Concept

To determine the requirements for a concept, the concept is expressed as an architecture in which the functional requirements are understood for each functional block. Then this architecture can be systematically analyzed to determine the safety requirements. A systematic analysis gives confidence that the requirements are complete. Such systematic analyses include the following:

1. Fault Tree Analysis (FTA)
2. Event Tree Analysis (ETA)
3. Diagnostic coverage
4. Requirements from other systems

Requirements from all other systems are always considered. An FTA is especially useful at the block level for determining what type of *failure combinations* may lead to a hazard. If a single failure may lead to a hazard, then it must be determined if the probability of such a failure is sufficiently remote, such as a mechanical failure where there is adequate design margin in a well-understood technology. For example, consider the strength of the rack in a rack-and-pinion steering system. If a single failure is not sufficiently remote, requirements may be elicited to create redundancies.

An ETA is particularly useful in determining the effect of functional failures. Each function of each block may be evaluated considering, for example, if it fails to execute, executes incorrectly or with the wrong timing. If a hazard may result, then there is a requirement for a safety mechanism to *independently* prevent the hazard. The independence is required so that this failure fault does not also disable the safety mechanism.

Diagnostic coverage is similar. If a fault can lead to an unsafe or a hazardous failure, then a specific diagnostic needs to be implemented to detect the fault and prevent the unsafe failure by implementing a safe state of operation. The diagnostic type provides the required coverage. This leads to specific requirements.

There is confidence that these safety requirements are complete when the systematic analyses are complete. This requires review of the analyses. It may be by an *independent peer review*. Another means of performing the review is through *simulation of the requirements* and the response to inserted faults to determine if the faults are properly managed.

The *safety requirements* are then assigned to architectural blocks. These are the same architectural blocks that represent system functional requirements. Each safety requirement is *uniquely identified, atomic, and verifiable*. To avoid complexity, the safety requirements and architecture are hierarchical. Lower level safety requirements satisfy the parent safety requirements. These safety requirements are split between hardware and software safety requirements. In addition, safety requirements are assigned to other systems to document assumptions concerning the behavior of these systems to achieve safety. This supports subsequent verification.

5.2.7   Design

The design is made consistent to the architecture. This allows the design to be created to satisfy the safety requirements directly. Then *traceable hardware safety requirements* can be derived from the architectural requirements to enable requirements-based detailed hardware design. Further hardware safety analyses may be performed to derive further safety requirements that may emerge from the design chosen. Such analyses may include analyses of single point failures and dual point failures. Such analyses are described in Ref. [3].

In a similar manner, *traceable software safety requirements* can be derived from the architectural requirements to enable requirements-based detailed hardware design. Further software safety analyses may be performed to derive further safety requirements that may emerge from the design chosen. A potential analysis useful for this is an ETA as described in the concept discussion earlier. This is useful to elicit safety requirements to cope with the software reaction to the exception of a hardware failure. The design may be improved to meet these safety requirements. Systematic software errors can be controlled by following a mature software process. This is not discussed here. Sometimes diverse software is used.

After the design is complete, it is verified to meet the safety requirements. Appropriate methods are chosen for verification. For example, if Ref. [3] has been used, then methods may be chosen based on ASIL. The actual verification detail, such as the test case, is identified for each safety requirement. The verification method is executed. Verification is performed hierarchically from bottom to top. The result of each executed verification method is reviewed to determine if the pass criteria have been met, and the result of this review is recorded. All nonconformances are resolved. To ensure completeness of verification, a systematic review of the status of all requirements and verification is implemented. Sometimes automation may help determine status. This simplifies the review process.

5.2.8   Manufacturing

The intent of safety in manufacturing is to retain the safety designed, throughout component production and assembly and into the product when it is manufactured. To elicit the complete set of safety requirements to ensure this, systematic analyses are performed. These include the *design failure modes and effects analysis* (dFMEA) and the *process failure modes and effects analysis* (pFMEA). The dFMEA can elicit critical characteristics to be controlled in manufacturing. Appropriate process controls are implemented to achieve the critical characteristics. The pFMEA elicits safety requirements to mitigate any process errors that may affect safety. Again, process controls are mitigated. The manufacturing organization provides feedback to the product design organization if these requirements cannot be met. Appropriate changes are implemented.

The *manufacturing safety requirements* are documented and traced to the process. This includes any configurable software, for example. When a manufacturing process change is proposed, these safety requirements are taken into account. Thus it can be ensured that the improved process is as safe as the process it replaces. No unreasonable risk is introduced.

5.2.9 Maintenance

When considering safety in maintenance, the user's manual is also considered as well as the maintenance manual. Warnings are included about potential misuse as well as expected maintenance. For example, for a convenience system such as adaptive cruise control, any limitations such as weather or stationary object detection are explained. This calibrates the user's expectations or sets user expectations appropriately. This calibration can be further reinforced through the message center in the automobile. Then the appropriate message is repeatedly presented at the appropriate time to support the user's understanding.

The maintenance instructions take into account safety in installation. For some systems, misalignment may lead to potential hazards. A warning and instructions may be included. Likewise, for example, torque applied to bolts in the steering intermediate shaft may be critical. A warning and specification may be included. As needed, information concerning diagnostic tests or messages is included. If replacement is necessary for safety instead of repair, then this is made clear. Likewise, instructions may be needed for some foreseeable maintenance anomalies, for example, instructions on what to do if the system is accidently dropped. Is it possible to check for damage? May it be used?

In addition to maintaining safety of the system, safety of the maintenance personnel is also taken into account. Any kind of stored energy may require measures to ensure that the maintenance personnel are not injured by its release, for example. Warning labels and maintenance manual warnings may be appropriate. Also, inadvertent motion may be considered, such as movement of an electric steering system connected to a battery while on a hoist. Disconnection may be recommended.

For continuous improvement, field data from performed maintenance may be helpful. This may be especially important for new systems during its initial introduction. Instructions on what data to record and return may be included. In this way, improvement of the instructions and product is supported.

5.2.10 Disposal

Disposal is normally the final phase of the product's life cycle. Many of the comments made above for maintenance are also appropriate for disposal. In the case of stored energy, it may be appropriate to discharge this energy when disposed. Airbags may be discharged when the vehicle is disposed. If there is a possibility that a system may be salvaged for reuse as used equipment, any safety requirements may be considered such as requirements to prevent an inappropriate installation due to calibration for another vehicle. Design measures may be possible. In addition the useful lifetime may be specified. A warning may be included.

5.3 Management of Functional Safety

5.3.1 Purpose

To ensure that safety is properly considered throughout the product, life cycle requires diligence. Therefore a systematic process is established for this purpose. Then this process can be managed; the tasks identified, resourced, and executed. The process creates evidence, such as work products, that this systematic process is followed. This evidence together with a safety argument becomes the safety case: evidence that the safety requirements have been elicited and evidence of compliance. With no evidence, there is no case.

5.3.2 Pillars of a Safety Process

A safety process can have 3 pillars: policy, audit and assessment, and implementation. These can be established independently. For example, independence of the assessment activity from the implementation activity can help ensure diligence. Such independence is recommended in Ref. [3].

An overall organizational policy helps ensure consistency, helps ensure uniform diligence, and helps ensure that best practices for safety are adapted across the organization. These best practices may include both analysis methods to elicit safety requirements and methods to trace these requirements. Also the overall organizational safety policy can set forth the strategy of how the organization will integrate a safety process into the organization's development process. This integration is important to the developers. At the end of the development life cycle, the developers will have completed whatever process they were following. It is important that all considerations were taken into account, because closing gaps at the end may not be possible. This may be especially true for safety. Safety considerations start in the concept phase. Then they are implemented.

Audit and assessment are independent of the developers implementing the process. In Ref. [3] this is to include independence from the organization responsible to release the product. The audit is to ensure that the developers follow the process in the overall organizational safety policy. Nonconformances to this policy can then be independently escalated to executive management for action. Such audits ensure diligence.

Assessment is performed on the evidence that the process is being followed, such as work products. These work products are to show that the safety requirements have been systematically elicited. An example may be the single point fault metric of Ref. [3]. It is intended to contain all the safety-related hardware and have diagnostic measures appropriate for the ASIL. Again, independent assessment ensures diligence.

To control that the process is followed, it helps to measure what is expected. It is expected that the process delivers artifacts that demonstrate that the safety requirements have been elicited for each phase of the safety life cycle. It is also expected that compliance is demonstrated during each phase of the safety life cycle. For those requirements that fall within the scope of Ref. [3], the safety work products for each phase are defined in Ref. [3]. The requirements for these work products, and other safety requirements not in the scope of Ref. [3], can be satisfied by the work products of the organization's development process. Metrics can be developed to indicate that this is achieved when it needs to be achieved to follow the safety process. Then there is confidence or *assurance* that the resulting products will be safe. It should be noted that failure to follow the process does not mean that the product is defective. In this case the evidence may be missing. Favorable metrics improve the confidence. Diligence is demonstrated.

To implement the safety process, each project that will release a product to the general public, includes plans to implement the safety process. The tasks to produce meaningful artifacts required by the safety process are identified for each phase of the safety life cycle. These tasks are then resourced adequately and planned to be executed on time. This requires that the scope of work is identified, for example, using a change impact analysis to determine what is planned to be changed from a baseline product and if product safety could be affected. Then the tasks are planned for those phases that may have a safety impact. A supportive environment for carrying out these changes is established. This includes change control and documentation. Requirements management is supported.

The analysis planned to elicit the safety requirements for these affected life cycle phases is performed. For example, if potentially safety-related changes to software are planned, then an ETA may be performed on those software modules involved in the change. An independent assessment is performed of this analysis. The analysis may be improved if necessary for acceptance. Safety requirements may be identified for these software modules, other software modules, or safety requirements may be identified for hardware, the system, or other systems. These requirements are captured so that they may be included in the design. Then the design tasks are executed. Verification tasks are executed to ensure compliance of the design to the identified safety requirements. The report of this verification is reviewed. Any noncompliance is resolved. The results are recorded.

To implement a project in this way, a *safety culture* in needed. The importance of safety in the product development process is recognized throughout the organization. This includes executive management to approve resources, project management to plan and allocate resources, and the development personnel. To obtain this recognition requires the support of management. When this support is evident, then training is offered and this training will be embraced. The training also includes training for management. Expectations become consistent.

5.3.3 Organization

There are 5 key requirements for a successful safety organization:

1. The organization must have the talent to perform the safety tasks.
2. Safety must be integral to product engineering.

3. There must be a career path for Safety Personnel to retain them in a safety role.
4. The safety process must be owned by program management so that the tasks can be planned, resourced, and executed.
5. There needs to be a periodic executive review cadence to ensure that the process is followed.

There are different organizational implementations to satisfy these 5 requirements for a successful safety organization. Each different organizational implementation has advantages and disadvantages. Consider a central organization. In this implementation the Head of Safety either manages or may be the safety auditor. The safety auditor checks each project to determine if the safety process is being followed. The safety assessors may report to the safety auditor. The safety assessors determine if the artifacts generated by the safety process are adequate for their purpose, and timely in their creation. This puts the safety assessors in a position to collect the data necessary for the metrics used to measure safety process conformance. The safety managers and engineers may report to the safety assessors. The safety managers and engineers are deployed to engineering projects where they participate in the product development process, plan, and help create the safety artifacts, such as a hazard and risk analysis.

There are advantages for a central organization. Each level of management is skilled in safety. This helps to foster technical competence. There is a clear career path to retain safety personnel in a safety role. It can include management or may be structured to also include a purely technical path. Because it is central, there is a structural foundation to support consistency in implementation of the safety process across different products the organization is developing. This can be encouraged by job rotation. There can also be load leveling across products. This also helps consistency.

There can also be disadvantages to a central safety organization. Even though the resources are deployed to support engineering, the rest of engineering may tend to take less responsibility for implementation of the safety process. There are many tasks necessary to launch a product. Product engineering may prioritize those not perceived to have support from the central safety organization. Also, because there are different organizations, the communication paths may not be well established. This is important so that safety-related changes are evaluated promptly. Also, safety requirements need to be communicated. Effective communication is needed.

A decentralized organization may also implement the 5 requirements for a successful safety organization. In a decentralized organization the safety auditor and assessor are organized separately from product development engineering. This is needed to achieve the required independence. The safety managers and engineers are assigned and managed by product engineering. They report directly into product engineering. The decentralized organization has the advantage that safety personnel are integrated directly into product engineering organization without "deployment." Domain knowledge of the product is increased through normal maturing due to focused engineering experience. Organizational communication may be established.

There are also disadvantages in this case. A career path needs to be established to retain personnel in a safety role or turnover will result. This may be established by a technical career path or ladder for safety, a product engineering safety management path, or a combination. The management in product engineering that is responsible for the safety personnel may not be as skilled in safety management and analyses as the personnel being managed. Measures may need to be established for continuous training of the management and safety personnel. This may be from internal assessors or externally. An independent review and escalation path needs to be established. This may use internal or external assessors. Executives should always be included.

5.4 Conclusion

In this chapter the definition of safety used is *the state of no unreasonable risk*. There is risk present and generally assumed in any activity and the use of any product today. This risk includes the risk of harm to people. The "true north" for product safety is that safety is incremental. It is that this risk not be increased by the products being introduced over the risk of the products being replaced. If the risk of the products being renewed or replaced is viewed as reasonable, then the risk of the product being introduced may then be considered reasonable. The product may be considered safe. This point of view relies on our ability to measure risk while being sensitive to changes in the perception of risk. Over time society has tolerated, on the whole, less and less risk and periodically governments and authorities have codified growing risk intolerance in regulations intended to enforce a higher standard for concerns such as safety.

Normally, product safety cannot be proven or demonstrated absolutely. However the determination or assurance of safety may and does consider evidence and arguments for safety. The evidence is to demonstrate that the safety requirements have been elicited correctly and evidence of compliance to these requirements. Confidence that the requirements are complete is improved with the use of systematic analyses, guided by standards representing consensus. This is the stuff of which safety arguments are made. Independent assessment improves confidence.

This evidence and argument can comprehend the entire product life cycle. The evidence is systematically compiled while the product is conceived and developed. The requirements for each life cycle phase are elicited. This includes the concept, design, manufacture, use, maintenance, and disposal. The requirements are implemented and verified. Both play a critical role in the safety argument.

A safety process and organization may be established. They can be used to manage the resources needed to fulfill the demand for safety. All products are expected and demanded to be safe and ultimately business is a competition to meet all such demands on products.

References

[1] N.C. Leveson, Engineering a Safer World, MIT Press, January 2012.
[2] IEC 61508 (all parts), Functional Safety of Electrical/Electronic/Programmable Electronic Safety-Related Systems, International Electrotechnical Commission, April 2010.
[3] ISO 26262 (all parts), Road Vehicle—Functional Safety, International Standards Organization, November 2011.
[4] SAE J2980, Considerations for ISO 26262 ASIL Hazard Classification, SAE International, May 2015.

6

CYBERSECURITY FOR COMMERCIAL ADVANTAGE

J.M. Kaplan
McKinsey and Company, New York, NY, United States

Most senior management teams and board of directors are starting to understand how damaging cyberattacks can be to their business. On-line fraud and crime can cost a company tens or hundreds of millions of dollars. Loss of sensitive personal information upsets customers, and in some cases, can depress revenues and create massive legal and regulatory exposure. Exfiltration of intellectual property can diminish the value of billions of dollars' worth of investment in research and development. Theft of sensitive business plans can upend critical pricing or negotiation strategies. And, given that most companies cannot operate without access to core systems, destructive attacks can threaten the viability of the business itself.

No company is an island in dealing with these risks. Companies share sensitive data like production plans and product specifications with their vendors, and they accept sensitive data from their customers. Everyone understands that banks have sensitive personal financial data and hospital networks have sensitive patient medical records, but almost every type of company receives sensitive data from its customers. IT service provides have critical details about their customers' networks and technology environments. Commercial insurance carriers collect sensitive data about manufacturing facilities to perform underwriting. Many types of manufacturers receive sensitive product or operational information from their customers.

Moreover, in an increasingly digital world, companies are interconnecting their technology environments with suppliers and customers to create business processes that collect, analyze, and act on massive amounts of data in real time. Already medical device and industrial equipment manufacturers install

Handbook of System Safety and Security. DOI: http://dx.doi.org/10.1016/B978-0-12-803773-7.00006-1

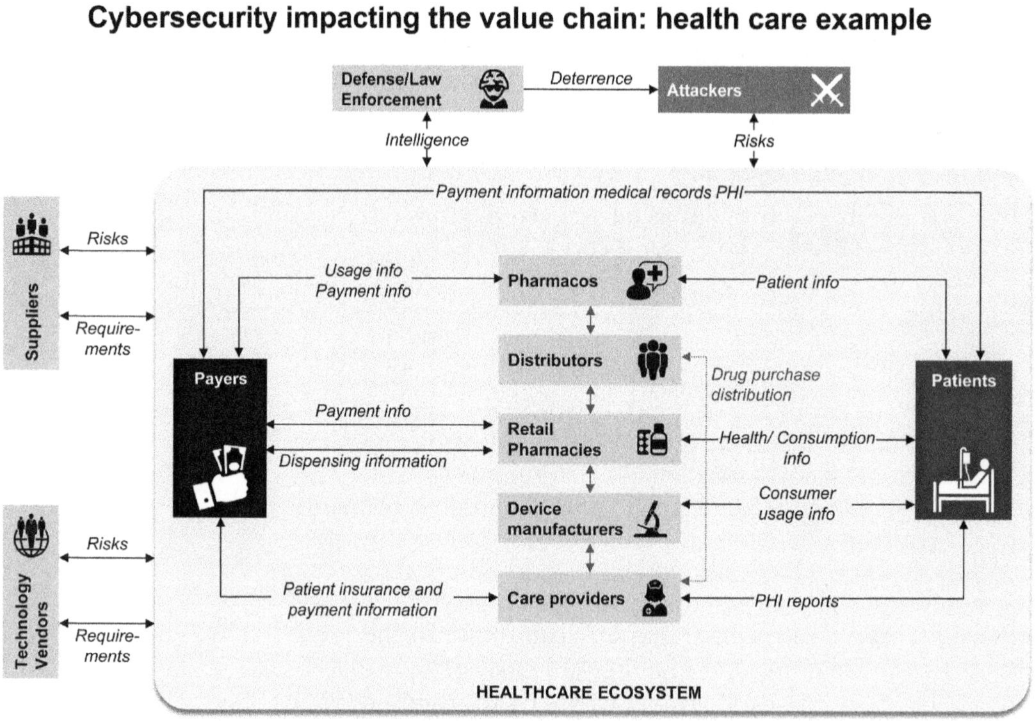

Cybersecurity impacting the value chain: health care example

Exhibit 1 Cybersecurity implications are pervasive across the value chain.

products that maintain real-time connections to aggregate performance and maintenance information.[1]

Given this, *cybersecurity concerns are starting to reshape value chains*, sometimes for better, sometimes for worse. As companies exchange sensitive data and interconnect their technology environments, cybersecurity necessarily becomes a commercial and contractual issue—companies are making cybersecurity capabilities an important criterion in sourcing decisions and conducting complex negotiations over the contractual terms and conditions mandating how their data will be handled. In some cases, this has been an enormously positive development. Commercial pressure can be a more compelling, and more surgically precise, incentive for improved cybersecurity capabilities than any regulatory mandate.

[1]J.M. Kaplan, T. Bailey, D. O'Halloran, A. Marcus, C. Rezek, *Beyond Cybersecurity: Protecting Your Digital Business*, Wiley, 2015.

However, given that most companies still treat cybersecurity as a "backoffice" or "control" functional, they have not yet been able to *integrate cybersecurity into their commercial interactions* either with suppliers or with customers. As a result, cybersecurity is already creating a significant turbulence in the value chain, slowing down collaboration between companies and, potentially, reducing competitiveness and innovation in some markets.

Companies need to place an explicitly commercial lens on cybersecurity, coolly assessing business risks and incorporating these risks' implications deeply into procurement, product development, sales, service, and procurement processes. The companies that do this most aggressively will not only reduce their risk but also *increase their operating efficiency and improve their value* proposition with customers.

6.1 Turbulence Along the Value Chain

It would slightly unfair to say that nobody cared about cybersecurity a decade ago, but only by a little bit. Outside of a few sectors like aerospace and defense, even Chief Information Officers (CIOs) devoted little time and attention to protecting information assets from attackers. Not only did many organizations not have Chief Information Security Officers (CISOs), but for them "IT security" meant the tech support staff who ran the antivirus or remote access environment. Basic protections for the network perimeter might be in place, but, insecure application architectures and infrastructure configurations were pervasive—and consequences for flouting security policies all but nonexistent. Threats and risks that followed legitimate entry across the network perimeter or asynchronous attacks were all but ignored. Needless to say, senior business managers considered security to be a "back office" function—requiring far less of their time than other IT issues.[2]

[2]J.M. Kaplan, T. Bailey, D. O'Halloran, A. Marcus, C. Rezek, *Beyond Cybersecurity: Protecting Your Digital Business*, Wiley, 2015.

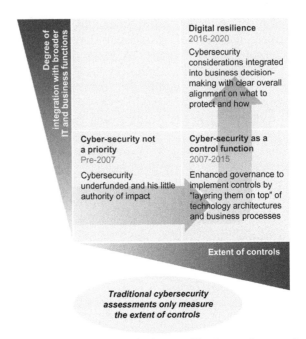

Exhibit 2 Most companies have made the transition from cybersecurity not being a priority to managing it via a "control function."

Over time, increasingly aggressive cyberattackers forced companies to revise their model. They vastly expanded the extent of controls, even if they failed to integrate security considerations more deeply into business processes and technology environments. Companies hired CISOs and enhanced the governance and oversight authority for the cybersecurity team. At their CISOs' direction, they disseminated policies, locked down end-user environments, and put in security architecture reviews for new applications. All this was necessary—without these steps there would have been many more breaches on the front pages of major newspapers. However these steps most often involved the security team saying "No" to certain initiatives and layering sometimes clunky and end-user-experience-detrimental security elements on top of new and existing applications. This has slowed innovation, reduced end-user productivity, and reduced resources available for business projects. It has also created turbulence in commercial interactions by slowing contracting processes, reducing vendor leverage, and attenuating customer experiences.

6.1.1 Slower Contracting Processes

Businesses entrust their vendors with tremendous amounts of sensitive data that could be extremely valuable to attackers, for example

- Employee data to payroll processes and other HR providers
- Customer data to ad agencies and marketing analytics companies
- Financial data to accountancies and investment banks
- Technology configuration information outsourced to service providers
- Product specifications and release dates to engineering or manufacturing partners

Some of the sensitive data may not be immediately obvious. Who thinks about the sensitive data concerned with facilities, for example, that companies provide to insurance carriers as part of the underwriting process. Large companies will often maintain relationships with thousands of vendors who have access to sensitive corporate data in one way or another.

Companies have responded with mechanisms they believe will reduce their exposure to vendor risks. They require new suppliers to fill out surveys with hundreds of questions, participate in architectural reviews, and submit to site visits. They also demand very specific terms and conditions for how data will be protected.

While necessary, all of this is not only resource and time consuming, but it also slows down the contracting processes both because of the time required to evaluate vendors and because of the time required for suppliers and customers to agree on such terms. For example, when we convened a group of entrepreneurial software companies' CEOs to talk about security, they told us that their sales cycle had doubled in length over the past 2 years because they first had to sell to the CIO or business owner and then conduct an equally involved process with the CISO. In some cases commitments of unlimited liability for the impact of data breaches they had made to get critical, early sales were complicating funding transactions—as venture capitalist or private equity firms discovered unlimited liability commitments in their due diligence processes. Likewise, executives at application services firms told us that commitments about liability for data breaches were often one of the "long poles in the tent" in coming to terms in for an outsourcing deal.

These types of impacts are not limited to the technology sector. In some cases investment banking transactions can get held up by data security concerns. One bank saw a large derivatives transaction held up for months because nobody fully understand all the parties who would receive the personal information associated with servicing the underlying mortgages and how that data would be protected. Sometimes customer demands about data protection conflict with regulatory mandates, creating further churn and delay. In negotiations, one bank demanded that its potential provider of mortgage insurance purge underlying customer data after 90 days. However, some (but not all) states required mortgage insurance providers to retain underlying personal data for the life of the mortgage.

6.1.2 Reducing Vendor Leverage and Reshaping Markets

In addition, mechanisms that companies have put in place to manage vendor risks can reduce vendor leverage and reshape markets.

In most companies, CISOs and security teams have succeeded in convincing procurement organizations that contracting processes have to take security requirements into account. However relatively simplistic and siloed interaction models between security and procurement teams can reduce vendor leverage and, may, over time reshape markets in ways the reduce competitiveness and slow the pace of innovation.

How does this happen? In drafting a request for proposal, the procurement organization will look to the security organization for "requirements" to be included in the document, just as they ask for requirements from the "business owner," who will use the product or service and other functional stakeholders, like the legal and compliance organizations. In this type of model, it is very easy for the CISO to throw all sorts of requirements "over the wall" to procurement for inclusion into an RFP based on a theoretical perspective on "best practices" (e.g., data can never be shared with subcontractors under any circumstances), without a practical discussion between security and procurement about what requirements really matter given the service in question, what vendors are likely to be able to do and how to make tradeoffs between requirements and ultimate cost impacts.

As a result, RFPs can get loaded up with noncritical security requirements that eliminate some vendors, reducing negotiating leverage, and bring others to increase their estimates of what it would cost to fulfill the contract. One large company saw 9 of 11 potential bidders disqualified for security reasons, dramatically attenuating its negotiating position and causing the ultimate contract to cost tens of millions of dollars more than expected.

However the impacts of security on procurement processes could become far more pernicious over time. Large companies can better bear the cost of security requirements because they can amortize them over a broader set of customers. They can invest in dedicated teams to respond to extensive security questionnaires. Incumbent vendors have an advantage in that they have already demonstrated their security capabilities to a company already.

As a company considers a new type software that it wants to implement quickly, say it can choose between an offering from one of its incumbent vendors and a relatively new attacker. Given the desire for speed, there could well be an organizational inclination to say "We have got to do this quickly. We understand the incumbent vendor's security model. It will take us a couple of months to get this startup to answer the hundreds of questions our security assessment requirements. Let us just go with the company we know." That is a perfectly rational decision, but over time, hundreds of perfectly rational decisions like that can harden markets, making it more difficult for new and innovative companies to gain traction.

6.1.3 Attenuating Customer Experiences

One capital markets CIO we know is fond of saying "In the past, for our customers, the API to our company was a phone call. In the future, the API for us will be an API." As companies seek to become digital businesses, more and more of their interactions with customers will take place on-line, either via a web portal, a mobile app or machine-to-machine communications. This on-line interaction includes everything from a consumer checking her bank balance to a jet engine "phoning home" so it can transmit usage and performance data to facilitate proactive maintenance.

However, any on-line process depends on authentication (validating that the user is who he, or it, claims to be) and authorization (checking that the user has the rights to access the data or undertake the transaction requested). Unfortunately, in the face of ever more sophisticated attackers the authentication model built up over the first two decades of the on-line economy is increasingly less tenable. Most companies realize that simple, static passwords that customers share across many sites provide little protection against sophisticated attackers—is utterly meaningless in a world where the "user" may be an automobile, a thermostat, a refrigerator, a jet engine, or a medical device.

Unfortunately, organizational silos between the marketing, product development, customer care, application development, and security functions often result in frustrating customer experiences as companies seek to better protect their customer interactions. As with procurement, the security team can load up a consumer-facing process with a list of "requirements," resulting in more complicated password rules, confusing interfaces, repeated requests for credentials and bewildering "challenge questions." Take just the last of these. Even if a customer remembers what he said was his favorite course when he opened the account, would he remember whether he entered the course name, the course number, or both together. This causes many customers to say, "This is too hard. Let me just dial the call center," slowing the adoption of digital processes and loading many companies with excess costs.

The same dynamic applies in business-to-business markets. CISOs at hospital networks will often express frustration at how medical device manufacturers address device security. They say that device manufacturers have not fully acknowledged that hospitals are highly sophisticated and integrated technology environments in their own right. As a result, the security model for many medical devices assumes that they will be deployed atomistically, rather than as part of a hospital network, making both authentication to the hospital network and connection to the manufacturers' network more complicated. As a result, many hospital network CISOs say that they often have to delay the introduction of connected medical devices by a year or more while they determine how to implement them securely.

6.2 Resilience for Commercial Advantage

If managing cybersecurity as a control function results in slower contracting processes, reduced vendor leverage, and more friction with customers, what can companies do to put in place a cybersecurity model that protects sensitive information while minimizing negative commercial impacts for their interactions with suppliers and customers? How can they turn protection of business information from a source of frustration to a source of commercial advantage?

The experience of the US auto manufacturers with quality management may provide something of an example and a direction. In the 1970s auto manufacturers tried to ensure quality by "inspecting it in." They examined shipments they received from vendors for flaws, and they placed quality inspectors at the end of production lines to check if, for example, the suspension had been appropriately attached to the chassis. This proved to be phenomenally ineffective and expensive. Even the most diligent inspector missed many problems, meaning that the average car had at least one production defect. Defects inspectors did find were equally problematic: they resulted in lots full of cars behind factories waiting for remediation—and tying up expensive working capital.

Eventually the auto manufacturers realized that to meet customer expectations about quality and cost, they would have to build quality into their business model. They started connecting plant managers with product engineers in order to design cars that were easier to manufacturer well. They started very interactive dialogs with their suppliers about how to collaborate in order to reduce defects. They started to redesign front-line activities so that it was difficult to attach a suspension to the chassis incorrectly. And they created a culture of quality throughout the organization, so that any worker was able to stop the line if he or she saw a problem.

Companies need to do the same thing in protecting their sensitive data. They need to move from layering security on top to achieving resilience by building security into their business model. In McKinsey's joint research with the World Economic Forum, we identified 7 levers for achieving Digital Resilience.

1. Prioritize information assets and related risks in a way that helps engage business leaders
2. Enlist front-line personnel—helping them understand value of information assets
3. Integrate cyberresilience into enterprise-wide management and governance processes
4. Integrated incident response across business functions, enhanced by realistic testing
5. Develop deep integration of security into the technology environment to drive scalability
6. Provide differentiated protection for most important assets
7. Deploy active defenses to be proactive in uncovering attacks early[3]

Interviews with executives at more than 100 institutions made it clear that collectively these levers would result in a step

[3]J.M. Kaplan, T. Bailey, D. O'Halloran, A. Marcus, C. Rezek, *Beyond Cybersecurity: Protecting Your Digital Business*, Wiley, 2015.

change improvement in companies' ability to protect critical information. More recently, our Digital Resilience assessment has made it clear that most companies are not progressing quickly enough in adopting these levers—the average company scores two points out of four in terms of overall maturity.

All of these levers are helpful for using cybersecurity for commercial advantage, but one more so than all of the others— integrate cyberresilience into enterprise-wide management and governance processes. This means conducting discussions across organizational silos to integrate considerations related to protecting information deeply, but also flexibly, into business processes like product development, marketing, sales, customer care, operations and procurement.

There are three places the companies can start to focus in doing this: in managing relationships with consumers, in managing relationships with enterprise customers, and in managing relations with suppliers.

6.2.1 Managing Relationships With Consumers

Most cybersecurity professionals believe that it is hard to communicate effectively with consumers about protecting information because any publically available advertising that speaks to a company's security capabilities immediately makes it a target for hackers looking to make name for themselves. There has also been a historic belief, among some executives, that consumers have not been particularly worried about protecting their information—that they are cheap and cheerful in this regard.

That said, there are still some very important actions that companies can take to make sure that they provide compelling experiences while also fulfilling their responsibilities to protect customer data.

6.2.1.1 Discover Consumer Preferences

Most companies have little information about how sensitive customers are to risks of information loss or disclosure. However there is at least anecdotal evidence that different customer segments have very different attitudes toward disclosure of information—for example, in financial services, mass affluent customers seem to be far more sensitized to the issue than customers in some other segments. Different types of customers also have very different perspectives on what constitutes an inconvenient security control. Getting real data from market surveys and focus groups enables organizations to understand what customers value and what frustrates them and incorporate those insights into customer-facing processes.

6.2.1.2 Apply Design Thinking to Security-Related Processes

Traditionally, many on-line experiences have been confusing and clunky, with complicated interfaces, vague instructions, requests for superfluous information and frustrating delays between what feels like an endless succession of screens. Increasingly, companies are using the discipline of "design thinking"—which truly requires business managers to take the view of what customers value in creating an experience—to many of their on-line processes. This should be no less true for security-related processes like authentication. In fact, one financial institution applied design thinking to their consumer authentication process. This allowed them to create a much smoother and less time-consuming customer experience. For example, customers told them they were much more concerned about fraud than the risk that someone might see their balance, so the bank delayed additional levels of authentication until the customer started to conduct transactions.

6.2.1.3 Allow Users to Customize Their Own Experiences

Once companies start to gather data on the impact of security controls, they find wide variations in what customers find to be inconvenient. One customer might have no objection to a complex passwords, but balk at changing it once a quarter. Another might prefer a simpler password, but find no inconvenience in entering a PIN texted to him on his phone every time he wants to log in. Several financial institutions are examining deploying portals that allow customers to pick from a menu of authentication-related controls—so long as they, in aggregate, combine to provide a sufficient level of protection. Over time, that minimum level of protection may vary by customer as well—with customers using products that are more "in the cross-hairs" for cybercriminals required to selected controls that provider a higher level of protections.

6.2.2 Managing Relationships With Enterprise Customers

Protection of critical data and cybersecurity considerations are an increasingly important part of relationships between companies and their enterprise customers. While marketing departments cannot create ad campaigns touting their cyberse-curity capabilities, client discussions and RFP responses hit very directly on cybersecurity capabilities in industries as diverse as business process outsourcing, enterprise software, wholesale financial services, contract manufacturing, medicals devices, group health insurance, and pharmacy benefits man-agement. As a result, there are a number of actions companies must be taking to improve their collaboration with enterprise customers in protecting critical information.

6.2.2.1 Treat the CISO and Team as Part of the Sales Channel

When security matters a lot, responses to a questionnaire only help so much. Customers feel more comfortable when they can spend time with the CISO and team to gauge their level of competence, test ideas, and problem solving on how to address thorny security issues that may exist at the seams between the two organizations. Some CISOs say they spend as much as 30% of their time with customers.

Others are not so effective in working with their sales teams and may spend almost no time with customers. Sometimes this is the result of CISO feeling that she just lacks the managerial bandwidth given other pressing responsibilities. Sometimes sales teams fail to recognize the importance of the issue. Sometimes there is an absence of trust between the sales and security functions, so account executives hesitate to pick up the phone and invite the CISO to a meeting. In any event, these are missed opportunities—in the absence of real dialog, questions about security get channeled into surveys and questionnaires that can bog down contracting processes.

6.2.2.2 Invest in Capabilities to Facilitate Vendor Security Assessments

For the foreseeable future, enterprise customers will require their suppliers to undergo vendor security assessments. They are painful, and they are inefficient, but until sectors can start to sort out standards for warranting the protection of informa-tion, they are also necessary. However, companies can make choices and investments that will dramatically improve their ability to address these assessments effectively. Instead of treat-ing each assessment as a one-off, they can start to analyze them for patterns in order to build the most important cus-tomer requirements into their security programs. They can cre-ate databases of information typically required for customer assessments, minimizing the grunt work of collecting data. And they can create a center of excellence to consolidate all activity required to respond to customer requests in one place.

6.2.2.3 Build Tight Connections Between Product Security and Cybersecurity

Not too long ago, product security and cybersecurity (or IT security or information security) were very distinct disciplines, with limited interaction in many companies. Specialists in engineering tried to make sure microcode in medical devices or other sophisticated equipment would not be compromised, and information security managers protected data on the company's internal systems.

Then the lines between products and enterprise networks started to blur. Customers integrated products into their own enterprise networks. Products started connecting to their manufacturers' enterprise networks to transmit diagnostic information—in effect they became endpoints on those networks. Customers started using applications running in manufacturers' data centers to configure products running in their facilities.

All of this creates new types of vectors for cyberattackers and makes it critical to take a holistic view across product security and IT security. Some companies have done this by unifying the responsibilities under one executive; others by cross-staffing teams and creating governance structures.

6.2.3 Managing Relationships With Suppliers

Just as companies must integrate cybersecurity considerations into their relationships with customers, when they are on the other side of the commercial transaction, they must integrate cybersecurity considerations into their relationships with suppliers.

6.2.3.1 Bring Together Vendor Security and Vendor Rationalization Programs

The only vendor that does not create cybersecurity risks is the vendor you do not do business with. Now, that does not mean that companies should jettison vendors who have a compelling proposition just because the security team thinks that there are too many vendors.

However, some companies have thousands of duplicative and subscale vendors who handle sensitive information. Yes, it is probably impossible to ascertain whether many vendors are treating sensitive data appropriately—a sourcing pattern like that may well represent an economically suboptimal vendor portfolio. In those cases, there is an opportunity for the CISO and the Chief Procurement Officer to join forces and make that case that vendor rationalization—while politically challenging— would have twin benefits of an improved cost structured and an enhanced security posture.

6.2.3.2   Improve Collaboration Between Security and Procurement

As notedearlier, security teams can easily load impractical requirements into procurement transactions. Avoiding this requires a very collaborative relationship between the security and the procurement teams. It starts with the CISO and team being willing to spend the time to educate procurement managers in each category about security implications associated with, for example, analytic services, accountancy, traditional IT outsourcing, or software-as-a-service. It continues with the security and procurement teams' problem solving on how to tier vendor relationships and types of procurement—so that both teams can focus their efforts on the highest risk relationships and transactions.

6.2.3.3   Examining Shared Standards and Utilities for Vendor Assessment

As many have noted, as necessary as they are, there is an element of insanity to vendor security assessments. A software or services vendor will spend weeks filling out an assessment survey and then, for its next sale, will receive another assessment survey that covers all the same topics—but just differently enough to require a wholly separate and substantial effort to complete.

From an enterprise customer's point of view they have to complete an assessment even they know an industry peer— with much the same risk posture—may have spent weeks looking at the same vendor very recently.

As a result, coalitions of companies—defined by sector or sometimes geography—are started to band together around common assessments. For example, a group of leading healthcare companies is launching a cybersecurity utility that will include a shared assessment capability. Members will be able to see vendor responses to a common set of questions and make an independent decision about comfort with that vendor based on a common, robust fact bases. As a result, they can repurpose scarce cybersecurity talent to higher value activities and introduce new products and services without waiting weeks or months for the completion of a custom questionnaire.

6.2.3.4 Establish Operational Linkages With Vendor Security Teams

For many types of commercial interactions, managing vendor risk does not stop with the vendor assessment or the signed contract. New types of information are share. New technology connections get provisioned. Adherence to agreed procedures for sharing data has to be managed—on both side of the transaction. Therefore maintaining day-to-day linkages with vendor's cybersecurity personnel becomes critical. It starts with having current contact information, but goes far beyond that. Some organizations conduct periodic checkpoints with key vendors to assess how they are jointly managing a deal against commitments and expectations. As few even incorporate vendor personnel in cybersecurity war games, they use to enhance their ability to respond to cyberattacks.

Given the amount of sensitive information shared in conducting business with customers and suppliers, cybersecurity is arguably a commercial issue. Already it is impacting contracting timelines, altering customer experience, and affecting which vendors win and lose business. When companies treat cybersecurity as a back office function that governs and places controls on the flow of information, and that creates commercial disadvantage, both in terms of reduced ability to leverage vendors and less intimate relationships with customers.

However, by building enhancing collaboration between the security team and the rest of the organization and building cybersecurity deeply into business processes, companies can source in a way that is secure and efficient and create customer relationships that both protect critical data and provide compelling experiences.

REASONING ABOUT SAFETY AND SECURITY: THE LOGIC OF ASSURANCE

A. Piovesan[1] and E. Griffor[2]

[1]*Diesel Jet, Castel Maggiore, Bologna, Italy* [2]*National Institute of Standards and Technology (NIST), Gaithersburg, MD, United States*

7.1 Introduction

An assurance case is a structured argument, supported by evidence, intended to justify that a system is acceptably assured relative to a concern (such as safety or security) in the intended operating environment. In this chapter we will use the example of software or functional safety of an automotive system as our example of a system concern that imposes requirements that require assurance. The "cases" for other system stakeholder concerns, such as security or reliability or timing, can be treated in a similar fashion. For a more comprehensive treatment of "concerns," the reader is referred to the NIST CPS Framework.[1]

Safety cases are often required as part of a regulatory process, a certificate of safety being granted only when the regulator is satisfied by the argument presented in a safety case. Example for automotive systems include crash safety and emissions regulations. Industries regulated in similar ways for safety include transportation (such as aviation, the automotive industry, and railways), energy and medical systems. As such there are strong parallels with the formal evaluation of risk used to prepare a *risk assessment*. A vehicle safety case may demonstrate the system to be acceptably safe to be driven on a road, but conclude that it may be unsuitable for operation under specific circumstances, if there would then be a greater risk of

---

[1]National Institute of Standards and Technology, Cyber-Physical Systems Draft Framework.

Handbook of System Safety and Security. DOI: http://dx.doi.org/10.1016/B978-0-12-803773-7.00007-3

harm, for example, a loss of control or an injury to the occupant. A safety case should be revisited when an existing system is to be repurposed.

In the context of ISO 26262,[2] a standard for software or functional safety for road vehicles, the safety case is defined as the "argument that the safety requirements for an item are complete and satisfied by evidence compiled from work products of the safety activities during development".

To state that the safety properties of a system are complete is to say that, for any *hazard* identified in the course of performing the *Hazard and Risk Assessment (HARA)* or *Hazard and Operability Study (HAZOP)* there are properties or requirements in the Safety Case intended to address that hazard. The assurance argumentation that the property of completeness is achieved for the system would make reference to completed HARA or HAZOP to justify the conclusion that *the safety properties of a system are complete.*

The intent of ISO 26262 is that the safety case should capture both the argumentation and the work products needed to establish confidence that "the system is safe for a given application in a given environment." This full potential of the safety case can only be achieved when it is planned at the outset of a project and updated throughout the product development process, capturing the argument at two levels:

- The relation between evidence and claims/propositions, i.e., judgments, about design elements or safety properties
- The basic assumptions, or structure, of safety case argumentation as described in ISO 26262

In this chapter we will provide the tools and formalism for capturing and enabling assurance case argumentation.

7.2 A Strategy for Safety Case Construction

To present the structure of Safety Case Logic in a graphic form, we introduce the notation of *goal structuring notation* (GSN) summarized in Fig. 7.1:

We will describe Safety Case Logic using a goal structure with the following assumptions:

- The Item under development's satisfaction of safety goals is taken as the primary goal of the safety case.

[2]ISO 26262:2011 Road vehicles. Functional safety.

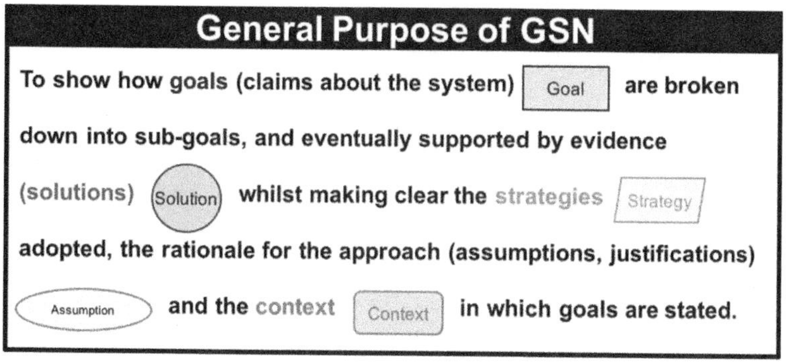

Figure 7.1 GSN terminology.

- Safety Standards' requirements (e.g., ISO 26262 Clauses) and best practices are used to argue (strategy) for the inference relationship that exists between a goal and its supporting goal (s), that is, those subgoals whose satisfaction is sufficient, in the sense of the standard, for satisfying the goal itself,
- Achievement of safety goals and subgoals is substantiated by proper solutions (evidences) documented by the work products listed in the Safety Plan or gathered from customer's (the entity that is the customer for the system) work products.
- Confirmation measures are included to argue correctness with respect to formality, contents, adequacy, and completeness regarding the Safety Standard's requirements.
- Verification reviews are included to argue correctness, completeness, and consistency of work products with respect to technical contents.

Each solution is linked to one more work products listed in the Safety Plan or Development Interface Agreement (DIA) documents (Fig. 7.2).

Again the primary goal of a Safety Case is to demonstrate the satisfaction of safety goals of the Item under development. Strategies are to be used to structure the argument that the inferences that exist between a goal and its supporting goal(s) or evidences are sound. These strategies typically are product-based or process-based arguments derived from requirements in the safety standard.

Evidence of goals' (safety properties) achievement is obtained through a progressive simplification of the safety properties based on the two-dimensional decomposition into subsystems and the logic of the standard all the way down to a set of "elementary" safety properties whose truth can be directly derived from the solutions practiced. Solutions are both product evidences and process evidences gathered from the ISO 26262 consistent work products.

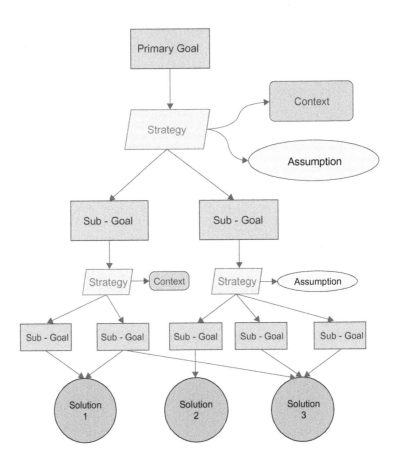

Figure 7.2 Strategy for a safety case logic.

An effective information exchange among managers and technical people involved in the project and the facilitation of recovery plans and problem-solving activities are further advantages derived from safety cases that are incrementally developed throughout the product life cycle and circulated inside the operative working groups in a framework that makes explicit work products, the relevant safety properties, and the argument that the work products provide evidence that these safety properties are true of the respective design elements.

This approach was originally developed at Fiat Powertrain Engineering to create a safety case implementation that demands minimal extra-effort in terms of time and resources and is easily understandable and is flexible in applications to a variety of projects, business models, and organizations.

This formal approach to the safety case uses process results and work products, generated during a development process consistent with ISO 26262, defines the broad notion of safety properties and provides a systematic approach to managing the inference relationship between intermediate safety properties, the safety goals defined for that product, and the supporting evidence that the design of the product satisfies those properties and finally satisfies the safety goals. The approach has been elaborated and refined to achieve a safety case framework which is project-independent, that is, depends only on the specifics of the product development plan being used.

A graphical notation is used here to represent the tree of steps in the argument. It is derived from the Kelly and Weaver [1] GSN. It gives an intuitive and clear representation of the "geometry" of inference relations between safety goals and the relevant "proofs" certifying their achievement. Finally, this graphic representation is transformed into a formal system for deriving "judgments" of the form "a set of work products is evidence sufficient for concluding that a safety property is true of a set of system elements". This is based on the formal system called Intuitionistic Type Theory [2], developed by P. Martin-Löf and later used to develop tools for deriving verified computer programs.

7.3 Decomposing the Functions of a Safety Critical System

The functions of a system can be decomposed and the decomposition can be represented in a *tree-like structure* where the branching corresponds to the relation that the function at a branching node is achieved or delivered using the functions at the nodes immediately below the given function.

An approach to decomposing a formal expression for a function is based on the notion of composition of functions $f(x) = g(h(x))$. The immediate successors in the *decomposition tree for f* are g and h and the immediate successors of g and h in that tree are defined by similarly decomposing their expressions. This approach gives a decomposition that depends on how f is expressed and is not intrinsic to the actual function performed by f. Function expressions are a special case of names for functions and their composition, often referred to as "terms" that are syntactic representations of functions.

We are interested in decomposing functions from the point of view of functions as transforms, typically of some form of energy, in the form of a verbal expression and organized hierarchically in levels as primary, secondary, tertiary, etc. Below is an

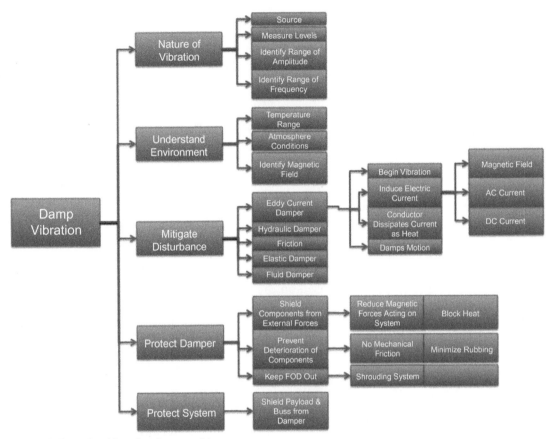

Figure 7.3 Example of function decomposition.

example of a "damping function." The primary is the damping function on the left and the secondary function level consists of "monitor nature of vibration," "understand environment," "mitigate disturbance," etc. (Fig. 7.3).

Let us consider now the structure of the Safety Case. We can make clear, using GSN, the kinds of properties or propositions and the kinds of reasoning or argumentation that are involved. If we follow the description in ISO 26262, we discover quickly that there are a distinct set of properties associated with the Safety Case.

3.1 Definition A property of a system s and the vehicle type v that arises in the course of working through the Safety Case for s and v is called a *safety property.*

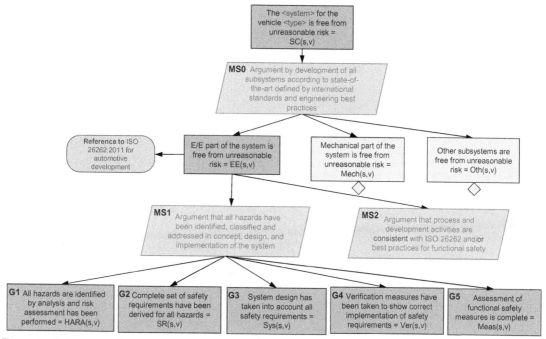

Figure 7.4 Safety properties.

An example of a safety property is provided in Fig. 7.4: SC $(s,v) := $ "The <system> for the vehicle <type> is free from unreasonable risk". Note that both "risk" and "unreasonable risk" are the attributes that need definition. This definition will be achieved by decomposing $SC(s,v)$, successively, into the *safety properties* involved and finally, using a notational convention for *safety case judgments*, relating instances of *work products* to the safety properties for which they are *evidence*.

Recall that this is a *two-dimensional decomposition* in the sense that each Safety Case proceeds both along the decomposition of the properties being asserted of the system in question and along the system *decomposition into subsystems.* An example of a *system decomposition branching* is MS0 in Fig. 7.4. An example of *ISO 26262 process branching* is MS1 in Fig. 7.4.

There is one final concept required to understand the structure of a safety case, that of the *system implementation.* The implementation of a system is the result of realizing all of the functions required to deliver the system function(s) in the physical components of the system.

7.3.1 Process Argumentation

A portion of the argumentation is related to the process dictated by the standard (Fig. 7.5).

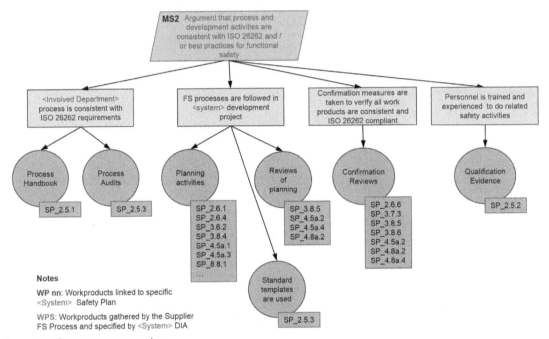

Figure 7.5 Process argumentation.

7.3.2 Hazard Argumentation

The argument that all hazards have been identified, classified, and addressed in the concept, design, and implementation of a system consists of several elements:

- All hazards are identified by analysis and a risk assessment has been performed.
- Complete set of safety requirements has been derived for all hazards.
- System design has taken into account all safety hazards.
- Verification measures have been taken to show correct implementation of safety requirements.
- Assessment of functional safety measures has been performed.
  - Functional safety assessment performed.
  - Validation report provided (Fig. 7.6).

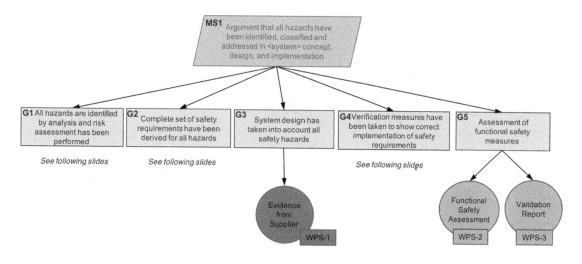

Figure 7.6 Hazard argumentation.

7.3.2.1 Hazard Identification

The hazard identification is accomplished by completing the steps of the *Hazard and Risk Assessment* (HARA), together with a list of operating situations for the system as well as evidence related to the *severity, exposure,* and *controllability* of the hazards. The flow shown in Figure 7.7 describes the elements of the reasoning associated with this process.

7.3.2.2 Requirements Elicitation

Once the system hazards have been identified, we must provide argumentation to the effect that a complete set of safety requirements have been derived, through the analysis and risk assessment of the system, for all hazards (Fig. 7.8).

7.3.2.3 System Design

Once the system hazard causes have been analyzed, safety measures have been implemented, and probabilities of random failures are sufficiently low. We must provide argumentation to the effect that the system design has taken into account the identified safety hazards (Fig. 7.9).

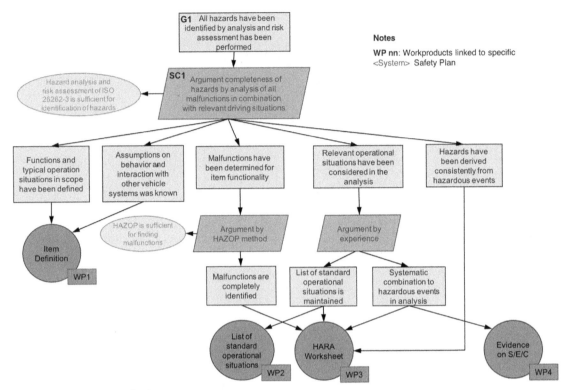

Figure 7.7 Hazard identification.

7.3.2.4 Verification Measures

Verification consists of the efforts dedicated to showing that the requirements for a system have been implemented or are met by the implementation of the system. In particular, safety-related verification measures are taken to show that safety requirements have been implemented correctly. Fig. 7.10 shows graphically how that goal (G4) is reached through reference to:

- Corporate or organization strategy derived from the standard
- Testing
- Subgoals for the Functional Safety Case (FSC), Technical Safety Case (TSC), and Integration Testing

7.4 Formal Reasoning for Safety Properties

Let w denote a work product, then the notion $w \in \psi(s,v)$ represent the *judgment* that "the work product w evidences

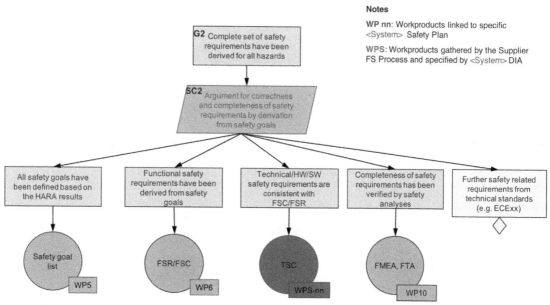

Figure 7.8 Requirements elicitation.

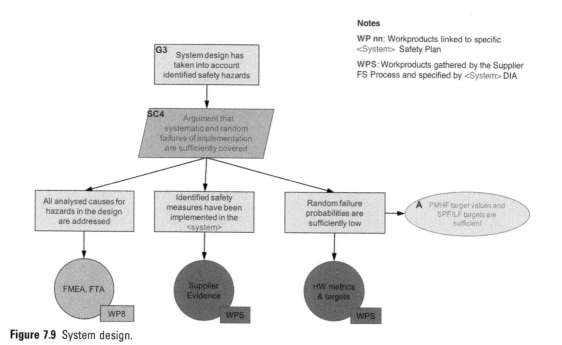

Figure 7.9 System design.

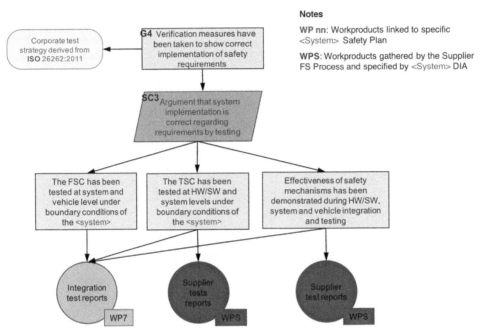

Figure 7.10 Verification measures.

that system s and vehicle type v have the property ψ." Judgments are not the same thing as propositions. Propositions or assertions that are fully specified are either "true" or "false." Judgments are either correct or incorrect—they capture in this context engineering judgment. What is regarded as evidence for the truth of an assertion can change over time, it is open ended.

The reasoning transitions in the GSN tree of a Safety Case represent what should be thought of as the *logical rules of a standard* (in this case of ISO 26262). MS0, for example, defines a rule for deriving the judgment SC(s,v) from the finitely many other judgments below it in the tree. In this sense the order of the GSN tree is the "reverse" of the order of a logical derivation. The judgment SC(s,v) is derived from the assumptions of the rule by a single use of the rule MS0, that is, from the judgments that there is evidence for $E(s,v)$, Mech (s,v) and Oth(s,v):

$$\frac{e \in E(s,y), \; m \in \mathrm{Mech}(s,y), \; o \in \mathrm{Oth}(s,v)}{<e,m> \, \in \mathrm{SC}(s,v)} \mathrm{MS0}$$

In a similar fashion, there are rules providing the derivation of each of the judgments. The judgments that appear above the line are the assumptions of the rule, while the one below the line is the conclusion of the rule. In future work, we will give the complete set of *Safety Case Rules* consistent with ISO 26262 as well as extend the methodology to other system stakeholder concerns, like security and reliability and others.

7.5 Assurance Case Logic

There are several use cases for a*ssurance case logic* (ACL). ACL can be used to demonstrate that a given system satisfies the assurance properties associated with a specific system concern and captured in an existing standard, through a detailed analysis of the system's development work products using that standard. ACL can also be used to derive an implementation of the system requirements, including those driven by concerns like safety, by using assurance case logic to analyze those requirements. The ontology of assurance cases consists of:

- goals/objectives and requirements (assurance properties)
- argumentation or reasoning
- evidence

An ACL is defined by providing the symbols and ways of composing them to build expressions for key properties of a system as well as for building expressions for the various sorts of evidence that is regarded as sufficient to be able to conclude that a system has one of these properties. In other words, an ACL begins with defining the *language of assurance* relative to a source of assurance like a standard or expert opinion. The intent of this language is to be able to express the relation that "the evidence e is sufficient to be able to conclude that a system S has a property P in the sense of a source of assurance." An assurance case judgement has the form:

$$J_1,\ldots,J_k \vdash e \in P\left[\frac{s_1}{x_1},\ldots,\frac{s_n}{x_n}\right]$$

which is read "from judgements $J_1,\ldots,J_k$ we can derive the judgement that evidence e is sufficient to conclude that the property P is true of system artefacts $s_1,\ldots,s_n$," where $x_1,\ldots,x_n$ are the variables in P.

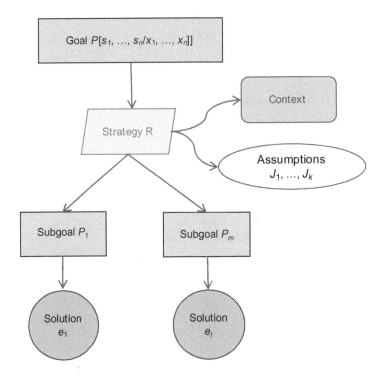

Figure 7.11 Assurance case strategy diagram.

The ACL then also included the *assurance case rules* that capture the principles for reasoning about or argumentation that are embodied in that source of assurance. Consider the assurance case strategy diagram ():

Fig. 7.11 represent inferences, individual, or compound, and are rendered in the assurance case logic as *assurance case rules*:

$$(\text{Rule } R) J_1, \ldots, J_k \vdash e \in P\left[\frac{s_1}{x_1}, \ldots, \frac{s_n}{x_n}\right]$$

where $e = <e_1, \ldots, e_n>$ is an encoding of evidence/solutions $e_1, \ldots, e_n$ and R is the inference rule of the assurance case logic, representing strategy R, for decomposing the assurance property P into $P_1, \ldots, P_m$.

Each instance of a source of assurance (such as standards, best practices/consensus, formal methods, regulation, or expert judgement) will give rise to its own assurance case logic.

7.6 Future Challenges

The perspective on assurance cases discussed in this chapter include assurance of properties of the development process and with advantage. The assurance of of a system relative to other concerns can be approached in a similar fashion. We have focused in this chapter on on systems that are *safety critical* (the system performs or delivers a *safety function*). Typically accomplishing this involves considering the development and the manufacturing and service processes. Additionally, we need to establish a similar level of confidence in the tools used to provide the work products.

An example of an important challenge facing designers of partially or fully autonomous automotive systems is the design of system human–machine interface (HMI). As the complexity of the functions performed by these systems increases the focus of concerns about human involvement is changing, from analyzing the ease with which the human provides inputs to the system to assuring the operator's continued engagement in the operating situation and the system's responses to that situation.

The development process must deliver all of the functions of the system reliably in order to meet the *intent of the system*. It does so by endeavoring to capture that intent in requirements, the design, development builds or preliminary implementation, and prototypes. In this way that process acquires an understanding of whether the design intent has been realized. Simulation and prototypes, assessing the design and revealing the design options, are assessed in terms of whether the *risk to intent* are acceptable. Thus there is an overall notion of defect relative to design intent and, specific to the *safety design*, defects relative to the subset of the design related to safety critical function.

In this chapter we have presented an approach to capture and analyze the activities/artifacts and the reasoning associated with the design of safety critical systems, with reference to best practices in standards like ISO 26262 for functional safety. This formal approach makes explicit what is common to the assurance practice for any safety critical system. Safety case logic is a methodology, presented here graphically with the help of GSN, that captures best practices of an assurance source and clarifies and optimizes it by exhibiting its meaning at each increment of the assurance effort.

7.7 Conclusion

This chapter outlines by example an approach to assurance of a concern developed to progressively create an assurance case using a formalism that captures that which is common to these assurance cases and that:

- Requires minimal extra-effort in terms of time and resources
- Makes easy reuse and adaptation for similar projects through the life cycle (change) and the inclusion of "carry-over" elements of the system
- Is easily understandable thanks to the notion of safety case logic and graphic representations (like GSN) that give an intuitive and clear representation of the inference processes and inference structure
- Is easily adapted for application to different projects, business models, and organizations

The approach uses process results and work products that are generated during a development process in a way that is consistent with standards (such as ISO 26262) in order to successfully represent and demonstrate the inferences that exists between the safety goals defined for that product and the supporting evidences.

From our preliminary assessment we expect a theoretical and relatively simple extension of this assurance case logic to any specific concern standard and technological domain (e.g., industry, aerospace, etc.) and, in particular, to the topic of system security.

References

[1] T. Kelly, R. Weaver, A systematic approach to safety case management, in: CAE Methods for Vehicle Crash Worthiness and Occupant Safety, and Safety Critical System, 2004 World Congress Special Publication SP-1879, Society of Automated Engineers, 2004.

[2] P. Martin-Löf, An intuitionistic theory of types, twenty-five years of constructive type theory (Venice,1995), Oxford Logic Guides, v. 36, Oxford Univ. Press, New York, NY, 1998, pp. 127−172.

Annex: Electronic Throttle Control (ETC)

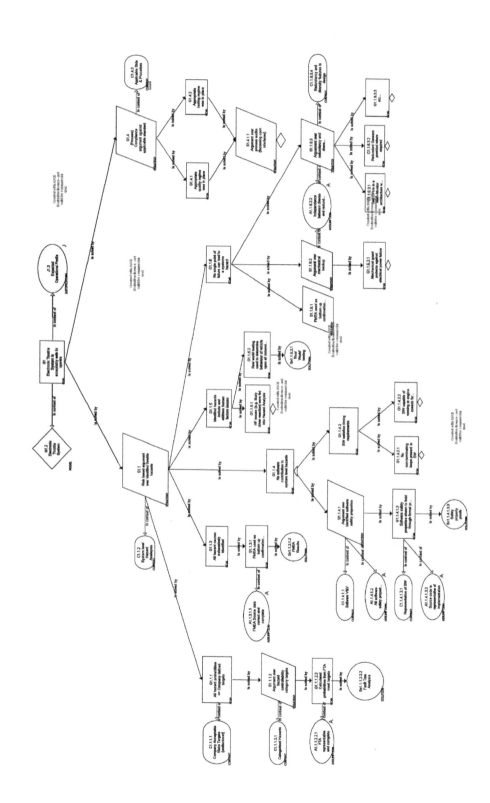

8

FROM RISK MANAGEMENT TO RISK ENGINEERING: CHALLENGES IN FUTURE ICT SYSTEMS

M. Huth[1], C. Vishik[2], and R. Masucci[2]

[1]Imperial College London, London, United Kingdom [2]Intel Corporation, Santa Clara, CA, United States

8.1 Introduction

Modern information and communications technology (ICT) environment is highly integrated and operates as a system of systems that share the same infrastructure and support the same processes. The ecosystem is very dynamic and diverse, and this diversity increases with the incorporation of every new generation of connected technologies. The evolution of the technology, including its usage models, is very rapid, resulting in an environment where legacy and cutting edge technologies coexist and situations where new devices, technologies, and frameworks are added to existing systems. All emerging technology contexts, from smart grid and connected automotive systems to Internet-enabled medical devices and industrial control systems, exhibit considerable complexity and diversity of operational requirements.

This dynamic and complex environment requires new strategies to evaluate and manage risks, and existing single-domain risk approaches are no longer sufficient for this task. Not only integrated risk models and viable approaches to risk composition are necessary, but also a modification of the system design and development processes to include integrated risk considerations at the earliest stages of the design process instead of being evaluated at a stage following system deployment. Incorporation of risk analysis in engineering processes requires the emergence of new design practices as well as creation of tools and mechanisms to support these practices.

Handbook of System Safety and Security. DOI: http://dx.doi.org/10.1016/B978-0-12-803773-7.00008-5

This chapter introduces the concept of *risk engineering*, describes its positioning in the modern technology environments, and provides a first view of tools and mechanisms necessary to support the proposed paradigm of risk engineering.

8.2   Key Aspects of Future ICT Systems

We start the discussion by describing key aspects of ICT systems that are relevant for developing fundamental concepts in risk engineering.

8.2.1   Ubiquitous Connectivity and Interoperability

Modern computing environments are characterized by their ubiquitous connectivity and interoperability among heterogeneous networks and diverse systems and devices. The numbers of connected devices today are extremely large. EMC Corporation estimates over 7 billion people will use 30 billion Internet-connected devices by 2020 [1], whereas Cisco and DHL predict a higher number—50 billion Internet-connected devices by the same date [2]. Disparate computing and network domains of 15 years ago have merged into an interconnected space that supports multiple models of usage, connectivity, and access via a shared infrastructure. The diversity of connected devices is enormous, including everything from data centers and full PC platforms to tablets, industrial control systems, disposable sensors, and RFID tags. This diversity of devices is matched by the diversity of supporting networks. Ubiquitous connectivity is beneficial for the users of the technologies and for the economy, leading to new efficiencies and increased productivity and providing a platform for widespread innovation. The challenges created by this environment are well known. Universal connectivity and interoperability complicate the analysis of threats and vulnerabilities, lead to uneven levels of protection in interconnected systems and elements of infrastructure, and, in many cases, can increase attack surfaces in yet-to-be understood ways.

The diversity of the environment makes it harder to evaluate and mitigate risks that such ICT systems either pose as components or services of other systems or that they themselves face in running and interacting with such complex environments. A major challenge that needs to be addressed is a methodology that can assess risk in a compositional way, so that risk analysis scales up; to develop such methods that can coherently examine risks pertaining to different aspects such as safety and security; and to their interaction.

8.2.2 Intrinsic Complexity and Dynamism of the Technology Environment

The modern computing environment is a combination of multiple frameworks, each using its own security and threat models. A framework is an abstraction providing generic functionality and a reusable environment, with specific use cases implemented via additional development. Example frameworks for software include Decision Support Systems or Web application environments. Hardware/software frameworks can include platforms such as PCs or Android mobile phones. The interoperability of frameworks forms the foundation of the modern technology environment and introduces new unknown vulnerabilities that are due to the effects of composition of security models associated with diverse frameworks. We expect connected cars to use the same infrastructure, standards, and protocols as other connected systems, but the introduction of new contexts of usage tends to increase attack surfaces, for example, using connected cars as self-driving engines or using connectivity in cars to enable ad hoc networks introduces a new class of potential vulnerabilities. Then, there is the issue of composition. To date, we have not developed methods that allow us to reliably analyze a composite security picture of the sort of infrastructure that is the reality of today's technology (Fig. 8.1).

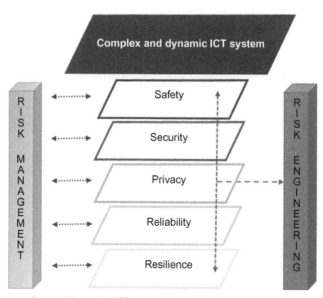

Figure 8.1 Analysis of a complex and dynamic ICT system through risk management or risk engineering models (separate management vs composition of risks).

Without any objective approaches to estimate security and adjacent risks of complex systems under operational conditions, and with neither standards or metrics to apply to diverse environments in which these systems operate, it is difficult to anticipate the consequences of system level or environmental changes for safety, security, dependability, privacy, or other salient risk domains. This complexity and ambiguity of environmental context also apply to data and data protection, making it necessary to rethink a number of fundamental concepts in computer and information science such as anonymity and data interoperability.

The increased complexity of the computing environment is the result of the aggregation of various frameworks and the often implicitly assumed composability of their underlying security, privacy, safety, and other aspects of risk that were designed in isolation and without a clear understanding of the aggregated operational contexts where they would be used during their life cycles. There are architectural patterns for composing systems that are often expressed in so-called architectural description languages. These languages help communicate system design decisions to both technical software developers and to end users. A structured technical description can facilitate early feasibility testing and analysis of design decisions. The architecture trade-off analysis method [3], for example, is a means of mitigating risk at an early design stage in order to maximize the business and technical value of the developed system. But such risk-mitigation techniques do not anticipate interaction within open and integrated systems, where business and technical considerations impact approaches to safety, security, or privacy. Conventional approaches to developing system architectures are not informed by the analysis of risk domains applicable to specific use cases. Thus standard architectural descriptions could provide structured approaches where integrated risks could be inserted, but research necessary to incorporate risk analysis into architectural description languages has not yet started. NIST Cyber-Physical Systems (CPS) Framework,[1] currently in a draft mode, represents an attempt to define fundamental concepts and their relationships for this complex space. This definitional work provides a solid foundation for the creation of a language capable of enabling a more integrated view of complex environments.

---

[1]Materials available at the Public Working Group website at: https://pages.nist.gov/cpspwg/.

8.2.3 Intermingling of Cyber and Physical Components

Another important characteristic of cyberspace is the connection between cyber and physical environments as exemplified in CPS, systems of systems that interact with the physical world, using computing components, communication capabilities, and physical subsystems [4]. CPS, now ubiquitous, require more complex and integrated security and risk models where the domains of safety, resilience, reliability, security, and privacy, which were traditionally separated at least to some degree, have to be analyzed together [4].

The Stuxnet attack was possible because sensor readings were trusted and not verified, allowing unauthorized changes that resulted in mechanical destruction of a centrifuge spinning beyond its safety margin [5]. The attack illustrates the need to verify and protect crucial system parameters and to develop risk models that link changes in one risk domain to a plethora of parameters affecting system operations. For example, insufficient care in protecting privacy of accounts can lead to security issues through unauthorized accesses that could result in safety issues if crucial operational parameters are altered in the process.

We need means of describing assumptions for prominent risk aspects of a system, for example, security and safety (such as security threats, vulnerabilities, safety critical failures, as well as detection and mitigation measures for safety or security critical events). These assumptions may pertain to the computational and physical environment. Additionally, we need to be able to understand and model the interaction or isolation of risk domains, for example, security and safety. Developing means to *verify* that a system handles safety and security correctly is a complicated task because the assumptions about environmental context contain stochastic or strict uncertainty and because expected residual risks benefit from a quantitative, metric-based evaluation and analysis.

System descriptions can better support such an approach if they are model-based, in order to use formal methods for analysis. One example of an architectural description language used to support modeling and formal analysis is the SAE Avionics Architecture Description Language (AADL) [6]. The AADL permits the developers to incorporate formal methods and engineering models into the analysis of systems and software architectures, thus enabling them to analyze the impact of composition on resulting complex environments.

8.2.4 Regulatory Approaches

An integrated risk model should also consider risks associated with the regulatory environment in countries where ICT and IoT technologies are developed and deployed. Business models and strategies which integrate policy implications can be more successful in seizing market opportunities and mitigating risks.

Literature acknowledges that regulatory risk arises whenever it affects the cost of capital of the regulated firm [7], and other authors distinguish between the impact of a given legislative scheme (regulatory impact) and the risk originating in discretionary behavior by regulatory agencies (regulatory risk) [8]. This section will describe compliance-related risks and also considers factors that influence negatively the lawmaking process and therefore increase legal uncertainty.

Deployment of innovative technologies depends on the success of technology commercialization, and this, in turn, is connected to the regulatory environments. A company that does not live up to regulatory compliance expectations of its investors, customers, consumers or market analysts undermines stakeholders' perception on the value of products and services and their reliability, therefore increasing risks. Market considers regulatory risks, and companies devote considerable resources to legislative monitoring and compliance activities, in order to maximize their understanding of the policy environment and minimize the impact of legislation and associated risks. Compliance has become a significant cost, in terms of dedicated compliance teams, internal audit, reporting mechanisms and impact assessments. However, the possibility of being exposed to fines proved to be costly both for financial losses and brand reputation damage. For this reason, compliance represents a key competitiveness factor as much as the adoption of the most advanced production techniques and new technologies. This is especially important for ICT products that support processes associated with a wide range of activities.

Overregulation or complex compliance requirements may constitute a reason for companies to relocate or establish a new business elsewhere, in order to limit the regulatory risk. Putting in place organizational compliance measures and ensuring full interaction of different functions within the company require solid management and legal expertise; it might constitute a real challenge for start-ups or for companies that want to expand in other geographies.

Uncertainty in the application of a regulatory instrument undermines the investments of a company and can be considered another element of regulatory risk related to the need for compliance.

The pace of lawmaking processes is not proportional to the fastest developments of technology. Moore's law has a cycle of 2 years [9], and modern technology development cycles can be even shorter, but the adoption of a piece of legislation can be far lengthier due to different procedural stages and political negotiations that slow down the overall outcome. In a scenario where legislation is a moving target, companies need to cope with legal uncertainty when they plan and take investment decisions while policymakers are still shaping new legislation or changing the existing one. In other cases, outdated, "technology retro-fitted" laws represent a drag for innovation, where industry is tied by provisions that do not reflect the state of the art in technology and do not allow expansion to new techniques and operations.

If pace asymmetry between regulatory decision-making processes and industrial investment planning contributes to increase the risk for companies, another factor is the information asymmetry between private sector and public sector (policymakers and regulators). The latter cannot anticipate better than the former the technology complexity described in the previous paragraphs.

Governments and public authorities draw their attention to several technology dimensions that concern all citizens: privacy, security, safety, and liability were previously addressed as different silos, but now that they are increasingly intertwined, their assessment needs to be done jointly to evaluate the overall reliability of information and communication devices. Sound awareness of technology and its ramifications is crucial for policymakers to keep regulation up-to-speed and to elaborate requirements based on objective and meaningful metrics. If regulators and policymakers aim to regulate new technologies, they need to develop a certain level of expertise on them, otherwise further risks for operational environments could arise from nonevidence-based provisions and requirements removed from industrial reality. Well-informed lawmakers could shape better regulation.

However, independent studies and figures on new technologies might not be available and some consequences of the technology deployment might not be clear yet (e.g., in terms of health or environmental sustainability) when policymakers draft regulation. In this case, decision-making process will be significantly driven by public perception of risks related to the adoption of a technology. Policymakers will be influenced by society—which is a "risk adverse society" [10]—in taking decisions regarding ICT systems: the precautionary principle will inspire their action, but this approach could represent another factor that leads to regulatory risk for companies, namely, once again, requirements removed from industrial state of art.

Risk aversion of governments and regulators could be translated also in an increase in liability for manufacturers. Unless accountability measures put in place by companies represent a real mitigating factor for limiting fines for companies in case of damage or harm to users and consumers of ICT and IoT technologies, increased liability would draw again the attention to compliance costs and might drain resources from R&D and innovation.

Moreover, another aspect that increasingly plays a role in creating regulatory risk for ICT and IoT systems is the posture of some governments around the world justifying an increase in control over data and technology as a form of sovereignty. The reason is twofold, economic and political: on the one hand, there is an attempt to protect trade secrets and develop local technologies; on the other, the idea is to limit foreign surveillance activities. However, the shift to local technology solutions or the creation of regional standards can be very harmful for the market in terms of fragmentation and competition. Likewise, proposals for data localization mandates do not seem effective in protecting against or preventing foreign surveillance. On the contrary, they might favor domestic surveillance and they surely impinge on the open internet and the free flow of data [11]. Following Snowden revelations in 2013 and the ECJ ruling invalidating Safe Harbor [12] in 2015, technology sovereignty and data sovereignty have been under the spotlight in Europe as strategies to pursue privacy and security. In an IoT environment, mandatory data localization could compromise business models, while technical measures like encryption could better serve the purpose.

Regulatory requirements have direct impacts on technology solutions and their adoption and therefore should be considered as another metrics necessary to model and evaluate risks in complex systems. Informing engineering processes with regard to regulatory requirements and associated risks, when the requirements are pending or unclear, or contradictory in different jurisdictions, will help create a consistent risk picture. Integrating regulatory risks with other risk aspects described earlier in the chapter is necessary in order to develop technologies ready for deployment (Fig. 8.2).

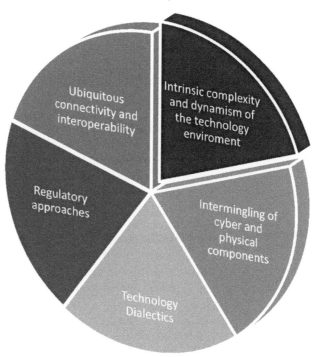

Figure 8.2 Integration of different domains of modern computing environments in risk engineering models.

8.2.5 Technology Dialectics

A number of technology and policy frameworks have been proposed to enable or facilitate the examination of multidisciplinary subjects in security and privacy. A good example is "Technology Dialectics" [13], a model proposed by Latanya Sweeney to mitigate conflicts between requirements of technology and context of use in society. The goal is to detect potential social and adoption issues early in the technology cycle and resolve them by creating tools to determine whether a technology is provably appropriate for a certain society or context. Although the framework focuses on privacy, it can be used for broader analysis and is easily applied to cybersecurity. Such frameworks may also be useful to explore potential risks to the reputation and brand value that the introduction of a particular piece of technology may pose, based on its correct functioning or based on uncertainty about its behavior. Technology dialectics and similar frameworks permit us to assess adoption and acceptability constraints and could become an additional dimension in a risk approach that combines technical, environmental, regulatory, and social aspects. Although quantifying societal risks is complex endeavor, such assessments are likely to have significant value in integrated risk analyses.

8.3 Evolution of Risk Approaches and Models

Different types of risks have been defined and considered for the analysis of operations in industry and government. Traditionally, risk models for security include three dimensions: people, processes, and technology. The increasing complexity of the technology environment rendered this model insufficient. To compensate for the shortcomings, additional dimensions were added, for example, organizational strategy and structural design.

Risk management approaches for more complex fields began to integrate additional risk domains, such as assurance and resilience [14], and risk assessment was integrated into the system development cycle. This risk aware development was first adopted in very structured environments, such as military technology development or aerospace systems, and cybersecurity was added to already rigorous risk-assessment models. In these cases, sophisticated programmatic risk models were already highly developed, and permitted to incorporate security as a new domain without modifying the existing framework as described in Ref [14]. Preexisting systems also permit the technologists to assess risks for evolving requirements, for example, a switch from password to PKI-based authentication, without jeopardizing the system of metrics embedded in the framework.

Although "people" have formed an evaluation area in the early risk analyses of organizational security, this aspect of risk has been significantly extended in recent approaches. In addition to sophisticated models of threat agents (e.g., as described in a model developed by Intel Corporation [15]) and their common use in mitigation processes, examination of insider threats became more detailed. Views on the role of human error have matured, and organizational behaviors have been studied in more detail.

As the risk domains are extended and integrated, a more detailed analysis of various threats and vulnerabilities is required, in order to build viable predictive models. Thus risk assessments with diverse mitigations for such varied areas as automotive security, electronic currencies, and airport security were among the contexts evaluated with a view to develop segment-based risk models. Later, the movement toward detailed assessments based on cross-cutting principles has allowed the risk community to create more nuanced risk postures in complex domains that are difficult to define unambiguously, such as privacy or safety or whole frameworks, such as cybersecurity or CPS.

An example of an integrated risk framework combining risk domains of security, privacy, safety, reliability, and resilience can be found in the draft deliverable of the Public Working Group on Cyber-Physical Systems [4].

Separate assessment of these domains is insufficient to address the risks because requirements optimized for one domain can be detrimental to the composite risk picture for a system or an area of infrastructure. Characteristics of CPS, such as the presence of a physical subsystem and real-time controls, may demand a departure from traditional views on security or privacy and instead put an emphasis on safety or reliability—for example, when developing risk models for a nuclear power station management where privacy concerns are minimal, but reliability requirements are crucial [4].

8.3.1 Shared Infrastructure, Economics, and Risk Modeling

The benefits of the shared global infrastructure are clear to all: we can use the same devices, applications, networks, and processes worldwide, with minimal issues. But compositional risk analysis of the shared infrastructure in conjunction with specific use cases has not yet been addressed by researchers.

The general consensus on the importance of the global shared infrastructure predates the commercial Internet, but concerns about its dependability have emerged early in the Internet history and crystallized into a separate area of research in the mid-1990s, as described by Hunker [16]. This infrastructure is shared in many different contexts that use cyberspace for transportation, energy, healthcare, or other activities in different geographic regions while always relying on the underlying functionality of generic systems and processes.

The operational contexts are organizationally, technologically, and geographically diverse, and the impact of failure is enormous due to the extremely large user populations of connected systems and processes. Around 40% of the world population used the Internet in 2014 [17]. Twenty years ago, in 1995, the level of connectivity stood only at 1% of the population. In 2014, 78% of the population of the developed countries and 31% of the population of the developing world were connected [18]. The global nature and scope of cyberspace and the multitude of its documented and spontaneous use cases suggest that we should acquire a strong understanding of the risk patterns that

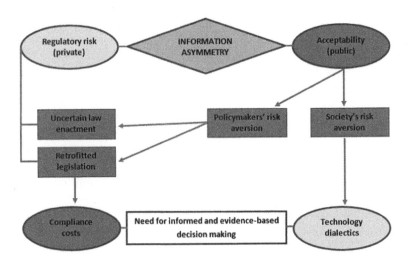

Figure 8.3 Consequences and challenges of information asymmetry.

underlie the use of these systems in diverse conditions and use this knowledge as an integral part of system design and development. Uneven availability of expertise and resources resulted in varying levels of cybersecurity and privacy protections in that infrastructure, which creates another need for revisiting the approaches to risk modeling and risk composition.

The ICT sector has a significant impact on the global economy. By 2010, it has represented 6% of global GDP and accounted for 20% of employment in OECD countries [19]. The sector is responsible for increasing overall productivity and for improving efficiency in other sectors. Moreover the impact of ICT on all aspects of everyday life and commerce is enormous. The digital economy allows the markets to create economies of scale and scope via intermediation and aggregation of resources. Novel usage models emerge and quickly become mainstream, providing a constant source of innovation and alleviating information asymmetry, as illustrated by Akerlof's model [20]. However, the process of building a unified economic theory for cybersecurity and providing recommendation on optimal economic models to achieve improved security coverage has been slow (see, e.g., [21,22]).

Fig. 8.3 provides an illustration for the connections between risk aspects of the computing and regulatory environment that are relevant for building a risk engineering paradigm.

8.4 Risk Engineering

The trend toward the integration of risk domains for modern systems means that premises are beginning to emerge for risk engineering, a concept we propose to denote the need for the incorporation of the risk approaches into engineering processes and development of tools that will allow the technologists to evaluate risks of future systems at the design stage, based on the techniques selected for the implementation.

We define risk engineering as "incorporation of integrated risk analysis into system design and engineering processes."

8.4.1 Challenges in Risk Engineering

The management of risk is only effective if there is a good understanding of the nature and extent of these risks in ICT systems or systems of systems. Traditionally, risk assessments are done for specific aspects of operations: for example, for the reputational risk that a new make of car and its marketing campaign may pose to the manufacturer or the security risk that software within that make of car may behave in unexpected, malicious, or fraudulent ways. These assessments are typically conducted in isolation from other categories of risks, in order to address specific practical concerns. In reality, various categories of risks are connected. For example, security flaws in home-connected appliances can result in privacy breaches, physical damage to the house, or operational safety attacks against the appliance management systems.

The management of complex risks can be greatly improved if ICT systems themselves could be engineered with consideration of risks of their future use in their operational contexts. Risk engineering therefore requires a process that enables the developers to articulate, define, and sometimes quantify risks. Such specifications may be informal, semiformal, or formal; they may be qualitative or quantitative; and they may be given in textual form or within a mathematical model. The communities of research and practice for safety, security, privacy, reliability, and resilience have developed methodologies for expressing such risk specifications, with the ability to analyze the consequences that such risks may bring. But there is relatively little work on making such specifications composable to scale, and on specifying risks that stem from the combination or interaction of different system aspects.

An interesting example of work on compositional specifications is found in Ref. [23], where probabilistic component automata model functional and nonfunctional behavior of software components and their composition—including the modeling of failure scenarios, the propagation of failures in the system, and failure handling. The resulting model is a discrete-time

Markov chain that can be analyzed, for example, at run-time to explore the reliability of a configuration change prior to its realization. Such foundational research, however, needs to find its way into broad industrial practice through the creation of appropriate pathways for knowledge and technology transfer.

8.4.1.1 Example: Interaction of Safety and Security Risks

Let us now focus on the interaction of safety and security in ICT systems to illustrate the complexity of risks in such interaction. The research and practitioner communities develop their own informal ontologies, methodologies, and best practices to address these issues. There is limited conversion of different points of view today: even the vocabulary is different. For example, "incident" refers to an event that has no safety-critical consequences in safety, whereas it usually denotes a serious breach in computer security—as noted in Ref. [24]. The lack of shared semantic context illustrates the diversity of approaches that results in challenges to integrated risk modeling. However, the flow of information between various risk domains already exists. For example, defense in depth is an established principle in computer security but it originated in the domain of safety in the design of nuclear power plants [25]. Similarly, fault trees in safety inspired the design of attack trees to understand security vulnerabilities at the system level. However, whereas fault trees allow for qualitative analysis (e.g., when may faults occur?) as well as quantitative analysis (e.g., how likely may this fault occur?), attack trees tend to be used for qualitative analysis.

The research and practitioner community would benefit from a better empirical analysis of the security risk domain, for example, through the analysis of big data, and from more research on the acceptance and adoption of technology where issues of privacy, security, safety or reliability may be codependent or conflicting. Frameworks such as the one developed in Ref. [13] could be extended to explore such issues during the engineering process. Risk engineering would also benefit from the development of theoretical models that have predictive power, for example, the number of security vulnerabilities in a code base as a function of its lifetime, studied in Ref. [26].

Another issue making risk integration study more complex is that quantitative information may span several orders of magnitudes. For example, probabilities in safety tend to be very small, whereas they are more significant in computer security due to an active, intelligent, and incentivized system adversary. Similarly, requirements for system availability typically incorporate very small risks for downtime due to a range of causes, whereas probabilities of attacks indirectly associated with system availability tend to be much larger. This discrepancy raises questions of how to compose such values, so that models and their analysis remain meaningful. A related problem is that the safety domain has a longer tradition of established procedures and standards encouraging rational behavior while computer security, in contrast, often involves irrational behaviors.

Even when analyzing risk domains in isolation, there is the need for resolving or managing conflicting conclusions. For example, in railway systems, the recommendations of safety experts may contradict those of the ICT and operational security experts; yet no tools were developed for dealing with conflicting requirements when designing, modifying, or operating a railway network.

8.4.1.2 Obstacles to Integration of Risk Aspects

In summary, we are encountering a strong need for the integration of different risk domains in order to incorporate them in the engineering process. But the integration is impeded by some obstacles, including:
- lack of common vocabulary and semantic context;
- absence of consistent metrics;
- lack of techniques for risk composition.

To overcome these challenges, we need to develop ontologies that span multiple system aspects and risk domains, supporting both the qualitative and quantitative analysis of system aspects and their interaction. It is also necessary to create methodologies to cope with numerical information spanning several orders of magnitude. In addition, we need to conduct more empirical research to gain reliable quantitative information for aspects that traditionally are expressed in qualitative terms only. Finally, it is necessary to devise approaches to integration of diverse risk domains (such as safety, security, or regulatory risks) and to risk composition from computed or assigned risks of different elements of the ecosystem.

Let us now explore, for illustration, an example of a model-based formalism, in which security and safety considerations can be analyzed, both quantitatively and qualitatively.

8.4.2 Case Study for Security Risk Quantification: Modeling Attacks, Their Cost, and Impact

We may think of security risks in at least two principled ways. In one approach, we are interested in the actual attack trace, the sequence of events that an attacker engages in that leads to a security breach. Techniques such as model checking [27] can be used to understand how such traces may be realized for known breaches. Another approach is inspired by fault tree analysis in safety, where we are interested in the capabilities that are required to realize a security breach, not in their actual operationalization as a sequence of attack, camouflage, or obfuscation events. Attack-countermeasure trees (ACTs) are a good example of the latter [28].

We note that both approaches have their strengths, and complement each other for analyzing and managing security vulnerabilities of systems: understanding attack traces is useful in the run-time monitoring of system security by potentially allowing the defenders to capture an attack "signature." The knowledge of the capabilities of attackers allows us to articulate the assumptions about their basic capabilities, and to anticipate likely consequences for the security of the system in question. In general, capability-based models inspired by fault tree analysis appear to be abstractions of operational models of attack traces; we believe that there is benefit in understanding such abstractions in order to automatically convert one approach into the other for complementary analysis. The richer information obtained by the combination of the two approaches could also be helpful in integrating other risk aspects, such as safety or privacy or influences of regulatory requirements on architectures.

8.4.2.1 Domain-Specific Modeling Language

Let us now discuss an example of a domain-specific language that has the ability to model the capabilities of an attacker with regard to a specific security breach, including cost and impact of a potential attack. ACTs [28] are graphical structures in which we may describe the interaction of attacks and countermeasures in a tree whose root is the attack goal and whose leaves are basic attacks or countermeasures. A countermeasure is a pair of detection and mitigation mechanisms. Fig. 8.4, reproduced from Refs. [28,29], shows such a model ACT for an attack of the border gateway protocol on the Internet: resetting a session of such a protocol, which we consider to be the specified security breach. While we can ignore the technical details of this particular model, we note that it specifies the probabilities of success for basic attacks, detection, and mitigation mechanisms as well as the cost of a basic attack to the attacker; and the impact a basic attack has on the system. For example, basic attack **Notify** has success probability .1, attack

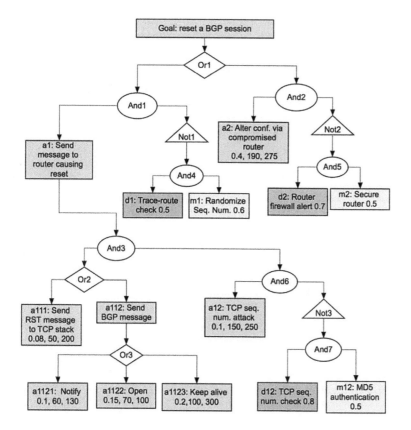

Figure 8.4 Example of ACT model.

cost 60, and system impact 130. It is up to the modeler to provide semantic content for these entities, such as an abstract mathematical value for impact, something in a discrete range of impact levels, or a specific cost in a currency.

8.4.2.2 Risk Metrics and Their Analysis

ACT models such as the one referenced above allow us to compute useful metrics, such as the probability of an attacker's to success in the security breach or the overall cost of an attack to the attacker. The tools for fault tree analysis developed in reliability theory [30] use completely different computational engines to answer these two types of questions: the probability of attack success is a quantitative computation from the bottom up on the ACT tree, whereas the attack cost is computed by enumerating all so called min-cut sets that make the goal node true when we interpret the ACT tree as a logical circuit. These are different algorithms that cannot interact directly to optimize measures that combine attack costs and probability of attack success. And such measures are of genuine interest.

For example, assume that we want to analyze the worst case, according to this model, of a security metric $f(p,i,c) = p *$ max $(0,2*i-c)$ where p denotes the probability of the attacker reaching the attack goal, i the overall impact of that attack to the system, and c the overall cost to the attacker of the attack that realizes this security breach. This metric multiplies the attacker's success probability p with a term that trades-off system impact with the attacker's cost—an established arithmetic pattern in risk metrics, including those used in the insurance business.

8.4.2.3   Analysis Support: SMT and MINLP Solvers

How can we compute a worst case value for the metric and develop a scenario that realizes this worst case and that modelers and decision-makers can comprehend? To do this, we can make use of advances in automated reasoning, for example, in Satisfiability Modulo Theories (SMT) [31] or Mixed Non-Linear Integer Programming (MINLP).

MINLP provides optimization over constraints that involve nonlinear arithmetic and where some variables need to be integral or binary. MINLP is an extension of linear Mixed Integer Programming (MILP) [32] to allow for nonlinear constraints. SMT combines decision procedures for a range of theories with SAT solving of propositional logic to perform automated reasoning. An SMT solver allows us to express functions, relations, and logical constraints and then computes whether all constraints can be satisfied at the same time. If this is the case, the SMT solver can supply information that provides evidence on how all constraints are satisfied; if not, then the solver either cannot answer the question (as the combination of theories may be undecidable) or concludes that the conjunction of all constraints is impossible to satisfy.

SMT solvers that can optimize linear objective functions exist today [33], so that evidence that satisfies all constraints can also minimize a linear objective in doing so. Alternatively, it is possible to use an SMT solver as a black box to compute minima or maxima for *nonlinear* objectives up to a desired accuracy (see, e.g., Ref. [34]). Such research outputs are attractive, since they permit us to formulate risk metrics for nonlinear composition of risk; moreover, they enable us to compute, through nonlinear optimization, worst case risk scenarios in the presence of nontrivial logical constraints. For example, regulatory or compliance regimes, privacy requirements, or safety-related laws may contain logical rules, constraining a model in a manner that is hard to represent in conventional optimization models using Linear Programming, MILP, or their nonlinear extensions.

8.4.2.4 *Analysis Tools and Interpretation by Analysts*

We can compile the ACT above into SMT, as described in Ref. [29], and compute 271.92 as the maximum of function f, using the optimization techniques on top of SMT as discussed in Ref. [34]. Moreover, the evidence that SMT presents for the maximal value tells us which events (basic attacks, detection mechanisms, and mitigation mechanisms) are operative in the scenario that realizes this value. The computation can potentially include constraints relevant to different risk aspects (e.g., safety, security, and privacy) as was described earlier.

Once the computations have been completed, an analyst may evaluate this scenario and, if necessary, add other logical constraints to the SMT model to rule out some of the events. It is also possible, in principle, to make some of the model information symbolic. For example, we may express the probability for basic attack *Notify* as variable x, and constraint x to be between 0.08 and 0.12 to determine whether this strict uncertainty in the success probability of basic attack *Notify* may modify the maximum of security metric f in unexpected ways. The feasibility of such symbolic sensitivity analyses using SMT has been demonstrated in Ref. [34] already in an application that has little prior data to inform the choice of numbers.

8.4.2.5 *Discussion*

As already discussed, the reliability of quantitative information in security may be hard to achieve. Therefore we think that symbolic approaches such as the one described above can lead to more robust optimization techniques [35] able to cope better with information asymmetry between the attackers and the defenders, between the developer and the influence of the complex operations environments, or even between the sellers and buyers in complex markets where information asymmetry is strong.

ACT provide a good formal method for modeling the interaction of probabilistic risk, costs to an attacker, and cost to the system under attack. It would be of interest to define domain-specific modeling languages (DSLs), in which such tree-like models can be enriched with logical constraints or with additional aspects such as the safety of the system. For example, we may consider "fault-resiliency" trees, where faults play a role similar to basic attacks, and resiliency may be represented by safety mechanisms that prevent or mitigate basic faults. We can then create a multidomain ontology to enable the trees to combine attacks, countermeasures, faults, and safety mechanisms in the same semantic framework. The approach to optimization proposed above would apply to this integrated model.

One limitation of the ACT ontology, however, is that it makes an implicit assumption that the probabilities of success of basic events are statistically independent. This, however, may not be the case in reality, especially with regard to fault considerations, and ACT-based optimization may therefore lead to results with limited validity. In such situations, it would be better to use alternative models able to accommodate the expression of probabilistic dependencies. Let us mention here causal networks such as Bayesian Belief Networks; see for example, Ref. [36], for more details on this approach. We refer to Ref. [37] for a survey on other approaches that combine safety and security considerations in the design and risk assessment in the context of industrial control systems.

Clearly, a better way to devise ontologies that can express the interaction of different system domains, such as safety, security, privacy, and resiliency, and more abstract aspects such as internal costs and reputational risk, is an important research area. Such ontologies should be constructed to support probabilistic and quantitative analysis of risk metrics of interest, regardless of whether the models are fully compositional such as ACTs described above, causal networks, or a combination of the two techniques. At the analysis level, more research is needed for the creation of more powerful tools for symbolic and automated reasoning such that these tools can combine compositional with noncompositional probabilistic inference in a coherent manner and with the ability to scale this up.

8.4.3 Model-Based Risk Engineering

Our presentation of MINLP and SMT reasoning engines suggests the following approach to modeling and analyzing risk composition, shown in Fig. 8.5: an analyst formulates models and queries about risk aspects in models, be they ACTs or any other suitable modeling formalism. A query may, for example, be whether the composed risk is always below a critical threshold. Reasoning engines would then analyze such queries and report back results. Ideally, these results would be both

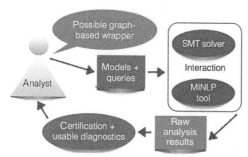

Figure 8.5 Analysis of queries through the interaction of different reasoning engines.

intelligible to the analyst—who is not an expert of the reasoning engines themselves—and independently certified, so that potential implementation flaws of reasoning engines are flagged up. Needless to say, the approach in that figure would not be committed to using MINLP or SMT as analysis engines; rather, we would imagine the use of several such engines to enhance the complementary value of their capabilities.

We think that the additional tools for the independent certification or confirmation of risk analysis results are also important when an analyst uses a DSL, as the translation from DSL to a reasoning engine may be flawed. Models written in such a DSL need to be translated into models that are suitable for the use of MINLP or SMT tools. Creating additional self-certification capabilities is complicated by technical challenges. For example, the reasoning in SMT may be complex and non-compositional when reinterpreted at the semantic level of the analyst's DSL. In Ref. [29], an approach is proposed to overcome such a challenge for a DSL, based on a language developed in Ref. [38], where raw analysis results are produced by an SMT solver: the satisfiability evidence for a query is postprocessed and then presented to the analyst in a compositional manner within the DSL, where this compositionality is achieved by potentially refining the witness with additional model information that was not strictly required for the reasoning conducted in the SMT solver.

We can see that mechanisms and modeling languages that can be adapted for integrated analysis of different aspects of risk already exist, and could potentially be used in operational environments when supported by multidomain ontologies describing semantics of these risks. However, additional research is necessary in several areas to define additional features and overcome intrinsic weaknesses in these approaches.

8.4.4 Ontology and Risk Engineering

One of the main goals of the field of Knowledge Representation (KR) is the development of methodologies and tools that enable the accurate capture of knowledge, enabling us to easily add and update information. Knowledge specifications can be formulated in a purely *declarative form* in order to specify the knowledge without any consideration for the algorithmic nature of such statements and their validation. The semantics of such a representation language defines the meaning of these specifications in a precise and unambiguous fashion. For computation, algorithms forming an inference engine can be separately defined to establish that a fact is true based on a given knowledge base [39].

An ontology is a hierarchical specification of a set of objects from a domain of interest, their properties, and their relationships. Ontological languages are associated with inference engines, enabling automated reasoning about the elements of an ontology. For example, an engine may expand the class–subclass relationships into an ancestor/descendant propagating properties and relationships through the hierarchy of an ontology. Inference engines can often derive information that was not immediately evident from the original specification of the ontology, while pinpointing repeatable algorithms for these derivations [39].

Work on ontologies and inference engines relies largely on logical languages and qualitative reasoning. Although this makes it possible to identify system flaws such as security breaches in access control, it does not automatically support the management of quantitative risk or the interaction of risk considerations across system aspects such as safety, security, and privacy. Nonetheless, the use of ontologies to manage quantitative or logistical interactions, for example, movements of robots, indicates that the development of qualitative inference engines is possible.

The development of quantitative inference engines would first require a thorough understanding of how to specify such interactions so that quantitative results are relevant to decision makers such as system designers (e.g., the level of risk of a planned design change) as well as to end users (e.g., the perceived privacy risk). However, the challenges in creating ontologies capable of supporting models and modeling languages used for integrated risk engineering do not appear to be insurmountable. Such ontologies require significant efforts to develop as well as participation of a multidisciplinary task force, to define different risk aspects and domains, but the benefit to the research and practitioner communities will be significant.

Ontologies have been used in the area of information security for at least two decades, for different purposes, including providing a broader analysis of the field, a way to codify and link diverse security and privacy requirements, or as a methodology to improve information-based models for security threats and mitigations. An early example of this work is Ref. [40] where a language (Telos) is proposed as a way to reason about components and properties of information systems, including security and part of a mechanism for creating security specifications. As security and privacy became increasingly prominent, ontologies dedicated to this area have been defined, including a multidomain technology–focused example created in Ref. [41] or a broader ontology put together in Ref. [42] that extends to non-technology components, such as organizational structures. In addition to descriptive ontologies, ontologies to be used in modeling have been created, such as Ref. [43] or [44], associated respectively with Tropos software development methodology and Toronto i* goal modeling language.

There is great diversity today in approaches to and uses of ontologies in security and risk areas, an indication of a still immature field. However, interesting and promising research, such as the examples provided in this section, forms a foundation for a more unified and broadly applicable approach that can facilitate more integrated models for risk and security analysis.

8.4.5   Risk Engineering: Challenges for the Development of Tools and Methodologies

Let us now discuss some tools and methodologies that may guide risk engineering and help overcome its major challenges. We have established that the use of semantic tools, such as an ontology, could be instrumental in this area. The use of an ontology suggests a preference for models in the form of graphs (the above ACT being an example), in the form of declarations in some logical formalism or in a combination of graph-based models and declarative constraints. One challenge is to devise support for multimodal annotations of such graphs that express constraints, expectations, assumptions or guarantees about risk, security, privacy, reliability, regulatory constraints, or resilience. Such annotations need to be devised in a form that is understandable to end users and system developers. These annotations need to define formal semantics necessary for the analysis of their interaction. In this regard, an important question is whether one can devise a modeling framework with such capabilities that can be instantiated to specific application domains (e.g., the instrument cluster of modern connected cars and the interplay of privacy, security, and safety therein). To address this question, it is necessary to capture common characteristics across application domains in appropriate form, for example, reference models or architectures.

The need for annotated models for communication and analysis is not confined to the design and implementation of a system or to the integration of a system into a complex environment. We also need to support risk engineering paradigm during the entire life cycle of a system, including its requirements capture, development, operational and change management, and retirement. It is unlikely that the same modeling formalism would apply to each of these stages or for expressing risk pertaining to the life cycle of the system itself.

Another challenge in creating tools and methodologies for risk engineering is the need to combine information and metrics from different risk domains, such as privacy, security, regulatory constraints, and safety, and to ensure that the result is meaningful for analysis. We already mentioned that metrics used for safety are often several orders of magnitudes smaller than similar metrics in the area of security. We need to develop "risk calculus," similar to David Grawrock's proposal for trust calculus found in Ref. [45]. In risk calculus, we could use algebraic and probabilistic operators so that we can combine diverse quantitative parameters in a manner that measures risk appropriately, while taking into consideration codependencies between different risk modalities (e.g., between privacy and security) and their potential conflicts (e.g., a conflict of high with tighter security controls at run-time). Any progress toward such a calculus would have real benefits for risk engineering. A purely compositional calculus, which an algebraic calculus would suggest, may not be expressive enough to capture noncompositional meaning, which the causal networks can do well.

Although calculi can play an important role in validating, monitoring, and controlling the risk in future ICT systems, we also need to develop a set of principles that can express risk and its management through policy. In the context of cybersecurity policies, Schneider and Mulligan have proposed the use of doctrines [46] as a "lens" to examine policy proposals or suggest new ones. Their Doctrine for Risk Management points out that there is insufficient data about threats and vulnerabilities to reliably inform the values of confidentiality, integrity, the cost of an attack to third parties and other metrics. For the same reason, actuarial models for cybersecurity do not have a strong foundation at present, as evidenced by several efforts currently under way to standardize underwriting practices in this area. As a result, cybersecurity insurance research seems to focus on aspects, for which more reliable such models exist, for example, the reputational risk inherent in a major security or privacy breach. Within their Doctrine of Public Cybersecurity (akin to "Public Health"), Schneider and Mulligan point out the need to manage insecurity and propose to use Diversity (akin to biodiversity, such as the adaptive immune system that is unique to each human individual) as a principle for such management: the systematic use of obfuscation and randomization to ensure that systems are not monocultures. Clearly, such diversification has benefits beyond security and is applicable, for example, to the study of privacy. While the approach is attractive, we need to assess the impact of such diversification on other system aspects, such as safety in industrial control systems. It would be of interest to formulate Doctrines of Risk Engineering using a similar approach.

A shared semantic context will be also beneficial to the creation of useful principles of risk engineering. Using the example of cybersecurity, comparison of cybersecurity strategies in a number of countries shows that there is considerable commonality in high-level principles and approaches used by diverse nations, as evidenced, for example, in Ref. [47]. However, transition from these principles to specific practices and associated risk analysis is complicated due to the lack of well-developed ontologies and risk models.

It is clear that, in order to create an area of study focusing on risk engineering, in addition to the work on adaptation of existing potentially applicable models and modeling languages, we need to develop a set of high-level principles to guide the solutions for significant technical and semantic challenges emerging in this area.

8.5 Case Study: Block-Chain Technology

We now present a case study to demonstrate how proposed risk engineering approaches can be used in connection with an emerging technology space, cryptocurrencies.

In 2009, Bitcoin [48] emerged as the first digital currency in which there is no need to trust a central third party. Instead, a distributed and therefore decentralized public ledger of transactions records the authentic history of approved transactions, and does so in a pseudo-anonymous manner. We refer here to Ref. [49] for a gentle introduction to this technology, and to Ref. [50] for a general discussion of the economics of digital currencies. We first introduce the ideas and concepts behind such cryptocurrencies, notably the block-chain technology and its concept of *Proof of Work*, before we discuss its implications for risk engineering.

Cryptocurrencies based on block-chain technology constitute a remarkable piece of innovation, solving a well-known coordination problem in Distributed Systems [51], known as the *Byzantine Generals*, that was thought by some not to have a feasible solution: how can $n > 1$ generals located on different hills coordinate so that their troops attack at the same time, given that all communication links are unreliable (in particular, broadcasts may not reach all at all times, and not at the same time)? Intuitively, it would suffice if they could elect a leader who would propose the attack time that all others would then follow. The challenge in this problem then is, faced with unreliable communications, to create a *unique* leader and that the identity of that leader becomes common knowledge among all generals.

8.5.1 Proof of Work

The innovation behind Bitcoin and its block-chain technology is a protocol that makes use of a concept called *Proof of Work*: the generals agreed, beforehand, that any general may announce an attack time, and that any general who hears a *first* such announcement, solves a difficult cryptographic problem based on a cryptographic hash function and dependent on the just heard announcement. We do not have to understand technical details of cryptographic hash functions here; it suffices to say that these are deterministic algorithms that take any message as input and produce a bit-string of fixed size, say 256 bits, as output; and, importantly, it is computationally hard to find two inputs with the same output, or to construct an input other than a given one that produces the same output as the given input.

The Proof-of-Work problem exploits these security properties of cryptographic hash functions and is designed to take, on average, 10 minutes to solve. A solution, a hash of the announcement, some random input, is then broadcast to all generals. The idea now is to compose such proofs produced by different generals so that Proof-of-Work problems work not just on a sole announcement but on a sequence of consistent such announcements (i.e., announcements that propose the same attack time), a so called *block-chain*. The agency and concurrency of this protocol imply that there may be more than one, competing, block-chains (each with a different proposal of attack time) that generals could work on—jeopardizing that a unique leader be elected. In simple terms, this threat to reaching a consensus is dealt with by the generals' agreement of always choosing the *longest* block-chain for the next Proof-of-Work problem. In other words, the chain that requires the most effort to produce, is interpreted as the current, authoritative version of "truth."

8.5.2 Consensus and Pseudoanonymity

One of the striking things about this solution is that it does not depend on the fact that the announcements made in each block are consistent. This technology may compose blocks containing any information, in particular information about a transaction; and the longest block-chain then represents the authoritative account of which transactions really did happen. And this works even though the parties participating in the construction of such chains are self-interested. In particular, block-chain technology may support novel trust infrastructures.

The core of decentralized cryptocurrencies such as Bitcoin is therefore a block-chain technology that enables the creation and maintenance of a public ledger that records the complete history of transactions, where it is difficult to insert a proven record of a transaction into the block-chain—as it involved Proof of Work—but where it is very easy to verify that such a record is authoritative, that is, that it was the subject of a solved Proof-of-Work problem. As already mentioned, this technology allows a transaction to be anything that can be expressed in a message—an attack time, a quote from a newspaper, payload data, a wire to transfer money, among others.

The design intent of this technology is that it also provides for *anonymity* of transactions. That is to say, while each transaction on the block-chain can in principle be inspected and verified by anyone, knowledge of the source and destination of a transaction is under the control of these transacting parties. The system also has built-in incentive mechanisms: people who attempt Proof-of-Work problems are referred to as *Miners*. If they solve a problem so that it gets added to the authoritative block-chain, they get rewarded in so-called bitcoins—with an optional transaction fee that the source of the verified transaction may offer as additional incentive. We may think of this as a game-theoretic means of ensuring that enough work is put into the system, so that transactions' verification will be attempted (without their verification they will not enter the block-chain and so they will not have "happened" according to that block-chain), and so that the block-chain will be maintained over time.

At the time of writing, miners get 25 bitcoins per block, an amount that will be halved about each 4 years. A block is understood to be a group of accepted transactions, where "accepted" implies that this indirectly also accepts all past transactions on the block-chain. The latter is achieved by making the hash of the previous block itself an input to the cryptographic problem that, if solved, makes this new block an accepted one. This means that a block that adds a group of transactions to the block-chain not only confirms the veracity of that group of transactions but, implicitly, also the veracity of all past transactions on that block-chain. From the perspective of a set of active adversaries, this means that attacking this system becomes harder: it may seem perhaps feasible to modify the most recently added block, by solving a related hard cryptographic problem of hash functions, in order to revise the history of its transaction, say by changing the addressee of a payment. But this is already hard to do, and it becomes harder and harder to extend such a capability to blocks that were added in the past: the block-chain gets extended about every 10 minutes, which seems too limiting a window of opportunity for adversaries to work effectively—even if the hash functions used in this technology may have security weaknesses.

8.5.3 Design Risks

In terms of risk engineering, the mining mechanism contains several challenges: the incentive for mining is a direct function of the prize of electricity in the Bitcoin currency, and the effort needed for a Proof of Work is designed to increase considerably over time. This may lead to pools of miners powerful enough to attack Bitcoin as discussed below. It also adds uncertainty as we know neither how energy prizes nor how the speed and energy efficiency of hashing hardware will evolve in the long-term. Understanding how to manage such risks is hard, and being able to engineer such risks is impossible using current methodologies.

To better define the problem, let us discuss how bitcoins act as a unit of account. The smallest unit of account in this system is 10^{-8} bitcoins. Coins, integral multiples of such a unit, can be seen as unspent outputs of transactions. Coins are authenticated because they are linked into the block-chain itself as a special transaction called a *coinbase*. The system provides a means of generating addresses for sending payments, and public-key cryptography is used so that the spending of coins is controlled by proof of ownership. The combination of public-key cryptography and the block-chain technology also solves the *double spending* problem: Alice cannot spend a coin for two different payments, say one to Bob and one to Claire: the block-chain will only allow one history in which that coin either went to Bob or to Claire.

Bitcoin has a number of system parameters, for which concrete values were chosen at system launch time and where some of these parameters can be adjusted dynamically as the system evolves over time. In particular, the system has a fixed limit on the number of bitcoins, 21 million, which can be created. That limit is expected to be reached by 2040. This means that any risk assessment made of Bitcoin needs to consider a timespan of about 25 years, which is challenging as we do not have good predictions of the nature of the technology space and we do not know how Bitcoin may be used, technologically and behaviorally, at that future point in time. Our limited predictive power for systems such as Bitcoin, in which security, reliability, privacy, and other aspects interact, is evidenced by numerous forecasts on Bitcoin future that have been proven wrong.

One interesting example of a dynamic system parameter in Bitcoin is how many blocks can be added to the chain before the difficulty level of the cryptographic problem is increased: the aim is to ensure that such problems can, on average, be solved by miners within 10 minutes. One may wonder how the designers came up with that value; it is clear that it is partly chosen to reflect latency in the peer-to-peer communication network. We may see the choice of 10 minutes as a form of risk engineering that, presumably, is the result of guesswork and experimentation with prototype implementations, to test various parameter choices and assess their suitability. However, risk analysts do not know whether the latency could be optimized for better performance or whether it is connected with increased safety, reliability, or security risks.

One effect of this decision to maintain a 10-minute average as a Proof-of-Work system invariant, however, is that Proof of Work will consume more and more energy over time. This raises obvious environmental concerns. But it also means that individual owners of modern computers with GPUs inside will have no value proposition for doing Proof of Work all by themselves: the energy cost of the computation already exceeds the revenue from the bitcoins earned in such computations at the time of writing. This then leads to the formation of powerful pools of miners (leading to what one may perhaps call Mining

Oligarchies), with the possibility of such pools to get close to the majority of network computing power. In the so-called "51% attack," a pool that were to have such a majority of computing power would literally be able to rewrite the transaction history: the ability to produce an alternative block-chain that is longer and verifies so that other nodes in the network would then switch to that block-chain as the authoritative one. This attack would have similar dramatic consequences to changes observed in human history, when new powers would refuse to honor existing contracts, property titles, and so forth—and might perhaps even rewrite the history books. In analyzing risks for Bitcoin, it is evident that probabilities of devastating attacks as well as safety, security, and privacy considerations need to be evaluated in concert.

8.5.4 Other Security Risks

Similar attacks may be feasible with <51% computing power of the network, for example, if one could exploit the interaction of the game-theoretic incentive mechanisms and the Proof-of-Work mechanism. Related to that, there was apparently a 6-hour period in 2013, in which a software bug led to two competing block-chains in Bitcoin that split the network roughly into two halves, each half believing in the authority of one of those two block-chains. This problem was solved by shutting down the system, and then asking network nodes to downgrade to a software version that did not have that bug. This was a rather drastic measure that may not be an option in some systems that have to remain operational at all costs.

This incident also illustrates that we need to trust the maintainers and developers of a particular cryptocurrency: we have very high trust in the authenticity of the longest block-chain (as a mathematical concept), but there is a legitimate question of whether the operators of a cryptocurrency are trustworthy. The issue of trustworthiness becomes even more pressing in dealing with service infrastructures built by others around a cryptocurrency. For example, a Bitcoin exchange is a service for buying or selling bitcoins with fiat money such as a US Dollar. Mt Gox was such an exchange that had a big market share among bitcoin exchanges in 2013. When it filed for bankruptcy, it appeared that it had lost about 800,000 bitcoins of which about 200,000 were later recovered. The actual reasons for this loss, be it mismanagement, theft, or something else, appear to be unclear at the time of writing.

This can be seen as a cautionary tale: while early regulation and legislation may hinder the innovation and development of such technology (e.g., as it is difficult to assess its future use contexts), lack of regulation or legislation creates considerable uncertainty to consumers and businesses that use services based on cryptocurrencies. This may be one reason why the retail sector has not seen much use of cryptocurrencies. A purchase with a credit card, for example, usually gives consumers certain rights and protection to return the goods within a certain time period for a full refund, say. Such rights and protections do not extent, at present, to purchases based on bitcoins, where it is also the customer and not the merchant who pays any possible transaction fees. One risk in regulating this technology, for example, through compliance regimes, is that is likely to drive up operational costs and so one of the key advantages of the technology, low transaction costs, may disappear.

A similar security problem to the one reported above occurred in an early version of a bitcoin client/wallet: a flaw allowed for the creation of many bitcoins; this was solved by creating another chain that eventually overtook that "bad" chain. We may think of this outcome as evidence of the resiliency of the block-chain technology (security in the absence of a 51% attack). But we may equally say that both of these examples raise interesting methodological questions about the interplay of software validation and the reliability and stability of complex systems such as Bitcoin that connect its core block-chain software with external services and infrastructures. We will articulate some of these questions further below.

Decentralized cryptocurrencies seem to possess good *pseudo-anonymity*: transactions are signed with a digital signature key, a private key known only to the signer. The corresponding public key and its association with that private key are public knowledge—yet the identity of the owner of these keys is not. In fact, an individual may produce a fresh such key pair for each of its bitcoin transactions to make it even harder for someone to identify the true source of a transaction. This, however, increases the complexity of key management where keys are stored in electronic wallets on the client side, offline, or on some server. In fact, some Bitcoin users have allegedly lost considerable assets by physically losing a private key for transactions: in the Bitcoin design losing the private key amounts to losing all value inherent in the transactions signed with those keys.

To assess risks of block-chain currencies, we need to understand how this technology connects with its operational context. Wallets, for example, provide an interface between the block-chain—with its security and resiliency—and the external world of online or offline financial and other transaction-based services, including the ICT infrastructure that supports the latter. As a consequence, adversaries gain attack surfaces for block-chains by attacking the digital credentials stored in such wallets and needed for interacting with the block-chain. Such attacks can be completed with conventional means, for example, malware that breaks into or steals such wallets by exploiting well-known security vulnerabilities in ICT systems (where these vulnerabilities reside outside of the block-chain and its design). But one may also attack the block-chain system itself: for example, there are documented cases [52] of botnets (a familiar means of getting control over a network of computers to use them for unauthorized and potentially illegal activity) that specialize in creating mining pools, which creates income for the controllers of these botnets without having to spend any cost on the energy needed for the mining (that bill is distributed to the owners of the hijacked computers of the botnet).

More speculatively, and more disconcertedly, what if the block-chain design of Bitcoin were to contain a serious flaw that would threaten its existence in terms of operability, credibility, or other measures? Such a flaw may be hard to find because it would require a subtle interplay of the game theory at work, choices of system parameters, and environmental trends such as the evolution of computing power or of the cost of energy, human psychology, and emergent use contexts of Bitcoin. Conspiracy theorists may also suggest that such flaws might be intentional design decisions, so that the creators of a cryptocurrency can exploit this flaw to their own benefit. At present, we do not have good risk engineering methodologies that could model and analyze this type of complexity to validate the design and implementation of a cryptocurrency with sufficiently high assurance. This inability raises serious issues of acceptability of such technology, be it for consumers and citizens, commercial and nongovernmental organizations or government agencies; and it suggests a compelling case for more funded research in that problem space—a case also made convincingly in Ref. [53].

There are also documented successful attempts of linking transactions to specific individuals [54]. Such threats to privacy can be countered by using a so-called mixing service [55], which swaps ownership of bitcoins randomly in order to obfuscate the linkage of coins to digital credentials; we refer to Ref. [53] for a detailed evaluation of anonymity techniques in this problem space. A related concern to privacy is that of fungibility of a currency: a cash bill of a currency such as the US

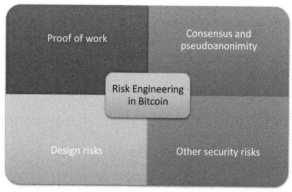

Figure 8.6 Risk engineering in Bitcoin: interplay of relevant challenges.

Dollar is basically anonymous in that we do not know the history of its usage: perhaps this bill was used for past transactions that we would not condone, but since we do not know that, we do not seem to care. However, in Proof-of-Work cryptocurrencies it seems possible in principle to provide links between coins and transactions in which they participated. So we can imagine that users may refuse to use some coins because, say, they were used in the past by a drug cartel (Fig. 8.6).

Finally, block-chain technology is expected to undergo *mission creep*: at the moment, it is defined with pseudoanonymity in mind. But the technology holds great promise as a tool used within an organization, where its identify management is linked with the block-chain and where the too costly Proof of Work is replaced by a more cost-effective alternative, for example, *Proof of Stake*. We then need solid means of composing risk (e.g., risk stemming from identity management with risk inherent in a Proof-of-Stake block-chain). We will discuss approaches to risk composition in section 8.6.2.

8.5.5 Risk Engineering of Cryptocurrencies

The discussion of pertinent features of block-chain technologies illustrated that there is no robust theoretical foundation for systems such as Bitcoin, and that it is unclear how existing approaches (e.g., Nash Equilibria) may be put to use to render predictive power for such. Creating such foundations is challenging. Although we indicated societal, regulatory, economic, and behavioral risk in evaluating elements of the risk picture in early sections of this chapter, the approaches to integrated risk engineering focused on system behavior, with less attention to human interaction or economic aspects of their operations.

For cryptocurrencies such as Bitcoin, however, it is vital to consider human behavior as a factor in analyzing risks for the privacy, availability, security, and correctness of systems that implement such block-chain technology. We need to develop appropriate abstractions of block-chain technologies and their deployment and adoption models. Such abstractions can help in engineering new methods for risk prevention, detection, and mitigation that inform risk management over the entire life cycle of such complex artifacts and to increase trust of the uses of such systems. As an example, in Bitcoin, low-cost transactions are not confirmed by one or more blocks within the block-chain at the time of transaction, limiting its trustworthiness. In addition to modeling and analysis capabilities, risk engineering could help deal with the tensions that could undermine the level of trust.

The economic aspect of cryptocurrencies would benefit from the use of conventional and new models analyzing asymmetric information in cryptocurrency markets, the evolved role of monetary economic models, and the impact of aggregation and intermediation. The use of multidomain ontologies coupled with appropriate reasoning methodologies and risk models as described in section 8.4.4 may help overcome these limitations.

A very long life cycle for cryptocurrencies-related system could also represent a limitation, but these issues have been addressed in emerging risk frameworks for cyber-physical and industrial control systems, which also have great variability of lifespans, ranging from one time use to several decades. A risk language proposed as an element of risk engineering foundational tools could be used to codify and quantify additional domain–specific risks as they appear at the initial stages of design and amend them with empirical metrics obtained during the operations of the framework.

Risk engineering approaches could be beneficial for cryptocurrencies. Appropriate multidomain ontologies could enable the analysis of the issues in a broader and more integrated context including reasoning about multiple applicable risk domains. Adaptation of compositional and other models used in traditional IT system spaces could be instrumental in modeling integrated risks for a variety of operational conditions; these models could be updated as the understanding of risk parameterization matures. A risk language could be used to manage risks in real time during operations and at the design stages. With risk engineering approaches, many risks can be addressed in context, quantitatively and qualitatively, and at the requirement elicitation stage, thus increasing security, safety, and reliability of such systems.

8.6 Model-Based and Language-Based Risk Engineering

In previous sections we summarized approaches to risk engineering using adaptations and integration of model-based and language-based methodologies available today. This section concludes the discussion providing additional insights in these two areas.

We believe that the use of models and declarative languages may help articulate risks in the design of complex systems such as cryptocurrencies, in particular in understanding the interaction of different aspects and their trade-offs. We already provided evidence for such utility in our discussion of ACTs in Section 8.4.2. Making such models automatically analyzable to scale, say for a model of Bitcoin, seems particularly challenging. Parameterized model checking can validate designs for a range of system parameters, and is often decidable [56]. But systems such as Bitcoin require its extension to both consensus algorithms (to model the block-chain) and different network topologies (to model peer-to-peer networks) or new formal methods with such capabilities.

8.6.1 Reasoning About Complex Fields Using Ontologies

We already discussed the applicability of ontologies to integrated risk analysis. The general-purpose, hierarchical nature of ontologies, and the fact that all relevant information is encoded in an explicit, machine-accessible way make ontologies prime candidates for formalizing multidisciplinary knowledge, reasoning about complex fields, and underlying connections between seemingly unrelated subjects, an especially useful feature for integrated risk analysis (e.g., Ref. [57]).

When describing multidisciplinary knowledge, as is the case for risk engineering, it is useful to use both an upper ontology and domain-specific ontologies. An upper ontology is an encoding of the concepts that are common across all domains included in the ontology, in an effort that mimics work to define cross-cutting characteristics of complex frameworks (Fig. 8.7).

A domain ontology formalizes a specific knowledge domain, with concepts from the domain ontologies describing the high-level concepts in the upper ontology. For example, an upper domain may capture the notion of a decision tree, where either the system or an adversary controls nodes. And a domain-specific

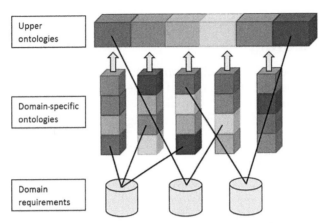

Figure 8.7 Risk engineering describes multidisciplinary knowledge: domain requirements can be described by specific domain ontologies and upper ontologies.

ontology may instantiate such a tree as an attack tree where a system tries to prevent an attack against an active adversary. In the safety domain, the adversary may be passive, modeling nature as a random process (e.g., corrosion of metals, failure of mechanical components, and so forth). When describing regulatory requirements, the concepts may be linked with the upper ontology and ontologies describing other domains. When addressing societal and economic issues, instantiation of concepts of the upper ontology for these domains could be used to clarify the connection, and linkages with other domains could inform other aspects of risk analysis. To specify privacy requirements, a decision tree for the use of privacy enhancing technologies or privacy compliance processes can be connected to the upper ontology and laterally to other risk domains.

This KR and reasoning framework becomes especially useful in situations in which knowledge from multiple fields must be taken into account at the same time, for example, assessing the vulnerabilities and safety requirements of a connected car or a smart meter. Using an ontology, one can study vulnerabilities that may come from coordinated exploits affecting both the power system and the braking system (or power management and data collection systems) or study risks in different environments.

One challenge is to understand how issues pertaining to different risk domains influence each other, for example, how safety or privacy influence issues pertaining to security or reliability. Approaches for such analyses have been already presented in section 8.2.3.

8.6.2 Risk Composition, Risk Language, and Metrics

Ontologies and their reasoning/inference engines are expressed in declarative formalisms, for example, Description Logics [58]. It is desirable that the inference problems that such engines aim to solve be decidable, so that algorithms can be devised, which always provide answers to reasoning queries. This is especially important when the answers to queries influence the behavior of a running system: the inability to answer is then an inability to influence. But reasoning about the design or implementation of a system may well benefit from considering inference problems that are more expressive and therefore generally undecidable. In the credit rating industry score cards [59] were developed to model the risk of providing a loan to clients. Ideally we would want such approaches to decision support for complex ICT systems. Let us illustrate how this approach might work by composing risk metrics in a declarative language, using an example discussed in Ref. [60]: a clerk of a rental company at a US location needs to decide whether a client may rent a car.

We can think of various policies informing this decision, where each policy has its own "score card," a numerical value. One policy may concern the risk of financial loss to the rental company should the car be damaged, where some vehicles have specific loss values, whereas others have a default one (e.g., to model effects on an insurance premium). Another policy may score the trust in a client's ability to drive the vehicle safely based on relevant considerations; this aspect also raises ethical and privacy issues. A third policy may concern the intended usage of the car, capturing, for example, different risk scores for off-road driving, city-only driving, and long-distance driving on two-lane motorways. This risk again needs to be analyzed in connection with potential privacy considerations, Finally, we may have a policy that accumulates trust evidence from a pool of drivers (without attribution), such as the number of years driven without accident (positive signal) or whether the client is traveling alone.

Apart from challenges in addressing such issues, there is the question of how such policies are best composed. We can imagine combining the score for financial loss with a probability of the loss occurring, where that probability may be inversely proportional to the level of trust we have in the client's safe driving. Technically this approach would aggregate policies into policy sets. Such aggregation may not be confined to weighted sums as familiar from the computation of probabilistic expectations.

We may also consider operators such as the minimum of two scores to model that one score acts as a hard constraint on any score returned by some other policy. For example, we may say that a client who is younger than 21 years may only rent specific car models; such a constraint may be enforceable in some territories, for example, those that issue driver's licenses with an initial learner status. But it may be illegal in other territories, illustrating that policy aggregation also needs to reflect such specificities accurately.

Let us call such aggregates policies "policy sets," which have numerical scores as meaning. We may therefore place such policy sets into logical conditions such as "The expected financial loss using Bitcoin will always be below a specific value." Ideally, we want to be able to analyze such declared conditions as formal expressions to explore whether they can give rise to cryptocurrency use scenarios that a risk engineer would not want to allow. This would then suggest refining the policies and conditions to rule out undesired scenarios. One important aspect in such analyses is the ability to incorporate domain-specific knowledge, for example, with regard to Bitcoin transactions.

The feasibility of such an approach for a different domain has been demonstrated in Ref. [29] and some of its usability issues are discussed in Ref. [60]. For a transfer of such a proof-of-concept approach into effective support for risk management, it would be desirable to create *patterns* of policies and score aggregations that reflect the particular needs of risk managers. The approach sketched above can already compose scores from different *levels* of risk, so that relative or absolute importance is taken into account. But there would be value in having dedicated top-level policies for different *types* of risk as well: risks that are known, risks that are unknown, risks that have been reasonably mitigated to name some example types. We note that these types and their score computations are also a function of domain-specific constraints and their variability. Constraint solvers such as the aforementioned SMT solvers and optimization tools are important resources for reflecting these dependencies so that a computed worst-case score for a type of risk is guaranteed to reflect *all* relevant scenarios. How to combine scores from policies of different types of risk, in order to better support decision making in risk assessment and management, is a question for more research.

More research is also needed for obtaining meaningful scores for scorecard-style policies in applications to future ICT systems. In the credit rating industry, computing scores is feasible since there are data on past credit decisions and on the outcomes of all positive decisions to give credit, say whether a given credit was not paid back, paid back late, or paid back in full and on time. From this, one can derive statistical models against which to compare an applicant's personal credit history. This is reliable if the personal information of the applicant is accurate enough, and if the behavior of the client base would not change dramatically in comparison to the existing statistical data. It is not immediately clear how such an approach can be adapted to engineering risk in systems such as a future ICT product platform for cars. But the fact that such products will collect much more data in the future will certainly help in the long term, as such "big data" can then render meaningful scores based on machine-learning techniques.

To summarize this discussion, the creation of trust and risk languages to provide semantic explanations of risk considerations is very important for the success of risk engineering. These languages can provide a foundation for integrated risk analysis as well as annotation of risk expectations at the time of system design. These languages can be linked to ontologies, thus providing mechanisms capable of analyzing specific operational contexts based on common considerations in the ICT space.

8.7 Summary and Conclusions

The complexity and dynamic nature of the modern ICT environment makes it imperative to analyze operational and other risks of ICT systems in an integrated manner. The risk domains of security, privacy, safety, reliability, resilience, and the influence of regulatory environments all combine to determine the risks of security or privacy breach, system failure, or safety issues. Moreover, different operational contexts, such as cryptocurrency, organizational use of IT, or driving a connected car, further complicates the analysis of these risks, especially since a system could be used in a variety of operational contexts over its lifetime. For example, the use of a smart phone as a GPS device in a moving connected car could provide information about the location of individual, a potential breach of privacy, thus altering the risk picture.

In addition to the need to form an integrated risk picture where privacy, security, safety, and other domains are jointly considered, we also need to define methodologies for risk composition, thus enabling us to assess the *combined risks of multiple systems used in an ecosystem*. Due to the integrated and complex nature of the computing environment, its dependence on the shared infrastructure, and the ability of ICT systems to produce significant economic impacts, managing risks associated with the use of one system taken in isolation is no longer sufficient.

The complexity of the environment also makes it impossible to assess risks in operational context only; it is imperative today to *inform the system development processes of the integrated acceptable risk requirements*. Thus, risk engineering is an area that should become a focus of research and practical evaluation, in order to usher in a new generation of systems that are *risk conscious by design*.

We think that the approaches necessary to build these systems already exist, but need to be adjusted for risk engineering. The major components of risk engineering methodologies include:

- Multidomain ontology to capture risk semantics and comprising an upper and multiple domain–specific ontologies linked together.
- Modeling approaches that could be combined with such an ontology, including graph-based models and declarative constraints.
- Risk languages that can be used to both annotate and analyze risks and are capable of supporting specific use cases.

Numerous challenges exist to creating a risk engineering framework. They include limitation of the existing approaches; need for broadly applicable metrics; differences in terminology and metrics used in different risk domains; limited inventory of approaches to risk composition; difficulties in developing a comprehensive multidomain ontology for risk engineering, and several other areas of concern. These challenges are significant, but probably not unsurmountable. More research should focus on these issues to improve our understanding of risks and to build stronger foundations of risk engineering.

Acknowledgments

We thank Leif-Nissen Lundbaek, a PhD student at Imperial College London, for comments and suggestions pertaining to the case study on block-chain technology. Andrea Callia D'Iddio and Ruth Misener collaborated with Michael Huth on research at the junction of MINLP and SMT; their work informed in part the material in Section 7.3.

References

[1] EMC Corporation, Press Release: New EMC Innovations Redefine IT Performance and Efficiency. <http://www.emc.com/about/news/press/2015/20150504-01.htm>, May 4, 2015 (accessed 11.08.15).

[2] Cisco, Seize New IoT Opportunities With the Cisco IoT System. <http://www.cisco.com/web/solutions/trends/iot/portfolio.html> (accessed 26.08.15).

[3] Software Engineering Institute, Carnegie Mellon University, Architecture Tradeoff Analysis Method. Available from: <http://www.sei.cmu.edu/architecture/tools/evaluate/atam.cfm>.

[4] Cyber-Physical Systems Public Working Group, Framework for Cyber-Physical Systems, Release 0.8. DRAFT, September 2015.

[5] Kushner, D., The Real Story of Stuxnet Spectrum. IEEE.Org (North American). <http://spectrum.ieee.org/telecom/security/the-real-story-of-stuxnet#>, March 2013, pp. 49–53.

[6] P.H. Feiler, Steve Vestal (Honeywell Technology Center), The SAE Avionics Architecture Description Language (AADL) Standard: A Basis for Model-Based Architecture-Driven Embedded Systems Engineering. Available from: <http://resources.sei.cmu.edu/library/asset-view.cfm?assetid=29547>, May 2003.

[7] S. Wright, R. Mason, D. Miles, A Study Into Certain Aspects of the Cost of Capital for Regulated Utilities in the U.K, Report Commissioned by the U.K. Economic Regulators and the Office of Fair Trading, London, February 2003.

[8] G. Knieps, H.-J. Weiß. Reduction of Regulatory Risk: A Network Economic Approach. Discussion Paper Institut für Verkehrswissenschaft und Regionalpolitik No. 117, September 2007.

[9] G.E. Moore, Progress in digital integrated electronics, in: Electron Devices Meeting, vol. 21, IEEE Conference Publications, 1975, pp. 11–13. Retrieved at <http://ieeexplore.ieee.org/stamp/stamp.jsp?tp=&arnumber=1478174>.

[10] A. Scott, Risk society or angst society? Two views of risk, consciousness and community, in: B. Adam, U. Beck, J. van Loon (Eds.), The Risk Society and Beyond: Critical Issues for Social Theory, Sage, London, 2000, pp. 33–46.

[11] T. Maurer, R. Morgus, I. Skierka, M. Hohmann, Technological sovereignty: missing the point? Report by New America's Open Technology Institute and the Global Public Policy Institute (GPPi) Funded With the Support of the European Commission, November 2014.

[12] Court of Justice of the European Union, *Judgment in Case C-362/14 Maximillian Schrems v Data Protection Commissioner*, October 2015. Retrieved at <http://curia.europa.eu/juris/document/document.jsf?text=&docid=172254&pageIndex=0&doclang=en&mode=req&dir=&occ=first&part=1&cid=191575>.

[13] L. Sweeney, Technology Dialectics: Constructing Provably Appropriate Technology, Data Privacy Lab. <http://dataprivacylab.org/dataprivacy/projects/dialectics/index.html>, Fall 2006 (accessed on 26.08.15).

[14] P. Katsumata, J. Hemenway, W. Gavins, Cybersecurity risk management, in: Military Communications Conference, 2010-Milcom 2010. IEEE, 2010.

[15] Intel Corporation, Prioritizing Information Security Risks With Threat Agent Risk Assessment, Information Technology White Paper. Available from: <http://www.intel.com/Assets/en_US/PDF/whitepaper/wp_IT_Security_RiskAssessment.pdf>, 2009.

[16] J. Hunker, Policy challenges in building dependability in global infrastructures, Comput Security 21.8 (2002) 705–711.

[17] InternetLiveStats.com, data available at: <http://www.internetlivestats.com/internet-users/>.

[18] International Telecommunication Union, Estimation Found At Estimate, at <https://en.wikipedia.org/wiki/Global_Internet_usage>.

[19] BSA|Software Alliance, et al., Moving Forward Together: Recommended Industry and Government Approaches for the Continued Growth and Security of Cyberspace, October 2013.

[20] G.A. Akerlof, The market for "lemons": quality uncertainty and the market mechanism, Q J Econ (1970) 488–500.

[21] J.M. Bauer, M.J.G. Van Eeten, Cybersecurity: Stakeholder incentives, externalities, and policy options, Telecommunications Policy 33 (10) (2009) 706–719.

[22] H.A.M. Luiijf, et al., Empirical findings on European critical infrastructure dependencies, International Journal of System of Systems Engineering 2.1, 2010, pp. 3–18.

[23] P. Rodrigues, E. Lupu, J. Kramer, Compositional realibility analysis for probabilistic component automata, in: IEEE/ACM 7th International Workshop on Modeling in Software Engineering, IEEE Computer Society Press, 2015.

[24] L. Piètre-Cambacédès, M. Bouissou, Cross-fertilization between safety and security engineering, Rel. Eng. Sys. Safety 110 (2013) 110–126.

[25] International Atomic Energy Agency (IAEA), International Nuclear Safety Group (INSAG), Defence in Depth in Nuclear Safety, INSAG-10, STI/PUB/1013, 1996.

[26] Ozment A. Software security growth modeling: examining vulnerabilities with reliability growth models, in: Proceedings of the 1st Workshop on Quality of Protection (QoP'05), Milan, Italy, 2005. pp. 25–36.

[27] O. Sheyner, J.W. Haines, S. Jha, R. Lippmann, J.M. Wing: Automated generation and analysis of attack graphs, in: IEEE Symposium on Security and Privacy, 2002, pp. 273–284.

[28] A. Roy, D.S. Kim, K.S. Trivedi, Attack countermeasure trees (ACT): towards unifying the constructs of attack and defense trees, Secur Commun Netw 5 (8) (2012) 929–943 (John Riley & Sons).

[29] M. Huth, J.H.-P. Kuo. Quantitative Threat Analysis via a Logical Service. Technical Report 2014/14, Department of Computing, Imperial College, London.

[30] T. Bedford, R. Cooke, Probabilistic Risk Analysis: Foundations and Methods, Cambridge University Press, Cambridge, MA, 2001.

[31] L. De Moura, N. Bjørner, Satisfiability modulo theories: introduction and applications, Commun ACM 54 (9) (2011) 69–77, ACM Press.

[32] M. Jünger, T.M. Liebling, D. Naddef, G.L. Nemhauser, W.R. Pulleyblank, G. Reinelt, et al., 50 Years of Integer Programming 1958–2008—From the Early Years to the State-of-the-Art, Springer, Berlin, 2010, ISBN 978-3-540-68274-5.

[33] N. Bjørner, A.-D. Phan, L. Fleckenstein, vZ—An Optimizing SMT Solver, Proceedings of TACAS 2015, LNCS 9035, Springer Verlag, Berlin, 2015.

[34] P. Beaumont, N. Evans, M. Huth, T. Plant, Confidence analysis for nuclear arms control: SMT-abstractions of bayesian belief networks, in: Computer Security——ESORICS 2015, Springer 2015, pp. 521–540.

[35] A. Ben-Tal, L. El Ghaoui, A. Nemirovski, Robust Optimization, Princeton University Press, Princeton, NJ, 2009.

[36] J. Pearl, Belief networks revisited, Artif Intell 59 (1–2) (1993) 49–56.

[37] S. Kriaa, L. Pietre-Cambacedes, M. Bouissou, Y. Halgand, A survey of approaches combining safety and security for industrial control systems, Reliab Eng Syst Safety 139 (2015) 156–178.

[38] M. Huth, J.H.-P. Kuo. An automated reasoning tool for numerical aggregation of trust evidence, in: Proceedings of the 20th International Conference on Tools and Algorithms for the Analysis and Construction of Systems (TACAS 2014), Lecture Notes in Computer Science 8413, Springer Verlag, 2014, pp. 109–123.

[39] C. Vishik, M. Balduccini, Making Sense of Future Cybersecurity Technologies: Using Ontologies for Multidisciplinary Domain Analysis, ISSE 2015, Springer Fachmedien Wiesbaden, 2015, pp. 135–145.

[40] J. Mylopoulos, M. Jarke, M. Koubarakis, Telos—a language for representing knowledge about information systems., ACM Trans Inf Syst 8 (4) (1990) 327–362.

[41] A. Herzog, N. Shahmehri, C. Duma, An ontology of information security, Int J Inf Security 1 (4) (2007) 1–23.

[42] Fenz, S., Ekelhart, A. Formalizing information security knowledge, in: ASIACCS 2009, 2009, pp. 183–194.

[43] H. Mouratidis, P. Giorgini, G. Manson, An ontology for modeling security: the tropos approach, Knowledge-Based Intelligent Information and Engineering Systems, Springer, Heidelberg, 2003.

[44] Massacci, F., Mylopoulos, J., Paci, F., Tun, T., Yu, Y., An extended ontology for security requirements, in: WEISSE 2011, June 20–24, 2011.

[45] D. Grawrock, Expressing trust, in: Talk given at the Workshop on Addressing R&D Challenges in Cybersecurity: Innovation and Collaboration Strategy, Imperial College London, London, UK, 20 June 2013.

[46] F.B. Schneider, D. Mulligan. *Doctrine for Cybersecurity.* Daedalus. Fall 2011, pp. 70–92. Also available as a Cornell Computing and Information Science Technical Report, April 2011.

[47] Cybersecurity Policy Making at a Turning Point: Analysing a New Generation of National Cybersecurity Strategies for the Internet Economy and Non-governmental Perspectives on a New Generation of National Cybersecurity Strategies: Contributions from BIAC, CSISAC and ITAC, OECD, 2012, http://www.oecd.org/sti/ieconomy/cybersecurity%20policy%20making.pdf (accessed August 24, 2016).

[48] S. Nakamoto. A Peer-to-Peer Electronic Cash System. <https://bitcoin.org/bitcoin.pdf>.

[49] R. Ali, J. Barrdear, R. Clews, J. Southgate, Innovations in payment technologies and the emergence of digital currencies, Bank of England Quarterly Bulletin (2014) Q3.

[50] R. Ali, J. Barrdear, R. Clews, J. Southgate, The economics of digital currencies, Bank of England Quarterly Bulletin (2014) Q3.

[51] L. Lamport, R. Shostak, M. Pease, The Byzantine Generals Problem (PDF), ACM Trans Progr Lang Syst 4 (3) (1982) 382–401.

[52] Infosecurity: Researcher Discovers Distributed Bitcoin Cracking Trojan Malware. <http://www.infosecurity-magazine.com/news/researcher-discovers-distributed-bitcoin-cracking/>, 19 August 2011.

[53] J. Bonneau, A. Miller, J. Clark, A. Narayagan, J.A. Kroll, E.W. Felten. SoK: research perspectives and challenges for bitcoin and cryptocurrencies, in: IEEE Symposium on Security and Privacy, 2015.

[54] T. Simonite. Mapping the bitcoin economy could reveal users' identity. MIT Technology Review, Computing News. <http://www.infosecurity-magazine.com/news/researcher-discovers-distributed-bitcoin-cracking/>, 5 August 2013.

[55] J. Matonis. The Policitcs of Bitcoin Mixing Services. Forbes.com. <http://www.forbes.com/sites/jonmatonis/2013/06/05/the-politics-of-bitcoin-mixing-services/>, 5 June 2013.

[56] R. Bloem, S. Jacobs, A. Khalimov, I. Konnov, S. Rubin, H. Veith, et al., Decidability of parameterized verification, Synthesis Lect. on Dist. Comp. Theory, Morgan & Claypool Publishers, San Rafael, CA, USA, 2015.

[57] C. Pesquita, J.D. Ferreira, F.M. Couto, M.J. Silva, The epidemiology ontology: an ontology for the semantic annotation of epidemiological resources, J. Biomed Semantics 5 (4) (2014).

[58] I. Horrocks, Description logics in ontology applications, KI 2005: Advances in Artificial Intelligence, Lecture Notes in Computer Science, vol. 3698, Springer Verlag, 2005.

[59] N.G. Pavlidis, D.K. Tasoulis, N.M. Adams, D.J. Hand, Adaptive consumer credit classification, J Oper Res Soc 63 (12) (2012) 1645–1654.

[60] M. Huth, J.H.-P. Kuo, On designing usable policy languages for declarative trust aggregation, Second International Conference, HAS 2014, Held as Part of HCI International 2014, Heraklion, Crete, Greece, June 22-27, 2014. Proceedings, 2014, pp. 45–56.

APPLICATIONS OF SYSTEM SAFETY AND SECURITY

9

A DESIGN METHODOLOGY FOR DEVELOPING RESILIENT CLOUD SERVICES

C. Tunc[1], S. Hariri[1], and A. Battou[2]
[1]University of Arizona, Tucson, AZ, United States [2]National Institute of Standards and Technology (NIST), Gaithersburg, MD, United States

9.1 Motivations

Cloud computing is a "model for enabling ubiquitous, convenient, on demand network access to a shared pool of configurable computing resources that can be rapidly provisioned and delivered with minimal managerial effort or service provider interaction" [1]. The most widely accepted delivery models of Cloud Computing are Infrastructure as a Service (IaaS), Platform as a Service (PaaS), and Software as a Service (SaaS) [2]. In addition, there are several deployment models (public, private, and hybrid) [3] and several emerging delivery models such as Storage as a Service (StaaS) [4], Security as a Service [5], and Network as a Service [6].

The recent embrace of cloud computing and services due to their performance and cost considerations will further exacerbate the security problem.

In cloud computing, organizations relinquish direct control of many security aspects to the service providers such as trust, privacy preservation, identity management, data and software isolation, and service availability. In addition, cloud computing integrates many technologies including virtualization, Web technologies, utility computing, and distributed data management, each with its own set of vulnerabilities. The adoption and proliferation of cloud computing and services will be severely impacted if cloud security is not adequately addressed. Traditional security approaches will not work effectively enough in a cloud environment due to many challenges related to the

Handbook of System Safety and Security. DOI: http://dx.doi.org/10.1016/B978-0-12-803773-7.00009-7

monoculture paradigm [7] that is widely used in configuring cloud resources and services, the rapid and dynamic changes in cloud environments, the use of social networking software tools that can lead to rapid spread of viruses and worms, the manually intensive management of security policies, and the use of heterogeneous and mobile tools and devices [8].

Cloud security suffers from a wide range of attacks targeting from physical machines to virtualized environment [9]. The dependency of cloud computing on the virtualized environment raises more security issues, like hypervisor exploitations [10,11]. In addition, one of the main security issues in cloud computing is the insider attacks, which has increased with the exchange of cloud data between different organizations.

Some previous works have presented classifications of Cloud Security [12–14]. In IaaS, since infrastructure resources such as computation, storage, network, etc., are shared among multiple users, IaaS services may not be designed to provide strong isolation among tenants, malicious insiders can gain access of legitimate user's data [14]. For PaaS, the providers offer platforms for development and deployment of clients' own applications on the cloud and abusive use of APIs can threaten all service-models [14]. In SaaS, customers remotely connect to cloud to use provided software applications. Cross-site scripting [15], access control weaknesses, OS and SQL injection flaws, cross-site request forgery [16], etc., are the threats to the SaaS cloud model and data [17].

Since in cloud the customers' data reside on the third-parties' data-centers, data security is a major concern for clients and some researchers have addressed data security in their works [18–20]. In addition, the insider attacks still remain a high-risk threat from employees inside the cloud provider company which potentially have access to a huge source of customers' information, especially for mission critical systems. Also, DDoS (Distributed Denial of Service) or network attacks can threaten the availability of cloud services. For such cases, intrusion detection approaches such as [21,22] have been used.

While various solutions have been proposed to solve cloud security issues [18,19], there is no comprehensive solution that covers all aspects of cloud security. Most of the offered solutions are partial and apply the detect-response model that fails with time. Furthermore, it is widely recognized that it is impossible to have cloud resources and services that cannot be penetrated and exploited. To address the cloud security challenges, we need an innovative design methodology based on resilience paradigm, moving target defense (MTD), and autonomic computing that will change the game to advantage the defender over the attacker.

9.2   Resilient Cloud Services Design Methodology

Our approach is based on using MTD concept to develop resilient cloud services (RCS) and algorithms that overcome the cloud security challenges [3]. The vision of MTD is defined as "Create, evaluate and deploy mechanisms and strategies that are diverse, continually shift, and change over time to increase complexity and costs for attackers, limit the exposure of vulnerabilities and opportunities for attack, and increase system resiliency" [23]. Our design methodology approach will make it much more difficult for any attacker to exploit vulnerability in a cloud service by changing the attack surface of the service randomly. Consequently, by the time an attacker probes, constructs, and launches an attack against the probed cloud service, that service will no longer exist or running; hence, the attack will become ineffective to disrupt the normal operations of the cloud service. Fig. 9.1 shows two scenarios: (1) *Successful Attack* when the cloud service environment stays static, as it is the case in most implementations/environments, giving the attacker plenty of time to study existing vulnerabilities by probing the services, and then constructing and launching an attack and (2) *Unsuccessful Attack* when the life span of one version of the cloud service is smaller than the time required to probe, construct, and launch an attack.

Our design methodology approach effectively utilizes the following capabilities:

1. *Redundancy*: It is a commonly used in fault tolerance technique [24] to continue to operate successfully in spite of software or hardware faults. In our approach, we combine the N-version programming [25] with hardware and virtual machine (VM) redundancy such that each cloud application

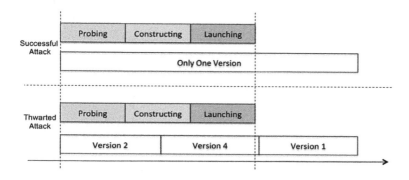

Figure 9.1 Attack window for moving target defense.

task runs on different physical nodes as well as on different VMs in the cloud infrastructure.

2. *Diversity*: This capability enables us to generate multiple functionally equivalent, behaviorally different software versions (e.g., each software task can have multiple versions, where each version can be a different algorithm implemented in a different programming language (e.g., C, Java, C++, etc.) that can run on different computing systems. We use the Compiler for Portable Checkpointing [26] to capture the current state of the cloud application such that it can be resumed on different cloud environments.

3. *Shuffling*: By randomly shuffling the use of diversified and redundant implementation of the cloud services, we obfuscate the execution environment of cloud services so that attackers will not be able to identify the type of execution environment and the resources used to run the cloud services. This approach will significantly reduce the ability of an attacker to disrupt the normal operations of a cloud service. Also, it allows adjusting the resilience level by dynamically increasing or decreasing the shuffling rate and their execution environments. A major advantage of this approach is that the dynamic change in the execution environment will hide the software flaws that would otherwise be exploited by a cyberattacker.

4. *Autonomic Management (AM)*: The primary task of the AM is to support dynamic decision among the various components such that the cloud resources and services. This way the services are dynamically configured to effectively exploit the current state of the cloud system and meet the application security requirements that might change at runtime.

9.3 RCS Architecture

Fig. 9.2 illustrates the architecture to implement the RCS development methodology using the following four main modules: Cloud Service Editor (CSE), Resilient Cloud Middleware (RCM), Configuration Engine (CE), Autonomic Service Manager (ASM) and Virtual Machines (VMs) to implement each resilient service managed by the ASM module.

9.3.1 Cloud Service Editor

The editor allows users and/or cloud service developers to specify the resiliency requirements of the cloud services by: (1) defining required diversity level (number of different versions

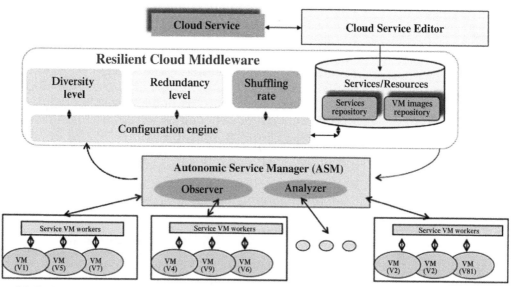

Figure 9.2 Resilient cloud service architecture.

and/or different platforms); (2) defining redundancy level (how many redundant physical machines are required); and (3) defining how often the execution environment and phases need to be changed.

9.3.2 Resilient Cloud Middleware

The RCM provides the control and management services to deploy and configure the software and hardware resources required to achieve the resiliency specified by the CSE. The resilient operation for any cloud application is achieved by randomly shuffling the versions and the resources used to run each service so that it can hide (analogous to data encryption) the execution environment. The dynamic change in the service behavior makes it extremely difficult for an attacker to generate a profile with the possible flaws and to launch a successful attack. The decisions regarding when to shuffle the current variant, shuffling frequency, and variant selection for the next shuffle are guided by a continuous monitoring and analysis of current execution state of cloud services and the desired resiliency requirements.

To speed up the process of selecting the appropriate resilient algorithms and execution environments, the RCM repository contains a set of BO algorithms and images of VMs that run different operating systems (e.g., Windows, Linux, etc.) to implement supported cloud services such as MapReduce, Web services, Request and Tracker applications, just to name a few.

The CE takes the resiliency requirements specified by the users using the editor and uses the RCM repository to build the execution environment for RCS. The selected BO algorithm runs each Cloud Application or service as a sequence of execution phases, where each phase is administered by the Autonomic Service Manager (ASM). The ASM controls the operations of redundant and diversified VMs such that it can be resilient to any type of attack against the managed cloud services. Furthermore, we use Master Virtual Machines (MVMs) and Worker Virtual Machines (WVMs) where each MVM manages the voting algorithm on the results produced by several MVMs.

9.3.3 Autonomic Service Management

We have successfully designed and implemented a general autonomic computing environment (Autonomia) that will be leveraged in this task to implement the AM module [27]. By adopting the Autonomic architecture shown in Fig. 9.3, we implement the ASM using two software modules: Observer and Controller modules. The Observer module monitors and analyzes the current state of the managed cloud resources or services.

The Controller module is delegated to manage the cloud operations and enforce the resilient operational policies. The Observer and Controller pair provides a unified management interface to implement the required RCS.

In what follows, through an example, we show how we achieve the resilient operations by obfuscating the versions and the resources used to run each service. Let us assume we have a service A that we like to run in three phases as $S_A = \{S_{A_1}, S_{A_2}, S_{A_3}\}$ as shown in Fig. 9.4.

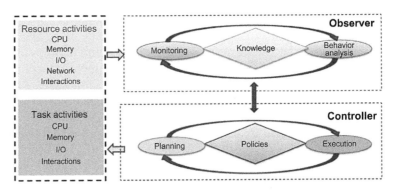

Figure 9.3 Autonomic service management architecture.

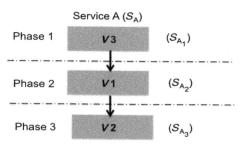

Figure 9.4 Service Behavior Obfuscation example.

The Service Behavior Obfuscation (SBO) algorithm that will be managed by the ASM hides the execution environment by dynamically changing the sequence of execution of service versions by shuffling the service version running after each execution phase. The decisions regarding when to shuffle the current version, the shuffling frequency, and the version selection for the next shuffle are guided by a continuous feedback from the autonomic service manager. The service S_A runs in three diversified phases: $V3$ in Phase 1, $V1$ in Phase 1, and $V2$ in Phase 3 of service S_A.

In addition to the shuffling of the execution of the service versions, we also apply hardware redundancy and software diversity to the implementation of the application tasks. The concept of design diversity is commonly used in software fault tolerance techniques to continue to operate successfully in spite of the software design faults. In our service obfuscation implementation approach, we combine N-version programming [25] and online anomaly behavior analysis techniques [28]. The multiversion implementation will prevent adversarial attacks from exploiting the monoculture problem. The anomaly behavior analysis approach will enable us to ensure that the operations of each task are completed correctly at the end of each execution phase; by using normal runtime models of the execution environment, we can detect any malicious changes in the execution environment, task variables, memory access range, etc.

To support the capability to resume the execution of different service versions on different platforms when they resume their execution, we use Compiler Portable Check-Pointing (CPPC) [26] technique in the service obfuscation algorithm. Checkpointing is widely used to recover from fault once it is detected as in fault-tolerance computing [29,30]. It periodically saves the computation state to a stable storage so that the application execution can be resumed by restoring such a state. The distinguishing characteristic of CPPC is that it allows for

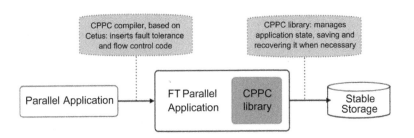

Figure 9.5 Compiler for portable checkpoint generation [26].

execution restart on different architectures and/or operating systems. It also attempts to optimize the amount of data saved to disk to improve efficiency and data transfers over the network. (CPPC is an open-source tool, available at http://cppc. des.udc.es under GPL license.) CPPC provides portable restart of applications in heterogeneous environments. Generated state files can be used to restart the computation on an architecture (or OS) different from the one that generated the file. The CPPC framework consists of a runtime library containing checkpoint-support routines, together with a compiler that automates the use of the library. The global process is presented in Fig. 9.5.

9.3.4 Resilience Analysis and Quantification

The process of quantifying the resilience that can be achieved by any SBO algorithm is a difficult process due to the heterogeneity of the environment, so a general and quantitative set of metrics for the resilience of cybersystems is impractical. In this section, we described an analytical approach to quantify the resilience that can be achieved using one configuration of the SBO algorithm. The method to quantify the resilience of a cloud application uses four important metrics: confidentiality, integrity, availability, and exposure.

The attack surface of a software system is an indicator of the system's vulnerability. So the higher the attack surface for a system, the lower the security is for that system [27]. The attack surface represents the area in which adversaries can exploit or attack the system through attack vectors. In our SBO-based resilient environment, the attack surface measurement can be used to quantify the resilience of the SBO algorithm with a given redundancy and redundancy level and number of phases. The goal of our analytical quantification approach is to show how the SBO algorithm can decrease the attack surface, and therefore, increase the resilience compared to a static execution environment. The first step in quantifying the attack surface is identifying the software modules and libraries that can be exploited by attacks; this includes the operating systems, programming languages, and the network. There are many tools that can be used to identify attack vectors that exploit vulnerabilities in these software modules, such as Microsoft Attack Surface Analyzer [31], Flawfinder [32], Nessus [33], Retina [34], and CVEChecker [35]. In addition to these software systems and modules, the cloud application will also have an attack surface less than or equal to the system attack surface because the application while it is running will utilize a subset of the system attack surface; not all of the system attack vectors will be utilized by the application execution environment.

Common Vulnerabilities and Exposures (CVE) [36], which is a public reference for information security, vulnerability and exposures, is used to determine the confidentiality, integrity, and availability of the software system. Common Vulnerability Scoring System (CVSS) [37] is used as a standard measurement system for industries, organizations, and governments that need accurate and consistent vulnerability impact scores. Cyber resilience depends on maintainability, dependability, safety, reliability, performability, and survivability which are all functions of confidentiality, integrity, and availability [38].

In our approach to determine the attack surface, the following steps are used:

1. Scanning the cloud system using multiple attack vectors which are built based on known attack scenarios.
2. CVSS is used for identifying the characteristics and impacts of the system vulnerabilities using three groups: Base, Temporal, and Environmental scores. The Base group represents the intrinsic qualities of vulnerability. The Temporal group reflects the characteristics of a vulnerability that changes over time. The Environmental group represents the characteristics of vulnerability that are unique to any user's environment. Each group produces a numeric score (showing a range from 0 to 10) and a vector (compressed representation of the attack values used to derive the score). Using the CVSS database, it is possible to obtain the corresponding score by comparing the attack vectors.
3. Determine the attack vector impact and its probability.
4. Finally, determine the probability of an attacker to successfully exploit the identified vulnerabilities in the cloud system as well as in the cloud application.

In what follows, we describe in further detail our approach to evaluate analytically the probability of successful attacks against existing vulnerabilities when the SBO methodology is used.

In this analysis, we define the resilience as follows:

Definition: The system resilience R is defined as the ability of the system to continue providing its Quality of Service as long as the impact of the attacks is below a minimum threshold R.

The impact $i_v(t)$ of a vulnerability v at an instant t is:

$$i_v(t) = \begin{cases} 0, t < T_v \\ I_v, t \geq T_v \end{cases}$$

where T_v is the time required for discovering the vulnerability and exploiting it, and I_v is the impact of exploiting the vulnerability.

The expected value of the impact of a vulnerability v is given by:

$$E[i_v] = I_v \cdot \Pr(A_v)$$

where A_v is the random variable that represents the occurrence of an attack exploiting vulnerability v. We can evaluate the probability of A_v as:

$$\Pr(A_v) = \Pr(A) \cdot \Pr(U_v)$$

A denotes the existence of an attacker who is trying to exploit the system, and U_v denotes the time needed to successfully exploit the vulnerability v. To simplify the problem, we will assume that there will always be an attacker, $\Pr(A) = 1$, and any attacker that spends more than T_v time in exploiting vulnerability v is successful, that is, assume that all attackers are expert attackers and can successfully launch the attack in a minimum time T_v. By using the application life cycle time T_f and assuming that U_v is a uniform random variable, the pdf (probability density function) for U_v is given by:

$$\Pr(U_v) = \begin{cases} 0, t < T_v \quad \text{or} \quad t > T_f \\ \dfrac{1}{T_f - T_v}, t \geq T_v \end{cases}$$

We define the impact of a system with N vulnerabilities to be:

$$i_{system} = E[i_{v_1} + i_{v_2} + \cdots + i_{v_N}]$$

Using the linearity property of the expected value, the previous equation can be re-written as:

$$
\begin{aligned}
i_{system} &= E[i_{v_1}] + E[i_{v_2}] + \cdots + E[i_{v_N}] \\
&= I_{v_1} \cdot \Pr(A) \cdot \Pr(U_{v_1}) + I_{v_2} \cdot \Pr(A) \cdot \Pr(U_{v_2}) \\
&\quad + \cdots + I_{v_N} \cdot \Pr(A) \cdot \Pr(U_{v_N}) \\
&= \sum_{k=1}^{N} I_{v_k} \cdot \Pr(A) \cdot \Pr(U_{v_k}) = \Pr(A) \cdot \sum_{k=1}^{N} I_{v_k} \cdot \Pr(U_{v_k})
\end{aligned}
$$

Since, we do not have a direct control over the $\Pr(A)$ or the impact value I_{v_k} of the kth vulnerability v_k, in our SBO technique, we continuously shuffle the application execution into multiple phases where we are basically reducing the execution time for each phase to be less than T_v for all or most vulnerabilities, which in turn forces $\Pr(U_v)$ for those vulnerabilities to be zero. We are currently using the CVEChecker tool to get the impact score I_{v_k}.

Using the multiple functionally equivalent variants to run a cloud application will significantly improve its resiliency to attacks because that will reduce the probability of a successful attack on the application execution environment. For example, by using L functionally equivalent versions of the application, the probability of successfully exploiting an existing vulnerability v_k is given by:

$$\Pr\left(U_{v_k}\right) = \Pr(U_{v_k,1} \cap U_{v_k,2} \cap \ldots \cap U_{v_k,L})$$

Since these versions are independent from one another:

$$\Pr\left(U_{v_k}\right) = \Pr\left(U_{v_k,1}\right) \cdot \Pr\left(U_{v_k,2}\right) \cdot \ldots \cdot Pr\left(U_{v_k,L}\right)$$

Assuming that all versions are equally likely to be attacked:

$$\Pr\left(U_{v_k}\right) = \frac{1}{L}\Pr\left(U_{v_k}\right) \cdot \frac{1}{L}\Pr\left(U_{v_k}\right) \cdot \ldots \cdot \frac{1}{L}\Pr\left(U_{v_k}\right) = \left(\frac{1}{L}\Pr\left(U_{v_k}\right)\right)^{L}$$

Fig. 9.6 shows the decrease in the probability of a successful attack as a function of the number of versions to be used in the SBO algorithm. For example, if we assume that the probability of an attacker to exploit a vulnerability equal to .5, by using two versions, this probability is reduced to .05 and by using three

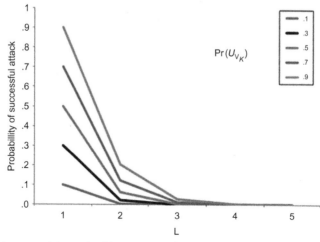

Figure 9.6 Probability of successful attack with respect to the number of versions.

versions, this probability is reduced to almost zero. Please note that the assumption if an attacker can exceed in exploiting existing vulnerability is very low using our SBO resilience approach, and consequently, a more a reasonable assumption is .1, and with that, we can see the probability of a successful attack against our approach drops to zero when we use only two versions.

From the previous discussion, it is clear that our technique will significantly reduce the ability of attackers to exploit existing vulnerabilities in cloud applications.

9.4 Experimental Results and Evaluation

9.4.1 Experimental Testbed Setup

Our testbed consists of IBM HS22 Bladecenter as our private cloud [39]. We have used three physical nodes on the Bladecenter for each of the applications that follow. On each of the three physical nodes, we have setup three VMs designated as follows:
- MVM: running Linux
- Slave 1 VM: running Linux
- Slave 2 VM: running Windows operating system

In addition, applications 2 and 3 consist of four additional VMs as follows:
- SBO Controller
- Supervisor (3 VMs are allocated where only one of them is active at any given time)
- Slave VMs: The two slaves contain functionally, equivalent, but behaviorally different versions of the same application. For example, in *Figure*, each slave contains a C++ and a Java version of the MapReduce Application.

9.4.2 Applications Tested

9.4.2.1 MapReduce

MapReduce [40] is widely used as a powerful parallel data processing model to solve a wide range of large-scale computing problems. With the MapReduce programming model, programmers need to specify two functions: Map and Reduce. The Map function receives a key/value pair as input and generates intermediate key/value pairs to be further processed. The Reduce function merges all the intermediate key/value pairs associated with the same (intermediate) key and then generates the final output. There are three main roles: the master, the mappers, and the reducers. The single master acts as the coordinator responsible for task scheduling, job management, etc. MapReduce is built upon a distributed file system (DFS), which provides distributed storage. The input data is split into a set of map (M) blocks, which will be read by M mappers through DFS I/O. Each mapper will process the data by parsing the key/value pair and then generate the intermediate result that is stored in its local file system. The intermediate result will be sorted by the keys so that all pairs with the same key will be grouped together. The locations of the intermediate results will be sent to the master who notifies the reducers to prepare to receive the intermediate results as their input. Reducers then use Remote Procedure Call (RPC) to read data from mappers. The user-defined reduce function is then applied to the sorted data; basically, key pairs with the same key will be reduced depending on the user defined reduce function. Finally the output will be written to DFS.

Hadoop [41] is an open source implementation of the MapReduce framework and is used in our experimental results to evaluate our system for the MapReduce application. Oracle Virtualbox [42] has been used as the virtualization software. To maintain consistency with the MapReduce parlance defined in Ref. [40], we will refer to each physical host machine as master and each guest machine as slave. To prevent any single point of failure, each guest machine is configured to run in a single node cluster [41]. The MapReduce Wordcount program [40] is available on each slave in C++ and Java. Thus, the combination of *< physical machine, operating system, programming language >* represents a single version. Fig. 9.7 provides details about the application diverse versions used in our implementation.

The MapReduce application in our experiment is divided into three phases as follows:
- Phase 1: First Map function
- Phase 2: Second Map function
- Phase 3: Final MapReduce function.

The outputs of Phases 1 and 2 are used as inputs to Phase 3. During runtime, the application execution is performed in parallel on each of the three machines. Also, at the beginning of each phase, each master runs a local shuffler program to determine the version to run at the current phase. For this experiment, we have used a random number generator to determine the version that will run on each machine. At the end of each phase, the three masters run local acceptance tests. If the acceptance test fails, the output is taken from one of the other masters.

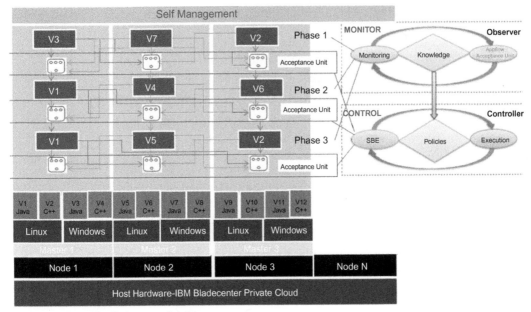

Figure 9.7 Resilient MapReduce application.

Fig. 9.8 shows an example of how to run the MapReduce application in a resilient manner using our methodology. At the beginning of Phase 1, the ASM runs a random number generator and selects versions V1, V8, and V10, respectively. After completion of the first Map on each physical machine, the output is checked for correctness by the acceptance test criteria. If this test fails, the ASM selects the output of Phase 1 from other physical machines and the first result that passes the acceptance test will be selected for the next phase of the application execution. Similar actions are performed in Phases 2 and 3.

9.4.2.1.1 Case 1: Resilience Against Denial of Service Attacks

In this scenario, we launched a DoS attack on one of the machines used to run the MapReduce application. The ASM detects the DoS attack and tolerates it. Although the DoS attack affected the attacked physical machine and increased its response time by 23%, since we took the output from the other physical machine the response time of the application with and without attack remained the same. An overhead time of 14% of response time was added by our approach.

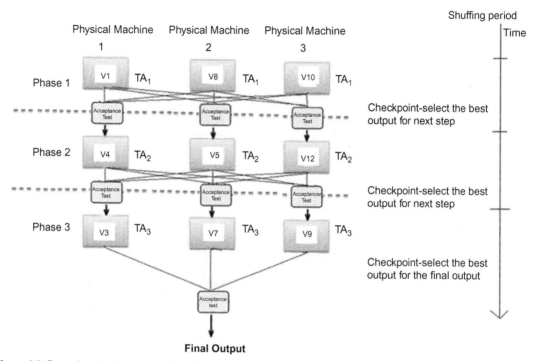

Figure 9.8 Example of achieving resilient MapReduce application.

9.4.2.1.2   Case 2: Resilience Against Insider Attacks

In this case, one of the machines (the fastest physical machine) is compromised by an insider attack and the computations running on that machine were changed by the internal attacker. Similar to the previous case, the application continued to operate normally in spite of the insider attack because the results from the compromised machine were ignored and the results from other versions were used instead. The performance impacts and overhead on the application performance are shown in Table 9.1.

As shown in Table 9.1, the average response time using the RCS approach increases by 14% (without attack) and 24% (with attack).

9.4.2.2   Jacobi's Iterative Linear Equation Solver

Linear equations are used to solve a wide range of real world scientific and engineering problems. The Jacobi technique is an

Table 9.1 MapReduce Result Summary

	Response Time	CPU Utilization per Physical Machine	Memory Utilization per Physical Machine	Network Utilization (%)
Without RCS	A	B	C	0
With RCS and no attack	1.14A	1.08B	1.02C	1
With RCS and attack	1.24A	1.12B	1.04C	2

Operating System/ Programming Language	Windows	Linux	Windows	Linux	Windows	Linux
C	V1	V4	V7	V10	V13	V16
C++	V2	V5	V8	V11	V14	V17
Fortran	V3	V6	V9	V12	V15	V18

Figure 9.9 Versions used in Application 2.

iterative technique for solving a set of linear equations under two assumptions [43]:

- The system given by $Ax = B$ has a unique solution
- The coefficient matrix A has no zeroes on its diagonal.

To solve a set of n equations, we solve the first equation for $x1$, second equation for $x2$ as follows: We first make an initial assumption of the values of x. We then substitute these values into the right-hand side of the above set of equations. This completes the first iteration. This process is repeated until convergence is reached on the values of x. The implementation runs on a three node cluster each hosting two VMs. One of these VMs is Windows based, while the other is Linux based. We have used VMware vSphere 5 [44] for the virtualization. The Jacobi Algorithm described above has been implemented in C, C++, and Fortran, thus creating multiple versions (see Fig. 9.9).

Table 9.2 summarizes the overhead in terms of the execution time and overhead percentage for five programs with a normal execution time ranging from 200 to 3600 seconds, respectively. The overhead is given as a function of the number of phases selected to run the application.

We calculated the overhead as the additional time taken with our algorithm compared to running the application without RCS. As shown in Table 9.2, for programs with higher execution

Table 9.2 Overhead in Application 2

Execution Time Without RCS(s)	Execution Time With RCS(s)					
	Two phases		Three phases		Four phases	
	Time	OH (%)	Time	OH (%)	Time	OH (%)
200	218	9	248	24	276	38
800	838	5	890	11	988	24
1500	1568	5	1624	8	1663	11
3600	3671	2	3847	7	3890	8

	Physical Machine Number					
	1		2		3	
Operating System	Linux	Windows	Linux	Windows	Linux	Windows
Version Number	V1	V2	V3	V4	V5	V6

Figure 9.10 Versions used with the MiBench suite.

times, the overhead due to RCS reduces significantly. For example, for a program with execution time of 3600 seconds, the overhead percentage for three phases is 7%. The number of phases to run each application can be chosen such that it meets the performance and resilient requirements of the application.

9.4.2.3 MiBench Benchmarks

The MiBench Benchmarks [45] consist of C programs from six categories each targeting a specific area of the embedded market. We used the following applications from the MiBench benchmark suite:

1. *Basicmath (Automotive and Industrial category):* This program performs mathematical calculations like cubic function solving, integer square root, and angle conversions from degrees to radians are all necessary calculations for calculating road speed or other vector values.

2. *Dijkstra's algorithm (Network category):* This program constructs a large graph in an adjacency matrix representation and then calculates the shortest path between every pair of nodes using repeated applications of Dijkstra's algorithm.

For each of the above available C programs, we used diversity in operating systems to have a total of six versions. The versions used are shown in Fig. 9.10. We calculated the overhead of our RCS

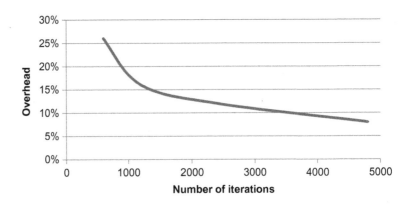

Figure 9.11 Basicmath—Overhead for RCS with three phases.

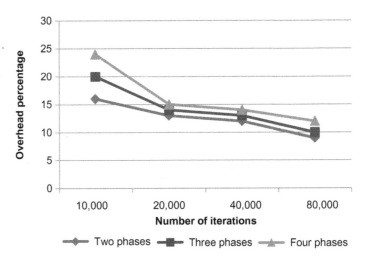

Figure 9.12 Dijkstra's Algorithm—Overhead for RCS with three phases.

approach for different number of iterations of the abovementioned benchmarks. The results are presented in Figs. 9.11 and 9.12. As seen in these figures, the overhead of our algorithm decreases as program size increases (Figs. 9.11 and 9.12).

9.5 Conclusions and Future Work

While cloud computing is emerging as a promising paradigm, security is a significant barrier to its adoption. In this chapter, we first presented an overview of the current security issues in cloud computing. We summarized previous works that classified cloud security issues on the basis of cloud delivery models and the components of the cloud. Further, we also observed that attacks on cloud systems cannot be prevented. We have presented a design methodology to develop RCS that based on the following capabilities: Redundancy, Diversity, Shuffling, and Autonomic Management. In the RCS methodology, we adopt diversity technique to the cloud execution environment, redundancy in the resources used to run the cloud services and randomly changing the versions and resources used to make it prohibitively expensive for attackers to figure the current cloud service execution environment and succeeding in exploiting vulnerabilities and launching attacks. We also presented a testbed to validate the RCS architecture and resilient algorithms using three applications (MapReduce, Jacobii's iterative linear equation solver, and some programs from the MiBench benchmark suite). Our experimental results showed that our RCS approach can tolerate a wide range of attack scenarios with around 7% of overhead time. As a future research direction, we are currently working on developing analytics techniques to quantify the resilience of different RCS implementation strategies, overhead, and performance of the cloud services.

Acknowledgments

This work is partly supported by the Air Force Office of Scientific Research (AFOSR) Dynamic Data-Driven Application Systems (DDDAS) award number FA95550-12-1-0241, National Science Foundation research projects NSF IIP-0758579, SES-1314631, and DUE-1303362, and Thomson Reuters in the framework of the Partner University Fund (PUF) project (PUF is a program of the French Embassy in the United States and the FACE Foundation and is supported by American donors and the French government).

References

[1] P. Mell, T. Grance, The NIST Definition of Cloud Computing, 2011.
[2] L. Savu. Cloud computing: deployment models, delivery models, risks and research challenges, in: International Conference on Computer and Management (CAMAN), Wuhan, China, 2011.
[3] S. Subashini, V. Kavitha, A survey on security issues in service delivery models of cloud computing, J Netw Comput Appl 34 (2011) 1–11.
[4] J. Wu, et al. Cloud storage as the infrastructure of cloud computing, in: Intelligent Computing and Cognitive Informatics (ICICCI), 2010 International Conference on, IEEE, 2010.
[5] C.P. Ram, G. Sreenivaasan, Security as a Service (SasS): securing user data by coprocessor and distributing the data, in: Trendz in Information Sciences & Computing (TISC), Chennai, 2010.

[6] P. Costa, et al. NaaS: network-as-a-service in the cloud, in: 2nd USENIX conference on Hot Topics in Management of Internet, Cloud, and Enterprise Networks and Services, San Jose, CA, 2012.

[7] K.P. Birman, F.B. Schneider, The monoculture risk put into context, in: Security and Privacy, IEEE, January–February 2009, pp. 14–17.

[8] S. Hariri, M. Eltoweissy, Y. Al-Nashif, Biorac: biologically inspired resilient autonomic cloud, in: Proceedings of the Seventh Annual Workshop on Cyber Security and Information Intelligence Research, ACM, 2011.

[9] Cloud Security Alliance. Security as a Service [online]. Available from: <https://cloudsecurityalliance.org/research/secaas/> (accessed January 2013).

[10] M. Schmidt, L. Baumgartner, P. Graubner, D. Bock, B. Freisleben, Malware detection and kernel rootkit prevention in cloud computing environments, in: 19th Euromicro International Conference on Parallel, Distributed and Network-Based Processing, 2011.

[11] D. Goodin, Webhost Hack Wipes Out Data for 100,000 Sites [Online]. Available from: <http://www.theregister.co.uk/2009/06/08/webhost_attack/> (accessed January 2013).

[12] V.S. Subashini, A survey on security issues in service delivery models of cloud computing, J Netw Comput Appl 34 (2011) 1–11.

[13] R. Bhadauria, S. Sanyal, Survey on security issues in cloud computing and associated mitigation techniques, Int J Comput Appl 47 (18) (2012) 47–66.

[14] C. Modi, D. Patel, B. Borisaniya, A. Patel, M. Rajarajan, A survey on security issues and solutions at different layers of Cloud computing, J Supercomput (2012) 1–32.

[15] H. Zeng, Research on developing an attack and defense lab environment for cross site scripting education in higher vocational colleges, in: Computational and Information Sciences (ICCIS), 2013 Fifth International Conference on, 21–23 June 2013, pp. 1971–1974.

[16] M.S. Siddiqui, D. Verma, Cross site request forgery: a common web application weakness, in: Communication Software and Networks (ICCSN), 2011 IEEE 3rd International Conference on, 27–29 May 2011, pp.538–543.

[17] G. Pék, L. Buttyán, B. Bencsáth, A survey of security issues in hardware virtualization, ACM Comput. Surv. 45 (3) (2013), Article 40 (July 2013), 34 pages.

[18] M. Abbasy, B. Shanmugam, Enabling data hiding for resource sharing in cloud computing environments based on DNA sequences, in: IEEE World Congress, 2011.

[19] J. Feng, Y. Chen, D. Summerville, W. Ku, Z. Su, Enhancing cloud storage security against roll-back attacks with a new fair multi-party non-repudiation protocol, in: Consumer Communications and Networking Conference, 2011.

[20] L. Kaufman, Data security in the world of cloud computing, IEEE Secur Priv 7 (4) (2009) 61–64.

[21] Y.B. Al-Nashif, A. Kumar, S. Hariri, Y. Luo, F. Szidarovszky, G. Qu, Multi-level intrusion detection system (ML-IDS), in: ICAC 2008, pp. 131–140, 2008.

[22] P. Satam, H. Alipour, Y. Al-Nashif, S. Hariri, Anomaly Behavior Analysis of DNS Protocol, Journal of Internet Services and Information Security (JISIS) 5 (no. 4) (2015) 85–97.

[23] www.nitrd.gov, [online] May 13, 2010. <http://www.nitrd.gov/pubs/CSIA_IWG_%20Cybersecurity_%20GameChange_RD_%20Recommendations_20100 513.pdf> (cited: 15.01.13).

[24] B. Randell, System structure for software fault tolerance, IEEE Trans Softw Eng 1 (1975) 220–232.

[25] A. Avizienis, The N-version approach to fault tolerant software, IEEE Trans Softw Eng SE-11 (12) (1985).

[26] G. Rodríguez, M.J. Martín, P. González, J. Touriño, R. Doallo, CPPC: a compiler-assisted tool for portable checkpointing of message-passing applications, Concurr Comput 22 (6) (April 2010) 749–766.

[27] X. Dong, S. Hariri, L. Xue, H. Chen, M. Zhang, S. Pavuluri, S. Rao Autonomia: an autonomic computing environment, in: Performance, Computing, and Communications Conference, Proceedings of the 2003 IEEE International, IEEE, 2003, pp. 61–68.

[28] S. Hariri, G. Qu, Anomaly-based self-protection against network attacks, Autonomic Computing: Concepts, Infrastructure, and Applications. s.l, CRC Press, Boco Raton, FL, 2007, pp. 493–521.

[29] A. Tyrrell, Recovery blocks and algorithm based fault tolerance, in: 22nd EUROMICRO Conference, 1996.

[30] K.H. Kim, H.O. Welch, Distributed execution of recovery blocks: an approach for uniform treatment of hardware and software faults in real-time applications, IEEE Trans Comput 38 (1989) 626–636.

[31] [Online]. Available from: <http://www.microsoft.com/en-us/download/details.aspx?id=24487>.

[32] [Online]. Available from: <http://www.dwheeler.com/flawfinder/>.

[33] [Online]. Available from: <http://www.tenable.com/products/nessus>.

[34] [Online]. <http://www.beyondtrust.com/Products/RetinaCSThreatManagementConsole/>.

[35] [Online]. Available from: <http://cvechecker.sourceforge.net>.

[36] [Online]. Available from: <https://cve.mitre.org/>.

[37] [Online]. Available from: <http://www.first.org/cvss/cvss-guide>.

[38] [Online]. Available from: <http://search.cpan.org/~nwclark/perl-5.8.9/utils/perlcc.PL>.

[39] [Online]. <http://www-03.ibm.com/systems/bladecenter/index.html>.

[40] D. Jeffrey, G. Sanjay, MapReduce: simplified data processing on large clusters, in: Sixth Symposium on Operating Systems Design and Implementation, 2008.

[41] Apache Hadoop [Online]. <http://hadoop.apache.org/>.

[42] Oracle VirtualBox [Online]. <http://www.oracle.com/technetwork/server-storage/virtualbox/overview/index.html>.

[43] [Online]. <http://college.cengage.com/mathematics/larson/elementary_linear/5e/students/ch08-10/chap_10_2.pdf>.

[44] [Online]. <http://www.vmware.com/products/vsphere/mid-size-and-enterprise-business/overview.html>.

[45] M.R. Guthaus, et al. Mibench: a free, commercially representative embedded benchmark suite, in: Proceedings of the Workload Characterization, Washington DC, 2001.

10

CLOUD AND MOBILE CLOUD ARCHITECTURE, SECURITY AND SAFETY

C. Mahmoudi
Algorithmic, Complexity and Logic Laboratory - Paris-Est Créteil University, Créteil, France

10.1 Introduction to Cloud Computing

Cloud computing has become a significant technology trend [1]. As anticipated by many experts, Cloud computing has reshaped information technology processes and the information technology marketplace as a whole. The most relevant Cloud computing definition [2] is a style of computing architecture that offers dynamic scalability and provides virtualized resources as services or as a container of services over the Internet. Cloud computing technology supports interaction with a variety of devices, including desktops, laptops, smartphones, and the Internet of Things to access services provided by the Cloud over the Internet. The Cloud services can be programs, storage, or application-development platforms offered by Cloud computing providers.

The Cloud computing paradigm introduces some advantages that include cost savings, high availability, and ease of scalability. These advantages help address the needs of the industry during the evolution of information technology architectures [3]. As illustrated in Fig. 10.1 the evolution of computing paradigms took place in five phases. In the first phase, called *mainframe computing*, many users were sharing powerful mainframes using terminal servers. In the second phase, called *desktop computing*, standalone computers became powerful enough to meet the majority of users' needs. In the third phase, *network computing*, computers and servers were interconnected through local networks. These connections aim to enable sharing of computing resources and data in order to increase performance. In the

Handbook of System Safety and Security. DOI: http://dx.doi.org/10.1016/B978-0-12-803773-7.00010-3

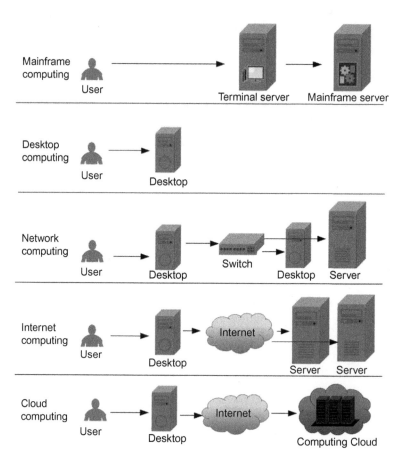

Figure 10.1 Evolution of the computing paradigms.

fourth phase, *Internet computing*, the technologies the Internet replaced the local networks. This global network emerged from the interconnection of different local networks in an effort to utilize remote applications and resources provided by other tiers. In the fifth phase, *Cloud computing*, the paradigm provides shared resources as services on the Internet where the Cloud provider manages the scalability and hides the complexity in a way that transparent to Cloud users. Comparing the Cloud computing paradigm to the other four computing paradigms, it appears that the Cloud computing model is very close to the one in the original mainframe computing paradigm. However several important differences differentiate these two computing paradigms. One of the differences lies in the fact that the computing power offered by Cloud computing is almost unlimited because of the scalable architecture behind it. Mainframe computing offers finite computing power because of the lack of scalability resulting from the isolation of the Mainframe back-end. Another notable difference relates to do with the access technology to the services. While Mainframe services are accessed using terminals with no computational power, Cloud computing uses powerful local computers those themselves can use Cloud services and execute applications built on top of such services.

10.1.1 What Problems Does Cloud Computing Solve?

Obviously Cloud computing has become a major trend that makes business processes more efficient in terms of service availability and scalability. This is driven by the fact that Cloud computing can solve many of the problems faced by businesses as well as academic and government institutions. We discuss in this section four examples of problems that can be solved using the Cloud.

The first example illustrates how Cloud computing can solve problems in academic information system. Let us suppose that a university needs to organize an international conference to be webcast to all students with access to the university network. The video stream is in full HD, 1080 pixels at 50 frames per second, with the rendering quality of the video stream being a key indicator of the success of this conference. The publicity chair of this conference done a very effective job. One week before the content was to take place on day one of the conference, and because of a good job by the publicity chair, the online registration shows an unexpectedly high number of registrants that was not anticipated by the technical infrastructure. The university technicians concluded that their local infrastructure was not powerful enough to support the webcast to all the subscribers. The main reason for this conclusion was that a single frame of the webcast would take 1 hour to render through their own data center. Rendering the whole conference webcast would take many years. Short of using the Cloud, the university would have to buy more hardware to support this event, which is a very expensive alternative knowing that the current infrastructure has plenty of resources to support the university's everyday activities. The Cloud solution for such problems is a very efficient one. The university can get all the server infrastructure needed to support the event in a very short time. Moreover, by using a Cloud provider for this event, the university will not adversely affect everyday operations because of this event. In addition, if the number of online attendees keeps increasing unexpectedly, the Cloud provider offers the needed scalability to adapt the Cloud services to the demand.

This second example discusses how the Cloud could solve the problem of data processing for a government laboratory attached to a US government department needs to carry out data-intensive processing in-house. This processing requires very expensive and extensive computer infrastructure that would need to run for an extended period to produce an output consisting of a small size report. As a specific instance of this example, consider what the National Institute of Standards and Technology would need to process the data collected for the analysis of Internet routing protocols like Border Gateway Protocol. Without any special arrangement, this analysis took in some cases more than a week. A solution that would set up a dedicated infrastructure and associated human resources to maintain it would cost more than $0.5 million per year. The decision was to migrate the analysis to the Cloud and use distributed computing power from a farm of processors turns out to be a cost-effective solution. Once the researchers ran the analysis in a Cloud-based platform, the results were impressive. Indeed, the same analysis that took more than a week to complete in-house now takes less than an hour in the Cloud. In addition the Cloud platform is available for sharing among other research teams that can use the same infrastructure for other kinds of analysis when it is available.

In the third example we consider an online florist that runs a small business. For 98% of the year, this kind of business needs relatively little information technology infrastructure requirement to support a limited volume of sales. A single machine can normally handle the infrastructure needed for a website for the e-commerce activities and management applications. However, at peaks like Valentine's Day and Mother's Day, their infrastructure requirements change drastically as their business increases by 4000–5000%. The Cloud offers two kinds of solutions to businesses with similar sales profile. The first one consists of a Cloud service with the scalability being managed by the Cloud provider. Under this solution the business owner has chosen to host all his services are hosted in the Cloud. An alternative solution known as *Cloud bursting*. This solution offers the business owners the ability to continue hosting their applications on their local infrastructure, but uses a Cloud environment to expand their infrastructure at peaks of activity. In this way consumers are on special occasions that experience peaks in sales volume. By operating in this fashion, the customers will always able to access the sales website and avoid any potential overload that can overwhelm the servers. By keeping its customers satisfied, the small business will not miss the opportunity to benefit from any seasonal increase in business volume.

The last example has to do with the availability of services in hostile environments or during major natural disasters. During events such as a tsunami or an earthquake, companies do not want to experience any loss of business data. Moreover, emergency response teams in affected areas need to have access to critical information to carry out their rescue missions. With Cloud computing adoption, companies should be able to recover the majority if not all of their data following a major disruption without having to pay for a backup facility. As most large Cloud providers have data centers deployed in multiple geographic locations, this deployment diversity allows them to provide backup and recovery. Cloud caching or Mobile Cloud Computing (MCC) [4] provides recovery and business continuity facilities even while basic infrastructures like the electricity grid or the optical fiber networks have not yet recovered from the disruption. Instead of building and managing a facility that will only be used in disaster situations, companies can now get the benefits of recovery and service continuity with a reasonably priced Cloud service.

10.1.2 Cloud Computing Is Not a Cure-All for Computing Challenges

Cloud computing introduces many features that help enterprises and government agencies build scalable and robust information technology systems. However Cloud computing cannot deal with every issue that these systems may face. In this section we discuss some problems for which the Cloud cannot offer a resolution.

One important issue that Cloud computing will not be able to improve is the performance of badly designed applications. The Cloud offers a well-defined architecture and patterns for Cloud services. Porting an application from a client/server architecture to the Cloud does not imply an automatic fix to any programming design deficiencies. Even if the Cloud platforms can mask the inefficiencies of the ported application, this does not mean that the application behavior and performance have been improved. The invoice from the Cloud provider will reveal those inefficiencies due to the excess consumption of Cloud resources due to inefficiencies of the deployed application will show up in terms of an excessive bill from the Cloud service provider.

Along the same theme of design issues, Cloud computing will not eliminate silos. In fact, it may even create new ones if the application design does not explicitly prevent this from happening. Silos may exist in information technology systems in terms of isolation of data, processes, and services. Using the Cloud may introduce new silos in companies' information systems as they create new entities that live in the Clouds.

10.2 Architecture: From the Cloud to the Mobile Cloud

In this section we present a "big picture" description of the concept of Cloud computing and we define the layers and the Cloud services provided by each layer. We introduce the differences between the types of the Cloud computing and present features, business benefits, metrics, and the key platforms from the vendors. We discuss also Cloud caching, as a base for *MCC*, and the integration of Cyber-Physical systems (CPSs) into the Cloud. We conclude the section with guidance as best practices to define a robust Cloud architecture.

The Cloud computing paradigm is based on a layered architecture. Each layer offers a collection of services, which can be presented as a layered *Cloud computing architecture* illustrated in Fig. 10.2. On the bottom of the stack, Infrastructure as a Service (IaaS) refers to computing resources as a service. This

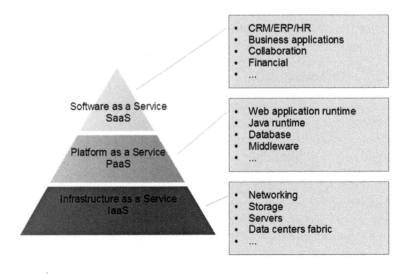

Figure 10.2 Cloud computing services' layers.

includes virtualized computers, processing power, reserved networking bandwidth, and storage services. IaaS services are offered by a variety of providers like Amazon AWS, Windows Azure, Google Compute Engine, Rackspace Open Cloud, and IBM SmartCloud Enterprise. Amazon Web Services [5], for example, offers a full range of computing and storage offerings in the IaaS layer. This offering includes on-demand instances such as virtual machines. Moreover it offers specialized services such as Cluster GPU instances, Amazon Elastic Map Reduce (EMR), high-performance SSDs on the storage side, and Elastic Block Storage (EBS). In addition the Amazon AWS IaaS solution offers infrastructure services such as archival storage called Amazon Glacier, in-memory caching services called ElastiCache, and both NoSQL and relational databases.

The middle layer of the stack is the Platform as a Service (PaaS) layer; this layer shows some similarities to IaaS. However, the PaaS includes required services, including the operating system needed for a particular application. The PaaS layer offers programming languages support for your application, server side technologies, and data storage options. The support for developer tools and applications integration is also very important. PaaS services are offered by a variety of providers like Engine Yard, Red Hat OpenShift, Google App Engine, Heroku, AppFog, Windows Azure Cloud Services, Amazon AWS, and Caspio. To illustrate the PaaS services, we give as example the services offered by Engine Yard. This provider is designed for web application developers using Ruby on Rails, PHP, and Node.js. Engine Yard allows developers to take advantage of Cloud computing without responsibility for the management operations in the infrastructure level. Engine Yard runs its PaaS platform on top of the Amazon Cloud and provides key operations tasks such as performing backups, load balancing, managing clusters, administering databases, and managing snapshots.

The top layer on the Cloud stack is Software as a Service (SaaS). At this level businesses delegate the hosting and the management of their applications to Cloud providers. The applications are available on-demand and typically paid for on a subscription basis. SaaS providers offer solutions including anywhere access, minimal administration, minimal maintenance, and improved communication.

When we talk about the Cloud layers, they may be implemented in three different ways [6]: as a public, private, or hybrid Cloud. An implementation on a public Cloud means that the complete computing infrastructure is located on an external Cloud computing provider that offers the Cloud service. In this type of Cloud the provider has the physical control over the infrastructure and the location of the resources allocated to the consumer. The advantages of the public Clouds are the usage of shared resources, they do excel mostly in performance. However, the drawback is vulnerability to various attacks. In the private Cloud, the infrastructure is used solely by one organization and those resources are not shared with any others. The organization acts at the same time as a Cloud producer and consumer. The resources may be local or remotely located. Some Cloud providers, such as a private Cloud externally hosted, offer solutions. To keep a physical control over the infrastructure, the organizations have an option of choosing an on-premise (or locally hosted) private Cloud as well which is more expensive. The advantages of the private Cloud reside in the usage of private network that introduces a higher level of security and control. The drawback is the cost of the infrastructure. Thus the cost reduction is minimal in such solution where the organization needs to invest in an on-premise Cloud infrastructure. In the hybrid Cloud the organization uses an environment that combines multiple public and private Cloud solutions. A typical usage of the hybrid Cloud is to use the public Cloud to interact with customers and keeps the data secured through an on-premise infrastructure in the private Cloud. However, this kind of usage introduces a drawback in the additional complexity of determining the distribution of applications across both a public and private Cloud.

The hybrid Cloud is used nowadays as a basis for the *MCC*. Mobile devices have more constraints on their processing power, battery life, and storage than regular computers. Cloud computing is used to provide an illusion of infinite computing resources for those devices. MCC is thus a platform combining the mobile devices and Cloud computing to create a new infrastructure and architecture for the development and the usage of the mobile applications. This architecture delegates the heavy lifting of computing-intensive tasks and storage of massive amounts of data to the Cloud infrastructure. Fig. 10.3 illustrates the architecture proposed for the MCC and its position in the general Cloud architecture.

Mobile devices are increasingly essential to everyday human life as the most effective and convenient communication tools. The unbounded time and place usage introduced by those devices allows mobile users to accumulate a rich experience of various services and applications. The execution of those services is not limited to the mobile device itself, more and more applications use nowadays remote servers via wireless networks

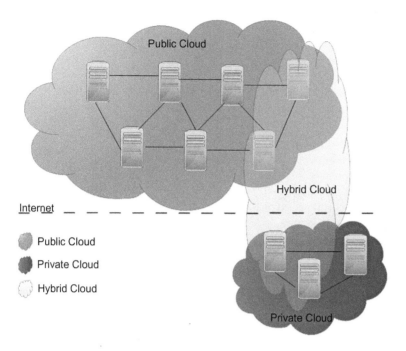

Figure 10.3 Cloud types.

to interact with services. Architectures based on *n-tier computing* have become a powerful trend in the development of information technology as well as in commerce and industry fields on mobile computing. Such systems can accept any (finite) number of layers (or tiers). Presentation, application processing, and data management tiers function is physically separated from the others.

However, mobile devices have considerable hardware limitations. Mobile computing faces many challenges in attempting to provide the various applications living on a single device with limited resources such as battery, storage, and bandwidth. Communication challenges like mobility and security arise, too. Those challenges motivate the delegation of the resource-consuming application modules to remote servers using Cloud service platforms. Google offers one of the major solutions called AppEngine allowing developers who do not need to have any previous understanding or knowledge of Cloud technology infrastructure to deploy services and use the Cloud. This platform executes the deployed services and exposes them as a remote service. This approach is used to delegate massive computation pieces of mobile software to the Cloud infrastructure.

Indeed, the mobile Cloud is a hybrid Cloud that offers services for mobile devices and CPSs [7] like *smart cars* and more

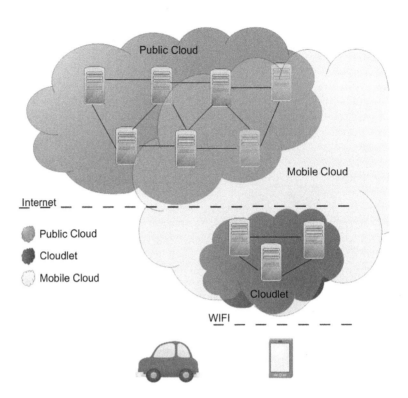

Figure 10.4 Mobile Cloud.

generally to smart devices in the transportation domain. Automobile makers are already in the process of migrating *navigation services* to the Cloud. This Cloud extends the processing capabilities for those devices using the Cloud paradigm. As illustrated in Fig. 10.4, the mobile Cloud uses a hybrid Cloud composed of a public Cloud and a private Cloud, sometimes referred to as a "Cloudlet." The Cloudlet is a private Cloud infrastructure directly accessible from the mobile devices and contains virtualization capabilities adapted to mobile systems. The mobile Cloud allows consumers to access the Cloudlet when possible—if the Cloudlet is not available, the public Cloud is used to run the mobile applications.

In the case of CPSs the mobile Cloud offers *virtually* unlimited resources to the "Cyber" part of the CPS. CPSs are systems that integrate decision/computation and the ability to sense or impact physical processes, where the measurement of physical processes may provide inputs to decisions or computations whose outputs may trigger actions that modify the energy and material flows that make up the physical world. The mobile Cloud offers a solution that extends these *feedback loops* to the

Cloud in a way that can integrate remote computing infrastructure with the sensors and actuators. Cloudlets offer a way to have an on-premise infrastructure that is available even if the remote access to the public Cloud is unavailable. Such mechanisms are very important for CPSs as they may be part of systems that help the rescue efforts to organize evacuation after an earthquake of in other situation in environments qualified as hostile. Because they operate in hostile environments, CPSs need to be agnostic to the global network, for example, in case of *emergency response systems*. Using mobile Cloud services for CPS gives many benefits. In addition to the security introduced by using a private network, the continuity of services is clear benefit of such a solution. Moreover the Cloud offers a level of scalability that cannot be achieved by using embedded microcontrollers for the CPS. In the case of important updates of the CPSs, the Cloud offers also the possibility to *remotely update* all the cyber parts at a vastly reduced cost.

10.2.1 Business Benefits

Building applications in the Cloud offers several benefits to organizations. One important benefit is related to the cost of installation. Building a large-scale system is a big investment in terms of cost and complexity. It requires investment in hardware infrastructure including racks, servers, routers, and backup power supplies. It also requires a location for the data center that requires investment in real estate and physical security. Moreover it necessitates recurring charges for hardware management and operations personnel. The delays to obtain approvals for this high upfront cost would typically involve several rounds of management approvals before the project could even get started. The Cloud-based solution bypasses such startup costs.

Even if the organization has an existing on-premise infrastructure, the scalability of an application could be a problem if this application became popular. In such cases you become a victim of your own success when the on-premise infrastructure does not scale to offer the resources needed by the application. The classical solution of this kind of problem is to invest heavily in infrastructure, hoping that the popularity of the application will be addressed by the size of the infrastructure. By using a Cloud infrastructure, the Cloud provider manages the infrastructure and you can rescale the infrastructure allocated to the deployed application in a just-in-time manner. This feature increases agility, helps the organization reduce risk, and lowers operational cost. That means that the organization can scale only as it grows. Moreover the organization only pays for their real resource usage.

To have a more efficient resource utilization, system administrators have to deal with ordering delays while procuring hardware components when the datacenter runs out of capacity. They also have to shut down some parts of the infrastructure when they have excess and idle capacity. By using the Cloud, the management of resources becomes more effective and efficient, since system administrators can have immediate resources *on-demand*.

Cost is one of the most important factors for businesses. With on-premise infrastructures, organizations have fixed costs, independent of their usage. Even if they are underutilizing their data center resources, they pay for the used and the unused infrastructure in their data centers. The Cloud introduces a new dimension of cost saving that is visible immediately on the next bill and provides cost feedback to support budget planning. The usage-based costing model is very interesting for organizations that actively practice application optimization. Applying an update that uses caching to reduce calls to their back office by 50% will have an immediate impact on costs. This savings will accrue immediately after the update. This on-demand costing model also affects organizations that have picks of activity. The picks will be reflected on their invoice as an additional charge.

Organizations where the business is *data analysis oriented* can get impressive results in term of the reduction of *time to market* by using the Cloud. Since the Cloud offers a scalable infrastructure, *parallelization* of data analytics is one effective way to accelerate time to results. Putting parallel analysis processes, which normally take 100 hours of effort on a machine, on 100 instances in the Cloud will reduce the overall processing time to 1 hour. Swapping machine instances is at the heart of the Cloud IaaS. Moreover Cloud providers offer specific solutions to exploit parallelization using big-data techniques. By using this elastic infrastructure provided by the Cloud, applications can reduce time-to-market *without any upfront investment*.

10.2.2 Metrics

This section introduces an approach to defining and representing the concepts and uses of measurement within the context of Cloud services and their underlying components. However *Cloud metrology* is not necessarily well understood by the stakeholders. Metrics and measurement artifacts often have several definitions, which make it very difficult for the service customer to use these metrics as a thrusted and standard measurement method. We propose a focus on Key Performance Indicators (KPIs) [8] as a framework to help organizations to define and measure progress toward organizational goals. The KPIs in Cloud services aim to be the measurement indicators for the adaptation and the progression of the Cloud services according to the organization's objectives.

Acquiring new customers and growing the business are the main challenges of organizations that are using the Cloud services to host their applications. These organizations need to consider seriously the metrics that show their ability to generate recurring revenue, retain customers, and to attract customers at a reasonable acquisition cost. Organizations nowadays use some common Cloud metric KPIs as described below.

One of the most important Cloud KPIs is the Customer Retention Rate (CRR). This KPI has three main impacts on subscription-based businesses. It affects the customer satisfaction levels, the recurring revenue, and the growth of the business. The value of the consumer retention is very hard to overstate and this holds for all the organizations, independent of their activity sector. According to research [9], an increase in consumer retention, even a modest increase, can have a big impact on the profits. This study shows that a 5% increase in consumer retention can bring an increase of more than 50% on the organization profits. The *consumer retention rate KPI* is interesting for organizations since they can anticipate the investment in marketing required to keep their sales rate stable. Indeed, generating revenue from loyal customers is less expensive than generating revenue by acquiring new consumers.

Financial institutions and telecommunication companies tend to have subscription-based businesses. The monthly recurring revenue is at the center of those organizations business model. One of the top priorities for these types of organizations is increasing the revenue from current customers. The *Monthly Recurring Revenue (MRR) KPI* helps those organizations to measure customer satisfaction and loyalty.

Indicators and metrics related to consumers and revenue are very important to the Cloud-based businesses. However they are not the only important metrics that organizations should monitor. KPIs related to the software development and deployment life cycle have a big impact on their businesses. The ability to deliver software updates faster to meet the consumer needs, with fewer malfunctions, and faster resolution of reported problems allows organizations to produce valuable software that will be deployed in the Cloud. DevOps [10] is a development methodology that helps organizations to achieve those objectives.

DevOps-related KPIs are used to define measurable goals that associate the development and the deployment life cycle to the organization's objectives. They are used to analyze what went wrong and allow teams to be transparent and share metrics with other teams on the organization like customer support and sales.

One important indicator for DevOps is the *Feature vs Bug (FVB) KPI* that monitors the number of bug issues as compared to the number of feature issues. This indicator allows the team to see how bugs, which are issues related to failure to meet specifications that teams have to fix, compare to feature issues that require changes to specifications. This indicator helps to adapt the speed of the team's efforts to fix these fundamentally different issue types. Teams use this indicator to monitor whether feature issues are within feature limits and that the current bug issues are within bug limits.

Another interesting indicator is the *Project Burndown (PBD) KPI*. Since Agile [11] methods recommend an *iterative and incremental cycle*, the PBD KPI is a metric that displays and compares project iteration projections to the number of iterations completed in the project. This metric allows you to keep a close eye on project iterations and, especially, on how they compare to the number of iterations that the DevOps team thinks they can complete.

10.3 Safety Concerns

Safety is a topic that is a challenge to Information and Communications Technology (ICT) in general. Safety is the concern about hazards that may result from malfunctioning behaviors of a system, whether they be from the cyber or the physical realizations of the system or from interactions between them. This challenge is also relevant to the Cloud since it has a prominent place in the organizations' ICT strategy. The organization that uses the Cloud needs protection from failures, damage, accidents, and harm. Moreover, they need to define boundaries and responsibilities in terms of harms and hazard against their Cloud provider. Indeed, the Cloud is used in many applications that enable sensing and actuation in the real world. Consider the emergency response example presented in Section 10.1.1. The Cloud is an active part of the emergency system and may affect the physical world through the actuators. Nevertheless the controllers of such systems are actually deployed in the Cloud, any dysfunction of the Cloud may introduce severe hazards into the system. Those hazards are directly related to the applications built on top of the Cloud. Those hazards are not related to the essence of the Cloud as it is used to host the virtual part of such a system. However they are relevant to the overall system where the Cloud deployed services are connected with the physical part of the system to build the CPS system.

The rest of this section discusses safety concerns related to the Cloud in order to help organizations define an efficient control of recognized hazards to achieve an acceptable level of risk. This section focus on two aspects of the Cloud where the risk is omnipresent: on-premise Cloud and Cloud storage.

The sections that follow deal with hazards for Cloud infrastructure for owners, operators and some hazards for Cloud customers. A complete safety analysis of Cloud computing should also examine hazards to owners and users of the systems 'connected by the Cloud' and would involve some kind of distributed interface agreement between Cloud and Cloud customer, at a minimum. This is little study of this topic currently but the reader should anticipate a much broader and deeper discussion of Cloud computing safety.

10.3.1 Data Centers

By opting for an on-premise Cloud solution, the organization has to manage server and hardware in data centers. To ensure a safe working environment in such space, the potential risks that hardware and the personnel may be exposed to need to be considered seriously. The risks include common risks such as fire and natural disasters. It also includes specific risks of information technology systems such as hardware failure, outages, electrocution, and physical injuries. To avoid and mitigate these risks, proper inspections, procedures, and training need to be part of the initial investment. Failure to prepare for such risks can be the main cause of outages in your data center. Moreover, the impact may be an Occupational Safety and Health Administration (OSHA) [12] noncompliance issue or injury to an employee. Organizations that choose an on-premise solution cannot expect that safe workplaces just happen, they have to put safety as a primary concern and plan and act to have a safe work environment.

Safety begins at the design level. Indeed, data center safety planning should be part of the initial design. This plan needs to take in consideration the analysis of the operations done to install and maintain the hardware. This includes the physical implementation steps that operators take to mount/relocate racks, load/unload servers, monitor the servers, and to perform the routine physical maintenance tasks. One of the actions that can be taken at the design level is the development of a well-designed floor plan that maximizes safety and simplifies emergency evacuation. In addition, improvement of the center's wiring contributes to data center safety. The organization should remove hardware hazards like the "spaghetti" of networking cables or holes in raised flooring those employees might trip on. Organizations should not minimize the impact of such simple and straightforward practices, neglecting those practices when facilitating server upgrades or network expansions may adversely impact the real possibility of physical injury.

Maintenance of the safety-related installations is an important item for the operating data centers safety. For business purposes, organizations focus the maintenance activities on testing the reliability of backup electrical systems like power distribution units and UPS's. However, fire detection and suppression systems deserve attention when it comes to maintenance. It is critical that these safety installations be regularly inspected and maintained. Nevertheless evacuation plans should be kept fully uptodate and available. Not only the evacuations plans, but also all the work instructions have to be clear and well defined. The employees working in data centers should know precisely what the organization expects of them. Providing thorough training, unmistakable diagrams, and clearly written instructions is the best way to help employees understand their responsibilities. Basic data center safety instructions for lifting hardware and operating a server lift should be included in the organization's work process documentation.

The safety process is not a one shot effort; the organization managers should watch and learn how each employee performs their everyday operations. This tracking has two objectives. The first is to have the assurance that the employees are following the safety procedures. Especially the assurance that they are not taking shortcuts that could compromise data center safety and expose them to injury or other risks. The second is to improve the existing procedures based on the employees' feedback. The safety process should not be limited to every day operations. The organization needs to include procedures for natural disasters in the safety process. Employees should be trained on preparedness for natural disasters that includes earthquakes, floods, hurricanes, and tornadoes. In some geographic areas, those who are most prone to these types of disasters, common practices verification such as anchoring equipment and storing materials in addition to the procedures for evacuation and holding areas should all be well-defined, tested, and well-understood by all the employees.

10.3.2   Cloud Data Storage

Multiple elements define just how safe Cloud storage is and which are the different security aspects that define safety. An organization that uses the Cloud, especially for critical data, needs to have assurance of the safety and the reliability of the infrastructure on which their information will be stored. The Cloud storage providers apply many safety mechanisms. Even with the hackers' attacks on those infrastructures, those of the Cloud providers, Cloud storage remains one of the safest and the most reliable ways to store data. The Safety of the stored data is one of the main reasons that encourage Cloud consumers to use such platforms. Thus Cloud storage providers use many techniques to assure this safety.

The storage safety involves keeping data out of the reach of hackers. For the data safety the providers use encryption as front line of defense to avoid hackers' attacks. The encryption methods used to transfer the data from/to the Cloud storage are based on complex ciphering algorithms for better protection. A key is shared between the Cloud provider and the consumer. This key allows both of them to cipher and decipher the transmitted data. Even if the hacker is able to get the data by sniffing the network, he will need the key to decipher the encrypted data. Although encrypted information may be cracked, decryption requires processing power that is not available everywhere, dedicated software for forensics, and enough time, all of which discourage malicious attackers. To achieve 100% safety assurance, relative to network-based attacks; the only solution is to keep the data offline. However Cloud storage providers utilize more complex security methods than average organizations [13]. Those methods allow the Cloud storage providers to achieve an acceptable safety assurance for the majority of businesses. Nevertheless the data stored in the Cloud profits from an added level of protection since organizations delegate safety to the providers that have this concern at the heart of their business.

When organizations use Cloud storage infrastructure from a provider, it implies that they delegate all the safety concerns related to the physical storage to the Cloud provider. The concerns that remain the responsibility of organizations are those related to the safety of data transfer and the robustness of the procedures implemented by the provider. Security is one of the decisive arguments for an organization in migrating to the Cloud. Safety is one of the top priorities of the majority of the institutions. Especially for government agencies and financial institutions, safety is paramount. The Cloud providers cannot assure a 0% risk on their platforms, the risk of a data breach is always a possibility.

Organizations need to evaluate this risk to enjoy the benefit of the Cloud without ruining their business. To evaluate the risk of data breaches, organizations need to realize that those data breaches occur on out-of-date online systems that are still using out-of-date security measures. Migration to the Cloud challenges organizations to rethink the design of their systems, embracing the latest technology means that the organization will avoid all known data breaches and assure the best state-of-the-art safety methods' usage. Organizations should not be afraid to upgrade their systems to use Cloud storage. The Cloud will encourage them to use safer technologies and methods that will not introduce new risk for security breaches. Cloud storage is safer than the legacy servers are. However migration to the Cloud should be accompanied by the employment of best practices to keep the business safe.

Mobile devices introduce new challenges [14] in addressing Cloud safety concerns. Bring Your Own Device (BYOD) is an Information technology policy where employees are encouraged to use their personal mobile devices to access the organization's data storage and systems. Organizations have to know the devices and the employees that are using those devices. Indeed, some employees do not prefer to have separate devices for personal use and for work. Especially on the modern workplaces where the teleworking is encouraged. From the organization's perspective, the BYOD may be efficient if everyone understands how to keep the devices and the systems safe. Safety procedures should be defined for the usage of all the personal devices in addition to a good monitoring solution to track the access of those devices to the system. Nevertheless holding frequent meetings to communicate and inform about safety concerns is important. For example, what applications are secure and which personal device is safe in addition to reminding employees about the mandatory protection rules whenever they are away from their desks.

Once again, a complete study of Cloud computing safety remains to be done and will surely be the topic of future publications on the topic.

10.4 Cloud Security

An organization that moves its applications to the Cloud will not make the application security responsibilities disappear by design. The organizations need to anticipate risks and develop creative ways to mitigate them. This section discusses why the organizations should not fear the switch to the Cloud, stresses the threat profile associated with the Cloud usage, and gives a list of the best practices that the organizations should apply to secure their deployed applications on the Cloud.

Indeed, information technology businesses are known for their propensity for innovation. However many of those businesses struggle with lingering apprehensions about switching to the Cloud. The hesitation is not caused by specific security concerns, but a limited number of common security issues. These common concerns cause them to overestimate the risks involved in switching to the Cloud. One of the main concerns that cause anxiety for decision makers of the organizations is the simple fact that the security means different things to different decision makers. The Cloud is associated by many with a convenient place to store music and photos online. However, for technically oriented employees, it means a complete software execution environment of an infrastructure for desktop-as-a-service desktop virtualization.

To establish security protocols [15] that allow organizations to stay protected while switching to the Cloud, the role that the Cloud should play has be clear and well-defined. Misunderstanding the role of the Cloud may have a negative impact on the security. Since the Cloud includes multiple concepts, designed to address many business needs, those concepts should not be merged into a solution without fully understanding the desired outcomes. Clearly articulating the needs and the Cloud concepts addressing those needs is the key to success in the switch to the Cloud.

Cloud migration changes the way that organizations manage the information technology infrastructure. Organizations need to give up some control of hardware to the Cloud providers and, relinquishin doing so, relinquish control over where their data are stored and who is accessing the servers where their data are stored. The organization needs to understand that once the data are transferred to the Cloud, their teams are no longer responsible for the data and it is instead the Cloud provider professional that is responsible for all the aspects of the data storage including the security and the isolation of the data.

Giving up the control to the Cloud provider may cause concern from the organization's employees. If the organization is migrating from an on-site infrastructure to an external Cloud provider for example, delegating the management and the control of the servers and the data storage to the Cloud may cause a fear of losing jobs. The managers need to explain that this drastic organizational change may be a good opportunity for the impacted employees to stay current and adopt new skills. The employees need to understand that maintaining outdated resources is not the interesting part of the organization's business and they need to focus on new skills that are of more value to the business. Moreover, since technology changes all the time, this is an opportunity to acquire and maintain state-of-the-art skills. This change will benefit at the same time the employees' resumes and the organization's business.

Potential for data loss is one of the most persistent and concrete fears associated with Cloud storage. There is no assurance of 100% security and safety for the data neither on traditional systems nor in the Cloud. However organizations can combat this fear by finding a Cloud provider that offers comparable assurance to the traditional system. Some Cloud providers offer back up, disaster recovery, etc.; those features can help the organization to determine if the provider is suitable for the criticality of their business needs.

10.4.1 Threat Profile

Security threats in the Cloud are real. However most of those threat concerns are overstated, unfounded, and easily managed. Organizations need to build a threat profile adapted to their business activities. To build a threat profile, organizations need to consider first the common threats that are known. Based on those threats, they may identify which threat constitutes a real risk depending on their activities.

The possibility of a data breach is one of the biggest fears related to working in a Cloud. External threats from hackers and malware may have their roots in many factors including the design, the implementation, and the configuration of the Cloud application. Since applications run in multitenant environment, organizations cannot control what the other users are doing. This concern is not a specific to the Cloud; even for traditional networked applications, the threat is real. However organizations need to estimate and manage the risks of exposing their applications on the network. The average attack of networked applications for organizations according to [16] is more than 15,000 attacks per year. The Cloud providers offer techniques to avoid such attacks, like Denial-of-service (DDoS) [17] that could compromise organizations' data and services.

The first line of defense for security in the Cloud is encryption. However traffic hijacking is a threat that involves the theft of security credentials. It allows the hijacker later gaining access to an organization's privileged information. Hijackers can use this stolen information to eavesdrop on transactions and perform modifications of data. The objective of the hijackers may be financial gain and it may be to disrupt the business. Even organizations that are big players in the Cloud may be affected by this threat. Amazon discovered a cross-scripting bug in 2010 that allowed Hijackers to steal the session IDs of certain users [18]. Amazon kept the number of affected accounts secret. Nevertheless all organizations that migrate to their Cloud might be vulnerable to this type of attack.

Threats do not come only from malicious attacks; hardware failure may cause severe damage to stored data and cause business damage to organizations. The policies regarding disaster management, the backup strategies, and datacenters' location have to be considered seriously by organizations as a part of their benchmarking to find the most suitable Cloud provider. Since they will delegate control over the physical location of the servers, they need to verify the provider's ability to handle emergencies and disasters.

Application programming interfaces (APIs) are exposed by the Cloud providers and used by organizations to access and control resources in the Cloud. Those APIs are designed for the application developers, they may suffer from a lack of documentation, or poor design. In some cases, third parties that adapt those APIs to a specific interface manipulate those APIs. The threat introduced by the APIs may affect the entire system. They are critical Cloud security vulnerabilities for many Cloud providers and consumers.

The DDoS attacks can have catastrophic implications for the organizations. As the pricing model for most Cloud providers is based on resource consumption, DDoS attacks may have a direct impact on costs. Even if Cloud providers have elastic resource allocation to avoid unavailability of the service, degradation of application performance may occur due to a centralized data management for example. The resulting downtime and other access problems due of the DDoS attacks may potentially leave the system open to other types of attacks.

As a multitenant environment, resources are shared between the organizations that are using the Cloud provider's infrastructure. Vulnerabilities may be introduced because of some isolation issues. The challenge in this context is to avoid this shared vulnerability. First, the organization needs to identify which Cloud provider uses the most sophisticated isolation technology to minimize the risk. Second, the organization needs to adopt additional security protocols to enforce the security and mitigate the shared vulnerability. For example, file system encryption for the data stored in the Cloud could avoid the risk of access to this data by malware introduced into the datacenter by other Cloud consumers.

The threat of attack is not only from outside hackers, malicious insiders constitute a growing risk in nowadays data centers. As the Cloud is becoming popular, the data centers are more implanted than ever. The Cloud providers have to manage multiple data centers. They contract freelancers to respond to some urgent demand on maintenance or upgrade on their data centers. The companies that are using the Cloud store their data and run their application on those data centers without any control over this infrastructure. Indeed, this complex task of managing the data centers has raised the possibility of an inside attack from an unscrupulous contractor. That makes insider attacks a growing Cloud security threat.

The Cloud is not only the target for the attacks; hackers use this infrastructure also as a vehicle for attacks. In the same way that the Cloud offers a scalable infrastructure for authorized business uses. Unlawful attacks can use the power of this anonymous infrastructure to launch session hijacking, complex DDoS attacks, spread malware, and share pirated material. The second-largest breach ever [18] was executed using Amazon infrastructure in April 2012 by an anonymous user against Sony's PlayStation Network. This attack allowed an anonymous user to access information of more than 100 million users. Even if these attacks do not affect directly the other applications running on the same Cloud. The Cloud providers cannot determine if the usage of their infrastructure is for authorized or unauthorized proposes. They can react only after checking for compliance for illegal or unethical uses of their infrastructure.

Failure of due diligence is the common characteristic among the majority of the treats related to the security of the Cloud. Organizations have the responsibility to ensure that the chosen Cloud meets their requirement in term of security. Moreover, they do not to rely on the Cloud provider for all aspects of security. They have to enforce the provider's security by adopting protocols and procedures to meet their specific requirements. Before the data or services are migrated to the Cloud, it is imperative to know the risks and understand the provider's security process. The providers have account specialists assigned to the organization to answer their questions. However, organizations need to be able to ask the right questions. Nevertheless organizations have the responsibility to know the legal obligations with regard to the confidentiality of their user's data. They have to be compliant with PCI, HIPAA, and other relevant regulations like data breach, backup failure, or insufficient record keeping.

10.4.2 Best Practices

Organizations outsource control when they move their data or their software to the Cloud environment. However they are able to maintain a perfectly safe and reliable secure system. The Cloud is an environment where the organization can benefit from the convenience and affordability in addition to the security and the safety. Knowing the Cloud security threats should encourage the organizations to implement control at the hardware, software, and procedural levels. This will help mitigate the risk and maintain tools to control and recover in the worst case. The organizations can adopt four main best practices to reduce concerns about the Cloud and make it safer and more secure.

The switch to the Cloud environment is not an arbitrary decision, an organization needs to plan this switch and begin with a thorough risk assessment. It should define how an outage would affect their business workflow, supply chain, and regulatory compliance. Even if the risk of outage exists, planning will help the organization to maintain business continuity in case of an outage or a security breach. The employees should be at the heart of the migration and Cloud-related operations. They should be consulted and informed of new protocols and rules for accessing to the Cloud resources.

The best defense against data and network-related threats is encryption. It assures the confidentiality of the information both on transfer and on the storage levels. The information should not be sent unencrypted to the Cloud. Important data should be encrypted before the transfer to the Cloud. In addition to regular encryption, the usage of an enterprise-grade protocol [19] is highly recommended for the most critical files and applications. Even if the data are encrypted, controlling and implementing privilege-based procedures for accessing data is a key for security. Employees should only access the information required to complete their job. These access policies prevent accidental security breaches and malicious insiders. The organization needs to define clear policies regarding authentication without over complicating [20] the procedure by using mechanisms like two-factor authentication.

The migration of the information technology system to the Cloud should be an integrative operation. Uncontrolled moves to the Cloud may introduce additional risk that is not need. The migration procedure should begin with the least-critical data. This will allow the organization to assess the policies and the procedures based on early feedback. Moreover in this manner employees will have time to become more comfortable with the new platform and to test for vulnerabilities. Some of the software is closely related to some specific data; the organization should determine which applications require interaction or rely on shared data. Those components have to be migrated at the same time to reduce latency issues. Nevertheless the migration to the Cloud is an opportunity for the organizations to update the software and operating systems and especially to update patches and licenses.

Cloud providers offer management and monitoring tools. The organization should take advantage of virtual management software that provides greater visibility into all the infrastructure activity, including networking and data storage. The majority of those tools offer notifications based on network events, suspicious behavior, and other correlations that may indicate an attack. This monitoring is not optional, many regulatory standards expect organizations to collect and monitor log data in order to be compliant with those standards.

The rewards associated with using the Cloud is worth the risk. Cloud computing is a technology that will be with us for a long time. Organizations are realizing the advantages of Cloud usage from the cost savings to scalability and monitoring. The failure of the Cloud migration is mostly due to the lack of preparation by organizations. The price of those failures may be high. Moving to the Cloud involves exchanging one set of responsibilities for another. The organizations give up the control over some aspects of security and they have to focus on other security aspects that are closer to their main business. For sure, it is possible to maintain an effective and proactive security posture after migrating business process to the Cloud.

References

[1] K.Y. Chung, J. Yoo, K.J. Kim, Recent trends on mobile computing and future networks, Pers Ubiquit Comput 18 (3) (2014) 489–491.
[2] P. Mell, T. Grance, The NIST definition of Cloud computing, Natl Inst Stand Technol 53 (6) (2009) 50.
[3] L. Wang, J. Tao, M. Kunze, A. Castellanos, D. Kramer, W. Karl, Scientific Cloud computing: early definition and experience, in: High Performance Computing and Communications, 2008. HPCC '08. 10th IEEE International Conference on, 2008.
[4] H.T. Dinh, C. Lee, D. Niyato, P. Wang, A survey of mobile Cloud computing: architecture, applications, and approaches, Wirel Commun Mob Comput 13 (18) (2013) 1587–1611.
[5] A. Wittig, M. Wittig, Amazon Web Services in Action, Manning Publications Co., 2015.

[6] M. Armbrust, A. Fox, R. Griffith, A.D. Joseph, R. Katz, A. Konwinski, et al., A view of Cloud computing, Commun ACM 53 (4) (2010) 50–58.

[7] R. Alur, Principles of Cyber-Physical Systems, MIT Press, Cambridge, MA, 2015.

[8] D. Parmenter, Key Performance Indicators: Developing, Implementing, and Using Winning KPIs, John Wiley& Sons, New York, NY, 2015.

[9] S.-C. Chen, A study of customer e-loyalty: the role of mediators, in: Proceedings of the 2010 Academy of Marketing Science (AMS) Annual Conference, 2015.

[10] W. John, C. Meirosu, P. Sköldström, F. Nemeth, A. Gulyas, M. Kind, et al., Initial Service Provider DevOps concept, capabilities and proposed tools, arXiv preprint arXiv:1510.02220, 2015.

[11] R. Levy, M. Short, P. Measey, Agile Foundations: Principles, Practices and Frameworks, London, UK, 2015.

[12] R. Administrators, D. Dougherty, Occupational Safety & Health Administration (OSHA), Washington, DC, 2015.

[13] S. Kamara, K. Lauter, Cryptographic Cloud storage, Financial Cryptography and Data Security, Springer, New York, NY, 2010, pp. 136–149.

[14] A. Bello Garba, J. Armarego, D. Murray, Bring your own device organizational information security and privacy, ARPN J Eng Appl Sci 10 (3) (2015) 1279–1287.

[15] U. Gupta, Survey on security issues in file management in Cloud computing environment, arXiv preprint arXiv:1505.00729, 2015.

[16] A. Potdar, P. Patil, R. Bagla, R. Pandey, Security solutions for Cloud computing, Int J Comput Appl 128 (16) (2015).

[17] J. Mirkovic, P. Reiher, A taxonomy of DDoS attack and DDoS defense mechanisms, ACM SIGCOMM Comput Commun Rev 34 (2) (2004) 39–53.

[18] P. Mosca, Y. Zhang, Z. Xiao, Y. Wang, others, Cloud Security: services, risks, and a case study on amazon cloud services, Intl J Commun Netw Syst Sci 7 (12) (2014) 529.

[19] A.H. Ranabahu, E.M. Maximilien, A.P. Sheth, K. Thirunarayan, A domain specific language for enterprise grade Cloud-mobile hybrid applications, in: Proceedings of the compilation of the co-located workshops on DSM'11, TMC'11, AGERE! 2011, AOOPES'11, NEAT'11, \& VMIL'11, 2011.

[20] B. Schneier, Two-factor authentication: too little, too late, Commun ACM 48 (4) (2005) 136.

11

A BRIEF INTRODUCTION TO SMART GRID SAFETY AND SECURITY

S. Khoussi[1] and A. Mattas[2]

[1]*The Mohammadia School of Engineers (EMI), Rabat, Morocco*
[2]*The School of Economic Sciences, Aristotle University of Thessaloniki, Thessaloniki, Greece*

11.1 Introduction to the Smart Grid

11.1.1 Overview

In recent years, many of us have heard the phrase *smart grid* used in a variety of contexts. Others may not be familiar with the terminology *smart grid* but may be aware that a new kind of electric power usage metering has been deployed. We all are aware of the times that our homes, businesses, and communities have "lost power," either due to a storm, a fallen tree, or simply "technical failures."

Problems with the electric power system are discussed on TV, in broadcast and print news, or even on the Internet. To understand what the smart grid is, we need to first comprehend better what is meant by the *grid* and by the term *smart*.

The grid or power grid refers to the electric power grid that delivers electricity around the clock to satisfy users' daily demand for energy. In fact, electricity is critical to most of modern technology. We rely on it for almost all our activities because most every device we have needs electric power in order to operate. Our phones, our home appliances (light bulbs, computers, televisions, ovens, HVAC, air-conditioning systems, etc.) and even our cars are dependent on electrical energy. Many of us take this precious utility for granted, thinking that all we need to do is to connect our devices to a wall outlet. Only when there is a blackout and the power grid goes down and electricity is no longer available, when the lights are off, and the

Handbook of System Safety and Security. DOI: http://dx.doi.org/10.1016/B978-0-12-803773-7.00011-5

Internet is no longer working, do we start to realize and appreciate its importance. One of the largest power outages in recent history occurred in northeast United States and Canada August 14–15 of 2003. This blackout caused serious inconveniences and risks for over 50 million people for almost two full days in which 11 people died and a lot of money estimated to billions of dollars in damages were reported [1].

Electricity supports the activities of our daily lives, it keeps us going, and it keeps businesses running and schools open, our streets safer, and our entertainment areas available. Nowadays the world we live in would definitely be in chaos without electricity, and our lives would come to a standstill without it. People from all over the world need reliable electrical energy to develop their societies and themselves. They need to learn how to maintain and manage this critical resource.

This is where the word, smart, in *smart grid* comes into the picture. The people who first used the word smart in conjunction with the word grid and who brought forth this concept were convinced that the current grid would be unable to fulfill the energy needs of future society and that to do so, some significant changes had to be made. The power grid of the future would need to meet changing demands efficiently and reliably. It would have to do so with minimal environmental impact and minimal waste. Thus the future grid would have to be responsive, adaptive, and be so in fractions of a second.

Among the proposed improvements to the existing grid is to make the grid *situationally aware*, more granularly than ever before, and be able to use that information to respond locally to meet the needs while coordinating regionally, and even globally, to maintain stability and efficiency. In short the improvements would require the grid to have some sort of intelligence or to be "smarter" than what we have today. Scientists, researchers, industrialists, and academics alike are all working together hand in hand to make a smarter and stronger electricity grid and "energy society" to achieve efficiency, resiliency, and a more environmentally sound approach to meeting our energy needs. Thus the smart grid has been called by many names including "electricity with a brain," "the energy Internet," and "the electro-net" [2].

In Section 11.1.2, we explore aspects of the traditional power grid, its components, its operations, as well as its problems.

11.1.2 The Traditional Power Grid

The power grid is one of the most complex engineered systems in modern world. It is an interconnected network consisting of power plants, transmission lines, substations, distribution lines, and users. The whole idea of the power grid is to deliver power from the generation sources to the service locations [3] (businesses and consumers) [4,5]. And this is accomplished today through these highlighted steps [6] of *energy conversion and delivery* [7,8]:

- **Generation**

  In 2014 there were about 19,745 individual generators, with nameplate generation capacities of at least 1 megawatt (MW) at about 7677 operational power plants in the United States. A power plant may have one or more generators, and some generators may use more than one type of fuel. Most of these plants are centralized and built away from extremely populated areas. These power plants contain electromechanical generators, steered by water or by heat engines driven by steam from chemical combustion of fossil fuel, including coal, petroleum, natural gas, and liquefied petroleum gas [9].

- **Transmission**

  To move the generated electric power over long distances and with less loss, it is stepped up to higher voltages to substations through *transmission lines*, since power plants are located in isolated and unpopulated regions away from consumers [10,11].

- **Distribution**

  Upon the arrival at a substation, usually near the users, the power must be stepped down from the transmission level voltage to a distribution level voltage. This step is called the distribution phase and this portion of the grid is called the *distribution grid* [12].

- **Consumption**

  By now, the power has arrived at the service location. Therefore it needs to be stepped down again from the distribution voltage to the required service voltage(s).

  Fig. 11.1 shows the different elements or components of the power delivery system in the traditional grid.

11.1.3 Problems With the Conventional Power Grid

It is important to mention that the conventional grid, the electrical grid of the past century, is a *unidirectional* network. This means that electricity flows unidirectionally from generators to substations, over transmissions lines, and eventually to consumers' outlets. Additionally it should be noted that most of

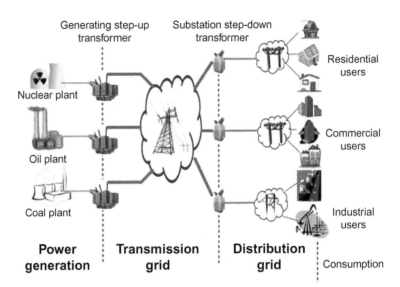

Figure 11.1 The different stages of delivering electricity in the conventional power grid [13].

the equipment and lines of the conventional power grid were installed many years ego. They are large investments and accordingly their provisioning typically takes years. As a result, these grid elements are outdated and need to be maintained and supervised frequently in order to keep the power flowing. Also, fossil fuels are constantly being depleted, through this and other uses, and are therefore generally getting more and more expensive based on market prices. But the conventional grid has challenges [14,15], (see Fig. 11.2). In fact:

- Conventional power generation plants are clustered and built up around communities, therefore delivering electricity to remote areas, intact with growth challenges our ability to estimate future needs for the capacity of the delivery infrastructure (the transmission and distribution lines).
- Installed grid elements were in many cases designed to meet historical energy demands rather than the current demand.
- Increased demand for power during peak demand can be a challenge to the existing grid infrastructure.
- Load balancing (generally electric power must be used as soon as it is generated). *Load balancing* is about keeping the demand curve within the generation curve. If demand exceeds supply, then grid collapse occurs and electric power is not available to any user on that grid. Whenever supply exceeds demand, then the result is unused energy or waste. One alternative would be to employ energy storage when excess power is available to avoid waste and provide one

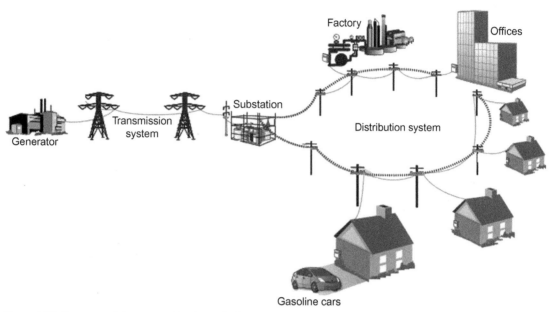

Figure 11.2 Elements of the conventional grid [16].

more way to *size the grid*. Though present power storage technology is more expensive than the benefit, this can change with the cost of energy and with advances in those technologies.

- One-way interaction: both energy and communication flow in the conventional grid is from the generation source to users. This means that the conventional power grid might not be able to adjust to the growing energy demands, faces challenges in locating grid failures, cannot spontaneously reroute electricity, and faces potential overheating of power lines (again energy loss or waste).
- Monitoring electricity flows remains largely manual.
- Frequent failures and blackouts: outages have become common due to natural disasters, weather, and technical issues with grid controls; these outages increase risks of harm and loss.

To address these issues, advanced teams are trying to replace and modify the current grid to make it a smarter and more adaptive power grid. *The smart grid* offers solutions to many of the problems described above.

In the next subsection, we will review the components of the smart grid and how they interact as we explore more of the drivers, motivations, and solutions for a more adaptive power grid.

11.1.4 Drivers and Motivations

When first conceived, the purpose of a smarter power grid [17,18] was:

- Improving demand side management: because electricity demand was and is increasing exponentially with population growth (each new user represents a potential for interactions with each existing user most of which correspond to energy usage)
- Improving energy efficiency and reducing greenhouse gas emissions that are a result of chemical combustion, by using renewable sources of energy instead of the traditional sources of energy, which are more often dependent on reserves of fossil fuel with. Those reserves are decreasing and expected to reach a critical level in a relatively short time.
- Building a stronger, more reliable, and self-healing grid against natural disasters as well as malicious attacks

However the *Smart Grid Framework* released in 2014 by the National Institute of Standards and Technology (NIST) states that a Smart Grid (SG) should be able to meet the following additional requirements [19,20]:

- *Improves the reliability of the power delivery system;*
- *Optimizes facility utilization and averts construction of backup (peak load) power plants;*
- *Enhances capacity and efficiency of existing electric power networks;*
- *Improves resilience to disruption;*
- *Enables predictive maintenance and self-healing responses to system disturbances;*
- *Facilitates expanded deployment of renewable energy sources;*
- *Accommodates distributed power generation resources;*
- *Automates maintenance and operation;*
- *Reduces greenhouse gas emissions by, for example, enabling the use of electric vehicles and new power sources*
- *Reduces oil consumption by reducing the need for inefficient generation during peak usage periods;*
- *Presents opportunities to improve grid security;*
- *Enables new energy storage options;*
- *Increases consumer choice;*
- *Enables new products, services, and market [19]*

So far, we have provided an overview of the historical context for smart grid as well as the drivers and motivations that have led engineers, researchers, industry leaders, and university faculty to promote and study the concept of a smart grid. However we still are developing smart grid best practices. Now we will explore the definition of smart grid and the features and functions it offers.

11.1.5   The "Smart Grid"

A basic definition of a smart grid is [21,22] that it is an evolving network of components for generation, distribution as well as components for communications, controls, automation, computers, new technologies, and management tools, all working together to make the grid efficient, reliable, secure, and greener. A more comprehensive definition, offered by NIST in its Smart Grid Framework [19], is "a modernized grid that enables bidirectional flows of energy and uses two-way communication and control capabilities that will lead to an array of new functionalities and applications."

The terminology "modernized grid" conveys the idea that smart grid is an enhancement to the conventional grid; it is not replacing all the past technologies and tools at once since it would be practically and financially impossible. Instead, the smart grid offers significant and smart improvements that can be deployed *incrementally.* Nonetheless there are going to be some *big changes* in our energy usage.

A smarter grid will impact multiple aspects of our current energy production and usage:

- The Production of Power

    The world is depleting existing *reserves of oil and natural gas* [23], the amount of technically and economically recoverable oil and gas, so a need for alternative sources of energy is being expressed. Though a portion of the demand for energy is being satisfied by renewable resources such as wind, solar, tidal, and others, power stations will still be required to adjust their voltages (ramp their output voltage(s) up or down) to ensure a balance between production and demand. In the future conventional coal-based plants may be phased out and be replaced by or converted to power stations using alternative sources of energy.

- The Infrastructure of the Grid

    The traditional infrastructure of the grid, generation plants, and distribution facilities must be changed or enhanced to enable the efficient transport of large amounts of energy from the location where it is produced tithe service location. Therefore,

    - More power plants, substations, and lines need to be built and equipped with sensors and actuators to enable the localization of failure, the rerouting of electricity, and to avoid outages.
    - Most existing grid components are over 50 years old and need constant repair, so updating the infrastructure is required [24].

- This new infrastructure must allow for a two-way transfer of both electricity and information in a decentralized architecture. This gives consumers an opportunity to participate in the processes of generation and delivery of energy.
- There may be a need for new businesses responsible for energy storage and supply as backup for existing grid capabilities.
- Demand Response [25]

  Advanced information metering, monitoring, and management equipment can be embedded in the infrastructure. Customers may appreciate having the option to track their energy consumption and know when less costly energy is available so customers can manage their own energy usage. Therefore equipment for metering, monitoring, and management should be included in the infrastructure.

  In order to apply this concept and in response to a legislative mandate EISA (Energy Independence and Security Act of 2007) to US Department of Energy and NIST, NIST provided a conceptual model or *framework* for Smart Grid. This model can be used as a reference to gain a better understanding of the Smart Grid and its components (Fig. 11.3)

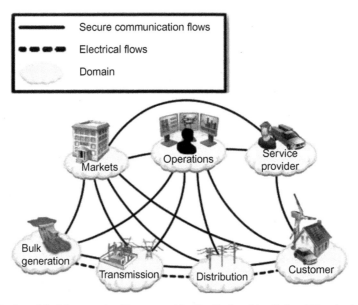

Figure 11.3 Conceptual model of the smart grid proposed by the National Institute of Standards and Technology (NIST) [19].

Now let us return to the concept of the conventional grid in Fig. 11.2 and explore the addition of these new components to it in order to clearly see the difference between the traditional power grid and the smart grid:

- In the conventional grid, power was provided by massive power plants that relyon coal and nuclear power to supply consumers' daily demands. But, as energy resources are not flexible in terms of adapting the generation to demand, these power plants are in general either operating, and producing a fixed output, or not. In the new grid, we have new or non-traditional sources, or so-called renewable energies; however renewable energy sources are intermittent [26] so for now they simply coexist with the previous power stations in the hope of a complete separation in the future. This collaborative generation is displayed in Fig. 11.4.
- Consumers are armed with appropriate monitoring and metering equipment (Smart meters and appliances' meters) to control and track their consumption of energy based on the current supply and market prices.

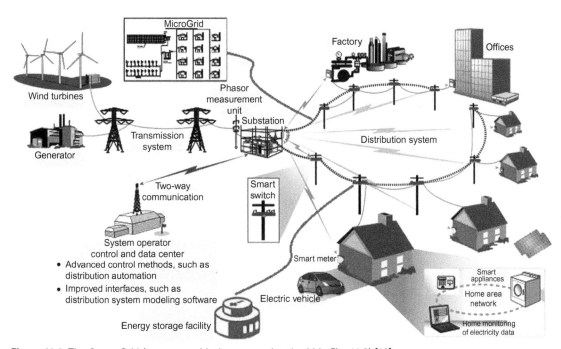

Figure 11.4 The Smart Grid (compare with the conventional grid in Fig. 11.2) [16].

- As electricity cannot be stored directly, instead it is being transformed into heat [27] or thermal energy in these facilities (gas turbines, pump storage, and others). This option provides a buffer during consumption peak and satisfies the increased load on the system.
- The smart grid concept offers a decentralized distribution of power centers: Microgrids [28–30]. These are self-sufficient, smaller scale distribution grids that are either connected to the grid or, in certain situations, can *island* themselves, that is, can disconnect from the grid. They have generation and/or storage capability of their own and can, as such, feed power back to the grid when connected.
- Two-way flows of electricity and information form the infrastructure for the *smart power management* of the Smart Grid [31]:
  - Information flow in the SG: The SG is obtained from the conventional grid by overlaying it with digital computers and communication devices. These devices help coordinate and link the delivery of energy from generators to consumers, reroute electricity in cases of failures, monitor the state of the grid, and control power stations depending on the loads on the grid;
  - Electricity flow: In a SG, electricity can also be fed back onto the grid by users. In fact, users may be able to participate in the generation process of electricity using, for example, solar panels at homes and feed it back into the grid. Electric vehicles [32], also, provide buffers for power when demand is high and/or when there is a favorable price differential.
- Two major monitoring and measurement approaches are being considered in the smart grid infrastructure, namely sensors, for example phasor measurement units (PMUs) [33,34]. Sensors are used for detecting mechanical failures in the system (conductor failures, tower collapses, hotspots, etc.). PMUs are there to provide a real-time measurement of electrical quantities across the power system. Both are there to help create a reliable power transmission and distribution infrastructure.

So after including some of these new grid elements in the picture, we end up with something like this:

To sum up, Table 11.1 gives a global view of why the Smart Grid is way better suited to meet our current and future electric power needs than the current grid:

Table 11.1 Difference Between the Old Grid and the Smart Grid [35]

Existing Grid	Smart Grid
Electromechanical	Digital
One-way communication	Two-way communication
Centralized generation	Distributed generation
Few sensors	Sensors throughout
Manual monitoring	Self-monitoring
Manual restoration	Self-healing
Failures and blackouts	Adaptive and islanding
Limited control	Pervasive control
Few customer choices	Many customer choices

11.2 Safety Analysis for the Grid

11.2.1 Why Do We Need a Safety Analysis and Why Is It Important

The purpose of this section is to outline an approach to the *safety analysis* of grid systems based on what is called a *Hazard Analysis and Risk Assessment* (HARA). Our summary is similar to the HARA used in standards that informs on how to approach electrical and power system safety, ranging from IEEE 3000 series of standards to US Department of Energy DOE-STD-1170-2007 on safety guidance for nuclear power generation to ISO 26262, and its predecessor IEC 61508, on *software or functional safety* for automotive electric/electronic systems. The HARA has two components. The first is an *identification of hazards* and is based on the analysis of malfunctioning behaviors of system functions using guidewords such as "too much function," "to little function," and so on. The second is a *risk assessment* that can be expressed in terms of a Safety Integrity Level (SIL). The SIL is an indication of the level of risk and is calculated based on the frequency and severity of worst-case scenarios or outcomes for that malfunctioning behavior while operating the system being analyzed.

One result of the SIL of the system is the formulation of safety goals for the system analyzed. These "goals" are called such since they are set as high-level *safety requirements* for any implementation of these functions of the system analyzed. At the same time the SIL of a critical function can serve to inform those involved in the development of the components of the system, involved in realizing the function, as to required or recommended practices during that development.

Hazard, risk, and safety are terms we hear expressed in a variety of ways and contexts: this product or that chemical agent has risks associated with its use, this task is a hazardous, or this behavior is inherently unsafe. Usually, during the development of a safe design, one designs and manages the activities of the process according to *safety best practices*. While these learnings are important, their application does not guarantee a safe functioning system. The purpose of the HARA is ultimately to anticipate and prevent risks that may lead to harm.

SIL classifications assess or estimate the level of risk and safety standards that usually indicate the mitigation efforts required in order to address the high-risk hazards that are identified. SILs are expressed as a discrete set of risk levels, from lowest to highest, and should capture the risk of harm due to failure of the mechanical or software systems that are used to realize the system function.

We will outline a HARA to indicate how one may approach the safety of the smart grid system. Although this outline is not detailed, it does describe the steps needed to identify the worst cases of risks for examples of critical Smart Grid functions.

11.2.2 Hazards, Risks, and HARA?

Before we get into our use case, it is better to explain the difference between the terms hazard and risk since so many people confuse hazard with risk and randomly use them to point to the same thing. Hazard is considered to be "the potential to cause harm" and a risk is the "likelihood of harm in defined circumstances" [36]. Finally, safety is the absence of both risks and hazards given a particular system.

The HARA model is composed of two different parts [37]: hazard analysis encompasses identifying the hazards potentially created by a product, process, application, or a system. The risk assessment, which is the step following the collection of potential hazards, is computing the probability and severity of each hazard and assigning a risk score/level.

11.2.3 Major Steps in a HARA Methodology

In order to achieve a safety analysis, it is recommended to follow these steps:

- Define primary functions related to the system under study.
- Identify the hazards associated with each function's forms of malfunction.
- Estimate the credible worst case scenario associated with each hazard.
- Estimate the severity of the harm that can occur in that scenario.
- Assess the risk or likelihood of this scenario (or its frequency)
- Document results

11.2.4 Use Case

Our use case is based on the example of and the corresponding graphic describing the smart grid (see Fig. 11.4). Returning to this figure, representing a smart grid system, consider the result of performing the steps above full.

To begin with, let us define a primary function of the system under study: to deliver electricity to consumers. To identify malfunctions, with respect to this primary function, we use a list of "guidewords" to generate the set of potential hazards. In other words, we ask "what could go wrong?" with that function or "in what different ways might this function fail to perform as intended?" In doing so, we identify the hazards associated with this function's potential behaviors.

Historically, as in the nuclear reactor safety report of the 1970s [38], one has used as a starting point the *worst case accidents* based on our experience of the system [39]. The authors of that report then used a "causal tree" to decompose each of these accidents, ultimately into failures of the smallest or simplest components of the system. The likelihood of failure of those components is typically well-understood through trials and can be expressed as a probability of that failure. Once fully populated, one can calculate the probability of the critical accident chosen, using the probabilities associated with each node of the decomposition tree. This was the method used to develop the first nuclear power reactor safety report in the 1970s, the so-called Rasmussen Report. Its output is a probability of the accident type in question and the accuracy of this method is clearly sensitive to the completeness of the causal tree analysis. In the terminology of the HARA, these accidents would arise, as worst-case scenarios, in the hazard analysis of the critical function performed by the reactor cooling system.

Returning to the primary critical function of the smart grid and following the HARA methodology described earlier, here is a sample hazard list based on a simple set of guidewords:

- too much power delivered;
- too little power delivered;
- no power delivery at all;
- intermittent power delivery.

To each of these hazards, we might regard scenarios associated with these hazards to be:

- Injury and fatalities due to explosion and fire caused by too much power delivered
- Injury and fatalities due to overheating as a result of excessive demand
- Injury and fatalities in vehicle collisions, resulting from road lighting failures due to a power outage
- Injury and fatalities in traffic due to intermittent function of traffic control systems due to intermittent power delivery

We could extend this listing of hazards, based on a more refined list of function behaviors, but this list should suffice to convey the basic concepts of the analysis.

The next step is to classify these scenarios according to the severity (S), indicating the severity of resulting injury or accident, and the exposure or frequency. Severity levels can be expressed in words and then assigned a "level" [40], for example:

- *S0 No Injuries*
- *S1 Light to moderate injuries*
- *S2 Severe to life-threatening (survival probable) injuries*
- *S3 Life-threatening (survival uncertain) to fatal injuries*

Referring to the scenarios above, the most severe possible consequence of these hazards is a fatality and hence the severity level assigned to each scenario is **S3**.

The next thing we need to do is to conduct a risk assessment. This is based on exposure (the relative expected frequency of the scenarios) and controllability (the relative likelihood that a hazardous consequence can be prevented, either by operators or by protections built into the system) levels. Just like severity (S), they are described in words and assigned levels:

Exposure Classifications (E): (in practice numerical ranges would be provided for each of these levels based on data gathered from sufficient operating durations)

- *E0 Incredibly unlikely*
- *E1 Very low probability (injury could happen only in rare operating conditions)*

- **E2** *Low probability*
- **E3** *Medium probability*
- **E4** *High probability (injury could happen under most operating conditions)*

Controllability Classifications (C): (again large amounts of data would need to be gathered and analyzed based on documentation of operations)

- **C0** *Controllable in general*
- **C1** *Simply controllable*
- **C2** *Normally controllable*
- **C3** *Difficult to control or uncontrollable*

Referring back to our scenario, the figure shows that wind turbines are used for renewable power generation. This is an indicator suggesting that the city depicted in the figure is very windy and therefore severe weather conditions can occur. Thus we can say that the exposure to the injury scenario has a high probability or an exposure level of **E4**.

As to controllability, it is obvious that such accident is difficult to manage once it happens. However it is most likely that operators would arrange a protective environment for the transmission area before installing the two poles, they might have installed a fence or other protective measures. But since nothing is displayed in Fig. 11.4 to indicate this, we can freely say that the controllability level is **C3**.

To summarize, we have obtained the following levels for the three classifications: severity (**S3**), exposure (**E4**), and controllability (**C3**), in this scenario. Keep in mind that the obtained classifications' definitions are informative and, most importantly, subjective. They are used to give an estimation of the SIL level that relates to the overall risk of hazardous scenarios associated with a function. One choice of possible SILs (used in automotive ISO 26262 and similar to the approach used in its predecessor in IEC 61508) is A, B, C, and D, where D corresponds to difficult to control, life-threatening, as well as highly probable scenario. The SIL level differs from one function to another. And as we have said, it is used to inform people about what kind of countermeasures they ought to take into consideration in order to avoid any malicious events. In this case, it is recommended to take action and try and think of how to secure the transmission area effectively to avoid fatalities and also stopping the process and wasting money.

Attached in Appendix A is a worksheet that reflects how the HARA can be conducted. In terms of these three classifications, a "Safety Integrity Level D" function (abbreviated "SIL D") is defined as a function whose most hazardous malfunctioning behaviors have a reasonable possibility of causing a life-threatening (survival uncertain) or fatal injury, with the injury being physically possible in most operating conditions, and with little chance the operator or user can do something to prevent the injury. That is, SIL D is the combination of **S3**, **E4**, and **C3** classifications. For each single reduction in any classification from its maximum value (excluding reduction of **C1** to **C0**), there is a single level reduction in the SIL from D to C, then B, and then A.

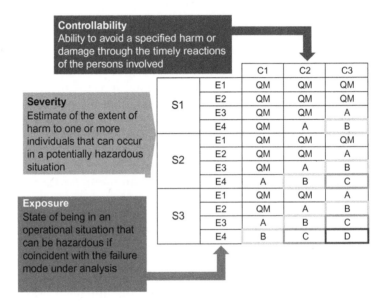

Controllability
Ability to avoid a specified harm or damage through the timely reactions of the persons involved

Severity
Estimate of the extent of harm to one or more individuals that can occur in a potentially hazardous situation

Exposure
State of being in an operational situation that can be hazardous if coincident with the failure mode under analysis

			C1	C2	C3
S1		E1	QM	QM	QM
		E2	QM	QM	QM
		E3	QM	QM	A
		E4	QM	A	B
S2		E1	QM	QM	QM
		E2	QM	QM	A
		E3	QM	A	B
		E4	A	B	C
S3		E1	QM	QM	A
		E2	QM	A	B
		E3	A	B	C
		E4	B	C	D

ASIL levels combined in terms of classifications described in previous sections [41].

11.3 A Security Analysis for the Smart Grid System

11.3.1 A New Approach to Smart Grid Security?

Smart Grid systems have emerged as an alternative platform for providing timely, efficient, and uninterrupted electric power to consumers. The Smart Grid offers innovations like smart tracking, monitoring tools, infrastructure for optimizing electricity generation, and usage for both providers and consumers. At the same time, the Smart Grid brings with it opportunities for new businesses. One of the expected benefits is our ability to maintain a satisfactory level of reliability. Failures and outages in any system may be the result of intrusions, either physical or cyber. A cyber intrusion is one accomplished through unauthorized access the information systems used in the system for purposes of modifying or altering that information. The consequence of such an intrusion may include adversely affecting its assets. Thus the cybersecurity of the electrical power grid is an important concern.

This section will discuss the concepts needed to address specifically the cybersecurity of Smart Grid. It is important to understand the ways in which Smart Grid systems differ from the information technology (IT) systems. Generally the Smart Grid is an industrial control system (ICS). An ICS has to meet all the security requirements of an IT system but the analysis of its security must also take in to account the Smart Grid's enormous physical layer. Furthermore the IT security of the resources of a smart grid should take into consideration the nature of parameters of an ICS environment in attempting to reach an acceptable levels of service. One challenge to maintaining adequate levels of service bearing in mind that the Smart Grid consists of an electrical network of thousands of miles of high-voltage lines that need intensive maintenance, continuous measurements and monitoring, as well as accurate controls. NIST Special Publication 800-82 emphasizes the differences between IT and ICS systems, giving a detailed analysis of their requirements, risk, communications, and their efficient management at both the cyber and the physical environment. For these reasons, we can view the grid's IT systems as a subset of its ICS systems. Hence the security of the grid's ICS system comprehends the security of its IT system as well as additional requirements and practices [42−44].

11.3.2 Background and Terminology

The research community of the information system has developed the cybersecurity or IT security which consists of policies, procedures, and associated activities. All these components contribute to the pursuit of protecting the cyber asset (hardware, software, and data) of any unwanted criminal action or damage. Similarly the security of smart grid has to deal with the same system protection, but with broadening concepts since its physical and cyber realm is even more enlarged and more complex. Nevertheless both systems share the same high-level security theory which is being discussed analytically in this chapter. Before any security aspect, we will highlight below the basic terminology of security theory.

This terminology is being provided by the International Organization for Standardization (ISO) was published on 2014 under the title of "Information Technology—Security Techniques—Information Security Management Systems—Overview and Vocabulary" and with a reference number ISO/IEC 27000:2016 [45]. ISO Organization is constantly in collaboration with universities, research institutions, and international businesses to provide accurate common standards among them. One of their main objectives is to publish a universal terminology for better understanding, and we highlight some of them below.

- *Information system: applications, services, IT assets, or other information handling components.*
- *Policy: intentions and direction of an organization as formally expressed by its top management.*
- *Reliability: property of consistent intended behavior and results.*
- *Process: set of interrelated or interacting activities which transforms inputs into outputs.*
- *Threat: potential cause of an unwanted incident, which may result in harm to a system or organization.*
- *Vulnerability: weakness of an asset or control that can be exploited by one or more threats.*
- *Attack: attempt to destroy, expose, alter disable, steal, or gain unauthorized access to or make unauthorized use of an asset.*
- *Audit: systematic, independent, and documented process for obtaining audit evidence and evaluating it objectively to determine the extent to which the audit criteria are fulfilled.*
- *Risk: effect of uncertainty on objectives. Risk is often characterized by reference to potential events and consequences or a combination of these.*
- *Control: measure that is modifying risk. Controls include any process, policy, device, practice, or other actions which modify risk.*
- *Risk analysis: process to comprehend the nature of risk and to determine the level of risk. Risk analysis provides the basis for risk evaluation and decision about risk treatment.*
- *Risk management process: systematic application of management policies, procedures, and practices to the activities of communicating, consulting, establishing the context and identifying, analyzing, evaluating, treating, monitoring, and reviewing risk.*
- *Information security: the preservation of confidentiality, integrity, availability and other properties, such as authenticity, accountability, nonrepudiation, and reliability.*

11.3.3   Principles and Requirements

From the ISO security definition [45], there are three essential concepts that recur throughout different areas of security, which are Confidentiality, Integrity, and Availability. Throughout the research literature [46–50], the security community refers those fundamental principles of security also as properties, security requirements, or even security dimensions. Moreover, they are broadly known as the CIA triad.

Integrity: property of accuracy and completeness.

The integrity supports the correctness and the completeness of the information. Information modification must be done from the corresponding authorize entity. Lack of integrity results in the unauthorized alteration or loss of information with subsequent results in the decision management of the smart grid.

Confidentiality: property that information is not made available or disclosed to unauthorized individuals, entities, or processes.

Confidentiality is imminently connected with the privacy concept. It regards any security decision on whether some information should be secured or open to the public. Specific at smart grid, confidentiality focuses more on protecting the personal privacy and the power market information.

Availability: property of being accessible and usable upon demand by an authorized entity.

Availability guarantees that a precise request of an authorized entity will continuously have access and use of information and services. It is obvious any unsuccessful fulfillment of availability concept in the smart grid will result in a short or long loss of the electrical power to an area.

The CIA security triad changes priority order (AIC) when is focused on ICT systems like the smart grid. Although IT systems are concerning more for their confidentiality and integrity of their information, ICT systems need first to ensure the availability to avoid any power blackouts' consequences (Fig. 11.5).

11.3.4   Vulnerabilities

One of the major goals of ITs and ICS security is to mitigate security risks and to protect the assets. A needed methodology of a system to protect its assets is to adapt a vulnerability threat control framework. Vulnerabilities can consider as weakness in

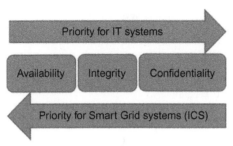

Figure 11.5 The principles' priority orders for both ITs and ICS.

some aspects of our system, and any vulnerability exploitation has the potential to cause harm or loss to our assets. The vulnerability threat control framework integration with the power grid using smart controls, computing devices, and communication networks, has a profound effect on the security of the smart grid [51–53]. Below are some of the main issues:

- Individual privacy: smart grid devices collect on a daily basis numerous amounts of information and make it available from the service providers to the individual customer. That information include personal information about consumers such as when, where, what, and how much energy they are using from which one might infer their private activities as well as when their house is vacant which, in turn, could lead to robbery or other serious crimes.

- Access control points: these so-called smart devices are responsible for managing, controlling, and monitoring both electricity power and users' demand which makes them vulnerable to tampering. Even entry points into the network, exposing it to a variety of physical and cyberattacks that may cause harm to a person or a property and severe economic loss.

- Outdated components: the smart grid will undoubtedly be deployed gradually or incrementally due to the costs. As a result, obsolete components will continue to participate in the system and might act as overall security weaknesses in the grid system since they will have to coexist with the new generation of devices.

- Physical sabotage: smart grid network consists of many new components which are installed during the routine daily maintenance. Any unsuccessful installation or faulty component can lead to the increased chances of physical access by strangers, wanting to sabotage the infrastructure, and cause local or global system failures.

- Conflicts of interest: different stakeholders, collaborating to provide disparate new elements of the smart grid, can be a source of conflicts of interest leading to dangerous attacks.
- Varying workers' backgrounds, as well as the lack of appropriate training of the staff, might be the cause of mistaken judgments and other faulty decisions.
- Failures of interoperability: with the looser collaboration, at the stakeholder and grid component levels, interoperability failures between elements of the grid could be the source of additional vulnerabilities. Misinterpreted information transmitted from one part of the network to another, which could either be incorrect or interpreted inaccurately, can trigger actions that an attacker could leverage this vulnerability.
- Standardization of Internet protocols, computer programs, and physical devices: any standards for smart grid can provide certain flexibility, interoperability, and also decrease their cost. Nevertheless this may only result in all grid systems inheriting and accumulating vulnerabilities intrinsic to IP, the hardware, or the software standards. For example, the Internet protocols open to several kinds of attacks, including IP Spoofing, Denial of Service (DoS), and more.

So far, we have reviewed various types of security weaknesses, related to the "smartness" of the new grid system; that may be exploited by attackers, attempting to undermine the function of the network. What kinds of attacks and attackers is the subject of Section 11.3.5.

11.3.5 Threats

Because the effective provisioning of electric power is critical and the investment is substantial, securing the smart grid and addressing any threats to its functions are a high priority. These experts are continuously predicting, analyzing, and brainstorming different scenarios that might cause this system to fail, now or in the future [51,52,54].

A human being that intentionally exploits a vulnerability is perpetrating an attack on the system, so an attack can be defined as an intentional exploitation of a vulnerability in a system. On the other hand, a threat is a set of circumstance that has the potential to cause loss or harm. Examples of possible grid system threats are the below type of attackers:

- Terrorist attacks or attacks intending to disrupt the grid operations: these are some of the most dangerous attacks, and the consequences can be severe.

- Displeased employees who seek revenge through minor attacks and/or intentional errors.
- Business competitors who sabotage each other's companies or organizations to achieve financial gain.
- Criminal intended actions by misled consumers would have greater opportunity in a smart grid system to affect adversely other power users.
- Nonmalicious attackers or pranksters. These are highly unpredictable, and they are attacking the system either by unintended activities or by intended ones like financial gain.

With these examples of potential attackers, those who may want to mount attacks on the power system, let us discuss some of the most commonly reported attacks and focus the discussion on cybersecurity, security as it relates to the cyber portion of the smart grid system.

According to the NIST Smart Grid Framework [49], the three key cybersecurity requirements for the Smart Grid system are: availability, integrity, and confidentiality. The attackers listed above can bring about:

- Topology-based attacks: their purpose is to prevent operators from having a full view of the topology of the smart grid system by launching, for example, a DoS attack and thereby blinding the operators to all of the grid systems and causing them to make incorrect judgments and decisions. In other words, a topology-based attack on smart grid aims at misleading the control center with incorrect topology information.
- Protocol-based violations: in this case, attackers hijack the communication protocol using various engineering techniques or by false injecting of unauthorized information.
- Component-based attacks: since most of the devices are in the field and outside of the utility premises, and since they are used to control remotely, manage, and monitor the grid system from a distance, they can also be used audit any failures.

Numerous reports of attacks or intrusions on the existing grid have been issued by utilities [55], such as:

- Malware and virus are affecting smart meters, servers, and controllers to interrupt communication transfers.
- Accessing of grid databases and hijacking of consumers' personal information.

11.3.6 Proposed Solutions

There are different approaches to ICS defending that are similar to the methods of an information and communication system. The first approach is prevention that can be accomplished by blocking an orchestrated attack to our smart grid system or by entirely closing and eliminating a vulnerability. The attacks are taking place when there is an intentional exploitation of vulnerability. Thus, by closing the vulnerability, the attacks cannot occur. The second method of defense is when you can deter an attack. Deterrence involves different measures to make the offense harder to accomplish. One other method is to deflect one attack. Deflection requires a strategy where you provide another target to the attacker which seemed to be more attractive to the attacker but on the other hand less valuable to the system. Last but not least is the mitigation of attack. It is important because it is more applicable to systems like the smart grid. Mitigation is defense mechanism where the necessary steps are taken to make the impact of an attack less severe. Due to the size and the complexity of a smart grid, it is usually hard to prevent, deter, or deflect an attack. Thus the best strategy is to have mechanisms in place which will contain the damage from attacks.

We can classify possible smart grid threat mitigation solutions as either physical or IT-based fixes [51−54]. In closing, we enumerate some of the known threat mitigation solutions.

IT-based mitigation: some of the recommended IT-based countermeasures as they relate to the threats or Smart Grid are:

- Assuring malware protection.
- Frequently assessing grid systems' vulnerabilities to ensure closed and secure points of weakness.
- Deploying awareness programs of best practices for users.
- Offering frequent training for staff members.
- Monitoring outdated grid equipment.
- Embedding security countermeasures such as security gateways and Hardware Security Modules.
- Attention to potential vendors' security mitigation incompatibilities.
- Securing network communications by using VPN architectures (Virtual Private Networks).
- Using smart devices to communicate only operations-critical data and not all consumers' private information.
- Using Public Key Infrastructure (PKI) to secure exchanges of information.
- Designing and implementing a Network Intrusion Prevention System.
- Permissions should not be guaranteed without identity verification proper authentication mechanisms and robust protocols.
- Privacy concerns with the Smarty Grid and privacy use cases.

Physical mitigation: Solutions addressing physical threats are fundamentally related to hardware protection and securing components and equipment of the infrastructure:

- Building a resilient physical network and safe infrastructure by securing off premises equipment or by adding fences.
- Securing components inside and outside of the utility's premises
- Protecting equipment and power lines.
- Constructing hard to break devices with embedded security by design.
- Making sure to install and maintain surveillance mechanisms.
- Making sure that the staff is well-trained and well-supervised.
- Frequently checking all the hardware and lines.

General speaking, we can say that there are two components to a comprehensive approach to smart grid security, security engineering, and threat mitigation. The former has elements related directly to discovering threats and the latter fixes or countermeasures. Optimally these two form an integrated whole that is fully integrated into the core system development process. Finally, it is well known that sustaining and increasing the funds in mitigation area will be critical for the business and academic security community to move forward. It is also essential for more effective security at any field of a smart grid to recruit and retain employees with expertises and highly technical security knowledge throughout its operating lifespan.

11.3.7 Standards and Guidelines for Smart Grid

The smart grid is arguably one of the most vital engineered systems of our modern times. Due to this fact, many documentation concerning the security of the smart grids are published and different organizations have provided guidelines and standard addressing smart grid cyber and physical security aspects. At the US level, the NIST has released NISTIR [42,50] and NIST SP1108 [42,49] where they consider smart grid as a complex and an extensive cyber-physical system. Specifically the NISTIR is separated into three different volumes where they address cybersecurity strategies, secure data exchange over smart grid and analysis of potential vulnerabilities on the physical and cyber layers.

On the other hand, the EU countries [56], through the decarbonized need of electricity power and the reduction of the imported fossil and oil fuel, led them to invest enormously mounts (it is estimated about 1.5 trillion euros [57,58]) on upgrading their electrical system to a smart grid.

The governments of the EU countries, using the help of robust stakeholder elicitation methods, publish numerous guidelines and regulatory documents for the smart grid. Such materials can be found at different European Organizations like ENISA [48,49], which is an agency of European Union that deals with improving network and information security, or at the Departments of Energy of the EU countries like United Kingdom's, Germany's, French's, and others. For example, Dutch Netbeheer Nederland Privacy and Security, Working Group has released the "Privacy and Security of the Advanced Metering Infrastructure" that describes a methodology for secure metering infrastructure. Another one is the UK smart grid Portal [59] that provides various information about the UK smart grid ensuring that everything is available for learning and exploring all the ongoing aspects of the smart grid development in the United Kingdom.

References

[1] <http://www.cbsnews.com/news/biggest-blackout-in-us-history/>.
[2] <http://www.nist.gov/smartgrid/beginnersguide.cfm>.
[3] <https://powergen.gepower.com/resources/knowledge-base/electricity-101. html>.
[4] <http://www.eia.gov/energy_in_brief/article/power_grid.cfm>.
[5] <https://www.youtube.com/watch?v=JwRTpWZReJk>.
[6] <http://anga.us/blog/2015/4/1/how-electricity-is-delivered-to-your-home-in-five-steps>.
[7] <http://www.eia.gov/Energyexplained/index.cfm? page=electricity_delivery>.
[8] <http://www.nap.edu/reports/energy/sources.html>] and [<http://caec. coop/electric-service/how-power-is-delivered-to-your-home/>.
[9] <http://www.fao.org/docrep/u2246e/u2246e02.htm>.
[10] <http://www.energyquest.ca.gov/story/chapter07.html>.
[11] <http://www.electrical4u.com/electrical-power-transmission-system-and-network/>.
[12] <http://www.science.smith.edu/~jcardell/Courses/EGR220/ElecPwr_HSW. html>.
[13] <http://www.intechopen.com/books/energy-efficiency-improvements-in-smart-grid-components/egyptian-wide-area-monitoring-system-ewams-based-on-smart-grid-system-solution>.
[14] H. Farhangi, The path of the smart grid, IEEE Power Energy Mag. 8 (1) (2010) 18–28.
[15] S.M. Kaplan, Electric Power Transmission: Background and Policy Issues, Congressional Research Service, Washington, DC, 2009.
[16] <http://www.inspirit-energy.com/article/3051461-a-building-block-of-the-smart>.
[17] C.-H. Lo, N. Ansari, The progressive smart grid system from both power and communications aspects, IEEE Commun. Surveys Power Tuts. (2011) 1–23.

[18] M. Hashmi, S. Hänninen, K. Mäki, Survey of smart grid concepts, architectures, and technological demonstrations worldwide, in: IEEE Innovative Smart Grid Technologies (ISGT Latin America), 2011 IEEE PES Conference on, pp. 1−7.

[19] National Institute of Standards and Technology, NIST Framework and Roadmap for Smart Grid Interoperability Standards, Release 1.0. <http://www.nist.gov/public affairs/releases/upload/smartgrid interoperability final.pdf>, January 2010.

[20] X. Fang, et al., Smart grid—the new and improved power grid: a survey, IEEE Commun. Surveys Tuts. 14 (4) (2012) 944−980.

[21] <http://energy.gov/oe/services/technology-development/smart-grid>.

[22] Hamed Mohsenian-Rad, Topic 2: Introduction to Smart Grid, Department of Electrical & Computer Engineering, Texas Tech University, Spring 2012.

[23] R.W. Bentley, Global oil & gas depletion:an overview, Energy Policy 30 (2002) 189−205.

[24] <http://www.forbes.com/sites/jamesconca/2015/05/21/its-our-aging-energy-infrastructure-stupid/#1a4787d77cd3>.

[25] <http://energy.gov/oe/technology-development/smart-grid/demand-response>.

[26] Renewable and Sustainable Energy Reviews.

[27] F. Nieuwenhout, J. Dogger, R. Kamphuis, Electricity storage for distributed generation in the built environment, in: 2005 International Conference on Future Power Systems, 18 November 2005, IEEE, Amsterdam, pp. 5.

[28] Z.H. Yang, L. Shan De, Research on microgrid, in: The International Conference on Advanced Power System Automation and Protection Research, 2011.

[29] Y. Li, et al., Design, analysis, and real-time testing of a controller for multibus microgrid system, IEEE Trans. Power Electron. 19 (5) (2004) 1195−1204.

[30] F. Katiraei, Micro-grid autonomous operation during and subsequent to islanding process, IEEE Trans. Power Deliv. 20 (1) (2005) 248−257.

[31] Y. Yan, et al., A survey on smart grid communication infrastructures: motivations, requirements and challenges, IEEE Commun. Surveys Tuts. 15 (1) (2013) 5−20.

[32] D.P. Tuttle, R. Baldick, The evolution of plug-in electric vehicle-grid interactions, IEEE Trans. Smart Grid 3 (1) (2012) 500−505.

[33] A. Bose, Smart transmission grid applications and their supporting infrastructure, IEEE Trans. Smart Grid 1 (1) (2010) 11−19.

[34] T.L. Baldwin, et al., Power system observability with minimal phasor measurement placement, IEEE Trans. Power Syst. 8 (2) (1993) 707−715.

[35] X. Fang, S. Misra, G. Xue, D. Yang, Smart grid—the new and improved power grid: a survey, IEEE Commun. Surveys Tuts. 14 (4) (2012) 944−980.

[36] <http://www.agius.com/hew/resource/hazard.htm>.

[37] <uspas.fnal.gov/materials/12UTA/08_hazard_assessment.pdf>.

[38] WASH-1400: Reactor Safety Study, An Assessment of Accident Risks in the US. Commercial Nuclear Power Plants.

[39] An Assessment of Accident Risks in U.S. Commercial Nuclear Power Plants. U.S. Nuclear Regulatory Commission, October 1975.

[40] ISO 26262 in Practice—Resolving Myths with Hazard & Risk Analyses.

[41] <http://www.embedded.com/print/4236887>.

[42] NIST Security Publications. <http://csrc.nist.gov/publications/PubsNISTIRs.html>.

[43] Guide to Industrial Control Systems (ICS) Security. <http://csrc.nist.gov/publications/nistpubs/800-82/SP800-82-final.pdf>.

[44] S. Clements, H. Kirkham, Cyber-security considerations for the smart grid, in: Power and Energy Society General Meeting, 2010 IEEE, Minneapolis, MN. http://ieeexplore.ieee.org/stamp/stamp.jsp?tp=&arnumber=5589829 &isnumber=5588047, 2010, pp. 1–5.

[45] ISO/IEC 27000:2016 Information Technology—Security Techniques— Information Security Management Systems—Overview and Vocabulary.

[46] ENISA Smart Grid Security Recommendations. <https://www.enisa.europa. eu/activities/Resilience-and-CIIP/critical-infrastructure-and-services/smart-grids-and-smart-metering/ENISA-smart-grid-security-recommendations>.

[47] ENISA Smart Grid Security.<https://www.enisa.europa.eu/activities/ Resilience-and-CIIP/critical-infrastructure-and-services/smart-grids-and-smart-metering/ENISA_Annex%20II%20-%20Security%20Aspects%20of%20 Smart%20Grid.pdf>.

[48] European Union Agency for Network and Information Security. <https:// www.enisa.europa.eu>.

[49] NIST Framework and Roadmap for Smart Grid Interoperability Standards. <http://www.nist.gov/public_affairs/releases/upload/smartgrid_interoper-ability_final.pdf>.

[50] Introduction to NISTIR 7628 Guidelines for Smart Grid Cyber Security. <http://www.nist.gov/smartgrid/upload/nistir-7628_total.pdf>.

[51] F. Aloul, et al., Smart grid security: threats, vulnerabilities and solutions, Int. J. Smart Grid Clean Energy 1.1 (2012) 1–6.

[52] W. Wang, L. Zhuo, Cyber security in the Smart Grid: survey and challenges, Comput. Netw. 5 (2013) 1344–1371.

[53] M.B. Line, I.A. Tøndel, M.G. Jaatun. Cyber security challenges in Smart Grids, in: Innovative Smart Grid Technologies (ISGT Europe), 2011 2nd IEEE PES International Conference and Exhibition on, 5 December 2011, pp. 1–8.

[54] S. Tan, Cyber security research in smart grid, J. Telecommun. Syst. Manage. (2014). 2014.

[55] DTE Energy Co. (NYSE: DTE). <https://www.newlook.dteenergy.com/wps/ wcm/connect/dte-web/home>.

[56] D. Xenias, et al., UK smart grid development: an expert assessment of the benefits, pitfalls and functions, Renew. Energy 81 (2015) 89–102.

[57] IEA, World Energy Outlook 2008, OECD/International Energy Agency, Paris, 2008. Retrieved 05/06/2013 from: <http://www.worldenergyoutlook.org/ media/weowebsite/2008-1994/weo2008.pdf>.

[58] Privacy and Security of the Advanced Metering Infrastructure. <http://hes-standards.org/doc/SC25_WG1_N1538.pdf>.

[59] UK Smart Grid Portal. <http://uksmartgrid.org/>.

Appendix A An example of the Hazard Analysis and Risk Assessment Model Worksheet

Reviewed/comments
Hazard tracking number
Hazard description
Risk analysis   Hazard type
                       Hazard target
                       Exposure
                       Severity
                       Likelihood
                       Risk code
Risk mitigation   Hazard controls
                       Control method
                       Control risk reduction

THE ALGEBRA OF SYSTEMS AND SYSTEM INTERACTIONS WITH AN APPLICATION TO SMART GRID

C. Mahmoudi[1,3], H. Bilil[2,3], and E. Griffor[3]

[1]*Algorithmic, Complexity and Logic Laboratory - Paris-Est Créteil University, Créteil, France* [2]*Mohammadia School of Engineers, Mohammed V University, Rabat, Morocco* [3]*National Institute of Standards and Technology (NIST), Gaithersburg, MD, United States*

12.1 Design Behind Success of a Smart Grid

The current state of the grid may be described as extremely sophisticated; it is already carefully designed as a critical facility to modern society. However this grid remains very sensitive to integration with the new concepts involved an open power market. Additionally an important percentage of the power generation is encouraged to be based on renewable energy sources (RESs). Hence utilities need to carefully weigh the effects of the integration of such systems when designing the composite smart grid. In particular, they should take into account the factors that go beyond their own grids and that influence their operating stability. Indeed the communication with grid partners is an important factor in the new grid design in order to allow actions beyond the local grid boundaries. The grid has to know whether there consumers are "plugging into" another electric provider or installing new solar panels in order to act like a producer. Following this logic, utilities are facing a real need to rethink, and redesign existing parts of the grid to accommodate these end-user changes and bidirectional power flows. Our proposed algebra helps the utilities' engineers to think about such challenges, design them, and verify the important design properties for their utilities.

Handbook of System Safety and Security. DOI: http://dx.doi.org/10.1016/B978-0-12-803773-7.00012-7

12.2 Trends in Renewable Energy Integration

The power grids are real-time energy delivery systems. Real time means that electricity is produced, transported, and delivered when we turn on the light switch. Power systems are not storage systems such as water and gas systems. Indeed, in a conventional power system, the generators produce the energy that the demand requires [1]. The system begins with the production, by which the electrical energy is produced in the power station and then transformed in the transformer station into high-voltage electrical energy that is more suitable for efficient long distance transport. The electrical plants transform other energy sources, in the process of generation, into electrical energy. For example, heat, mechanical energy, hydraulic, chemical, solar, wind, geothermal, nuclear, and others are used in the production of electrical energy. The power lines, in the transport segment of the electric power system, are intended to efficiently transport electrical energy over long distances to the points of consumption. Finally the transformer stations "step down" the high-voltage electrical energy into low voltage, which is, transmitted via the electrical distribution lines that are more appropriate for the distribution of electric power to its destination, where it is again stepped down to a voltage level appropriate for residential consumption, commercial, and industrial.

Unlike the tree structure of unidirectional descending power flow from generation toward consumption, the next generation of power systems integrates distributed RES generators and the *structure* becomes one of bidirectional power flow where each node in the system can either be producer and/or consumer. Fig. 12.1 shows the basic blocks of a next-generation electric power network.

In recent decades many studies have been done on designing hybrid renewable energy systems and proposing operation modes for its components. These systems can be classed according to the scale of designed network.

On one hand, the RES Integration can be into a microgrid or a *subgrid*. This class consists of small networks powered by a hybrid electric production system as microgrids. Several studies have been conducted in order to optimize the design of a hybrid system. In Ref. [2], the authors present a comparative study of different structures of hybrid renewable energy systems. Combinations of photovoltaic, wind, diesel generators, and batteries are regarded as presenting the system designer every

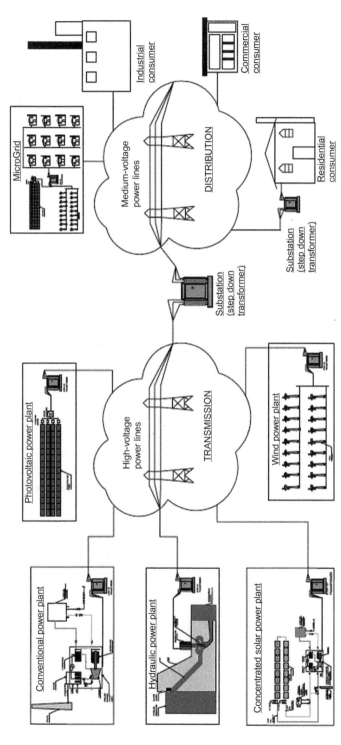

Figure 12.1 Smart grid components.

possibility that he/she might need to make the right decision when *sizing* the system for its intended use. For each of the scenarios, the study takes into account the annualized cost and reliability of the system as a multiobjective system. In fact the proportion of renewable energy, the probability of load loss, and the operating time of backup diesel generation represent the system reliability. The decision variables included in the optimization process are the power to install photovoltaic generator, wind power, number of batteries, and the diesel generator power. This approach has employed a multiobjective *genetic algorithm* [2] for solving the described optimization problem. Moreover, the study developed in Ref. [3] presents an overview on the design and implementation of hybrid RESs.

On the other hand, several studies have been conducted on the RESs integration into national networks on a large scale. For instance, the study presented in Ref. [4] addresses the penetration requirements of different RES technologies, which are assessed by considering, at the same time, other attenuation strategies aiming to reduce the global emissions of electricity networks and achieving the required objectives. Then the study of the impacts of the climate change attenuation strategies on the demand and the mix production has been envisaged to facilitate the RES penetration. As an application of this approach, marginal emissions associated with individual production technologies in the state of New South Wales (NSW) were modeled, and the total emissions associated with the electricity grid of NSW was evaluated. Furthermore, in Ref. [5], the authors present long-term strategies for transmission network infrastructure in order to integrate increasing amounts of renewable energy for the periods from 2030 to 2050. Another study developed in Ref. [6] points out the research problems whose solutions would allow us to prepare and to better manage the impact of RES integration into the German power system. This study was investigated in the framework of the German energy transition goals, called "Energiewende." Many solutions have been proposed as a network expansion and revision, more flexible production in conventional power plants, and demand control in the context of this new concept of smart grids and smart markets. In the same context, the United States has launched several studies, including a comparison of two studies ("Sunshot Vision" and "Renewable Energy Future") as presented in Ref. [7]. The study developed in the framework of "Sunshot Vision" evaluates the potential impact of solar technologies implementation with very low cost, while the "RE Future" study analyzes the benefits and impacts of providing up to 90% of the country's electricity from RES technologies. Both studies show that solar technologies could play a very important role in the US power system over the next 20–40 years. They also state that there are many challenges along the way to achieving such future results. Other countries have initiated research projects on the RES integration in order to increase penetration into their national grids such as Canada, Brazil, South Africa, to name a few.

12.3 Power Systems Laws

Power systems are constrained by many laws that must be considered in order to meet the widely varying electricity demands while ensuring the correct and safe operation of the whole system. However the most important power system constraint is "Power Balancing," which requires that the power produced be exactly the sum of the power consumed and the grid losses, as expressed in (12.1).

$$P_g = P_d + P_{loss} \tag{12.1}$$

where P_g is the produced power, P_d is the electricity demand, and P_{loss} is the power lost in the grid links. Since electricity cannot yet be economically stored in large quantities, the logistics of power production is done dynamically in order to maintain this power balance at any given moment. With the conventional production, generation adjustment was possible (primary, secondary, and tertiary) to maintain this balance of production power and demand power. However, with the distributed and intermittent generation sources associated with the smart grid concept, it will be necessary to develop system designs that will guarantee the power balance. We will need tools to produce, assess, and assure these system designs.

12.4 A Cyber-Physical System Algebra

The aim of this section is to present a formal framework that provides the underlying semantics for a high-level *cyber-physical system (CPS) design language*. This framework is defined as an algebra, that is, a mathematical structure with a set of elements and a set of operations on those elements. The operations of an algebra frequently satisfy properties such as commutativity, associativity, idempotency, and distributivity. Our proposed framework provides some built-in smart grid–related properties that use smart-/microgrids as processes. They are used as values for a *parallel composition* of a new CPS design. Parallel composition is defined to be a commutative and associative operation on CPS.

12.4.1 The π-Calculus as Root

In our approach, a CPS is regarded as a composition of concurrent parts. The overall behavior of the CPS is structured by the combination of the behaviors of its subsystems. We can assimilate each subsystem to a process or an agent within the overall CPS. The π-calculus [8] is a model of computation for concurrent systems. It is also a process calculus that lets a designer represent processes, parallel composition of processes, synchronous communication between processes through channels, fresh channel creation, processes replication, and nondeterminism. The extension of such an algebra, as proposed here, gives rise to a CPS Domain Specific Language (CPS-DSL). In this DSL, a CPS component is defined as a process. Indeed, in this framework, a smart grid component inherits properties from the π-calculus such as those of composition and communication. Those properties alone are not sufficient to address the specific case of CPS. The CPS-DSL introduces a *specialization model* for which the CPS under study being specified is modeled using the proposed modeling language. In order to enrich the semantics of the CPS-DSL, we define a framework where smart grid process is defined within the *specialization model* based on the general π-calculus processes. We use the higher order capabilities of the π-calculus to exchange agents that capture the specific behavior associated with smart grids.

The monadic π-calculus operations, between and on processes, are explained below. If P and Q denote two processes then:

- $P|Q$ denotes a process composed of P and Q running in parallel.
- $a(x).P$ denotes a process that waits to read a value x from the channel a and then, having received it, behaves like P.
- $\bar{a}\langle x \rangle. P$ denotes a process that first waits to send the value x along the channel a and then, after x has been accepted by some input process, behaves like P.
- $(\nu\, a)\, P$ ensures that a is a fresh new channel in P.
- $!P$ denotes an infinite number of copies of P, all running in parallel.
- $P + Q$ denotes a process that behaves like either P or Q.
- Ø denotes the inert process that does nothing.

The polyadic [9] form of the π-calculus introduces *vectors*, as parameters exchanged over the channels, of the form

$a(\vec{x}) \stackrel{\text{def}}{=} a(x_0, x_1, x_2, \ldots, x_n)$ where a is a channel, n is the arity if the vector x noted $n = \|x\|$. In addition to this notion, two other notions are introduced and they will be at the heart of our CPS-DSL:

- Abstraction on names for processes from a given process: $(\lambda \vec{x})P$.
    - This is the essence of the parametric definition. It may be used to define the parameters of a process inside its definition instead of writing the parameter on the process's name

        $-$We can write $K(\vec{x}) \stackrel{\text{def}}{=} P$ as an abstraction of $\vec{x}$ over P
        $K \stackrel{\text{def}}{=} (\lambda \vec{x})P$
    - This is the basis of the chaining combination between processes. Consider an example, as illustrated in Fig. 12.2 where $F \stackrel{\text{def}}{=} (\lambda\, a)(\nu\, x)\bar{a}\langle x\rangle$ and $G \stackrel{\text{def}}{=} (\lambda\, b)\ b(x)\cdot\tau$. In order to enable the chaining of those two processes, we can create a new channel c and use the renaming to obtain a chaining combination as

        $-(\nu\, c)(F|G) \equiv (\nu\, c)\{F\{c/a\}|G\{c/b\}\}$
- Concretion of names from a process: $[\vec{x}]P$. This is a way to treat output dually to input. The concretion is used in order to communicate datum already bound. Consider a process K that defined as $K(\vec{x}) \stackrel{\text{def}}{=} P$ and we have to send the output $\vec{x}$ over the channel a as $\bar{a}\langle\vec{x}\rangle \cdot K(\vec{x}) \stackrel{\text{def}}{=} P$. We can consider the output prefix $\bar{a}\langle\vec{x}\rangle$ by bypassing the need of the parametric definition as $\bar{a} \cdot K$ if $K \stackrel{\text{def}}{=} [\vec{x}]P$
    - $K \stackrel{\text{def}}{=} \bar{a}\langle\vec{x}\rangle \cdot P(\vec{x})$ can be represented using the concretion-based notation as $\bar{a} \cdot K \stackrel{\text{def}}{=} [\vec{x}]P$

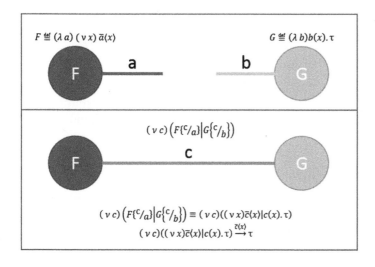

Figure 12.2 Abstraction used for chaining combination.

12.4.2 CPS-Specific Language

The CPS design framework, that we are proposing, offers the primitive structures built into the language to deal with CPS components and their composition operator. Two distinct categories of elements are modeled in this approach:

- *Components*: Components are atomic building blocks of the system. Those elements are characterized by their inputs, outputs, and behavior. They are considered by the system as a black box offering a function on the system. The components are used to model both the cyber objects and the physical objects.

- *Composites*: Composites are building blocks composed of components or other composites. They aim to provide a "Glue," which enable connecting the components to each other and offer a new feature. They may be considered complex components as they aim to provide a function, even if they are using component to provide that function. They are characterized by their inputs, outputs, and the components that they incorporate.

We introduce here *syntactic sugar* as a syntax within CPS-DSL to make the composition easier to read or to express. Indeed, the name $CPS(\vec{b})$ is used to refer to both the composite grid and the elements of the CPS. Therefore, we define the term *CPS* in (12.2) as a parallel deterministic choice between a *Composite* in (12.6) and a *Grid Component* in (12.5). The term *CPS* has a parameter vector $\vec{b}$ that stands for "behavior." This parameter is used to pass an agent as a higher order parameter. The agent will drive the behavior of the grid according to his specificities.

$$CPS(\vec{b}) \stackrel{\text{def}}{=} [||b|| = \underline{1}]Component(b_0)$$
$$+ [||b|| \neq \underline{1}]Composite((b_i \otimes)^{||b||}) \tag{12.2}$$

The definition of the term *CPS* calls *Component* if the arity of the vector $\vec{b}$ is equal to one. It calls the term *Composite* if the arity is greater than one. Before calling *Composite*, we apply the composition operator, defined in (12.10), to the elements of the vector $\vec{b}$ in order to *chain* them.

12.4.3 Application to the Smart Grid

The aim of our design framework is to provide a domain-specific language for CPS. The language needs to embrace the application domain of the CPS to provide relevant syntactic elements. In the smart grid domain of application we distinguish the composition operator that is used to build a structural composition between two elements that may be a macrogrid [11], microgrid [12], or a grid component [13].

The term *Component* is a generic term that represents the elements of the Smart Grid [13]. This term is a generic one for grid elements like:

- *Asset Management Systems*: elements used to help in the optimization if the OpEx and CapEx.
- *Building Automation and Control System*: elements including the control and management technology for building, plant, facilities, etc.
- *Decision Support Systems*: elements used to protect the equipment from fatal faults and avoid instabilities and blackouts in the power systems.
- *Distribution Automation*: elements that promote automatic self-configuration and self-healing features.
- *Distribution Management System*: elements used as the control center for the distribution grid.
- *Energy Management System*: elements used as the control center for the Transmission grid.
- *Power Monitoring Systems*: elements that supervise all activities and assets/electrical equipment.
- *Smart Consumption*: elements that lie at the interface between distribution management and building automation.
- *Smart Generation*: elements used for fluctuating generation from renewable energy.
- *Smart Homes*: elements representing houses that are equipped with a home automation system and may generate green energy.
- *Smart Meter*: remotely controllable electronic meters, also called Advanced Metering Infrastructure (AMI).

As this components list is not exhaustive terminology of standardization is still ongoing, the proposed composition language will evolve to meet the standardization effort under the leadership of NIST (United States National Institute of Standards and Technology) that is yielding good results as illustrated by the NIST Framework and Roadmap for Smart Grid Interoperability Standards (NIST-SP-1108, Release 3.0). Moreover, the behavior of each element varies depending on his physical and/or cyber properties, the proposed algebra allows the framework to decouple the behavior from the composition mechanism. In other words the composition of the grid components needs to be agnostic to the execution context. In order to be more concrete, let us consider the case of three agents, as shown in Fig. 12.3. In this example, three communication channels are connecting these agents. A consumption channel c, a production channel p, and a metering channel m. The definition of the tree agents'

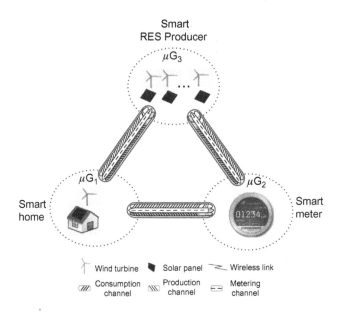

Smart
RES Producer

μG_3

μG_1
μG_2

Smart
home

Smart
meter

⊤ Wind turbine ◼ Solar panel ⌇ Wireless link

⬚ Consumption   ⬚ Production   ⬚ Metering
channel   channel   channel

Figure 12.3 Algebra of three components.

behavior that we using for our use case is given in (12.3), (12.4), and (12.5).

The agent *Smart Home*, as defined in (12.3), represents the behavior of a smart home that consumes energy reserved on the channel c, sends a message to the smart meter on the channel m and, if the home is not producing energy, it sends a null value $\overline{p}\langle\varnothing\rangle$ on the channel p.

$$Smart\ Home() \stackrel{\text{def}}{=} in(c, m, p) \cdot (c(unit) \cdot \overline{m}\langle unit\rangle \cdot \overline{p}\langle\varnothing\rangle)$$
$$\cdot (v\ p')\overline{out}\langle p, m, p'\rangle \tag{12.3}$$

The agent defined in (12.4) receives messages on the canal m about the usage and then executes a *nonobservable action*. That means that in this example, the metrics are not observable at this abstraction level, only the exchange of the information influences this system.

$$Smart\ Meter() \stackrel{\text{def}}{=} in(c, m, p) \cdot (m(unit) \cdot \tau) \cdot (v\ p')\overline{out}\langle p, m, p'\rangle \tag{12.4}$$

In (12.5), we present a *Smart Generation* agent that represents a power generation behavior, this component produces power, sends it on the channel p, and updates a smart meter using the channel m.

$$Smart\ Generation() \stackrel{\text{def}}{=} in(c, m, p) \cdot ((v\ unit)\overline{p}\langle unit\rangle \cdot \overline{m}\langle unit\rangle)$$
$$\cdot (v\ p')\overline{out}\langle p, m, p'\rangle \tag{12.5}$$

At this point, we define the term *Component* that is used as *wrapper* for a behavior agent. This term is used to manage the input channel in and the output channel out that are used by the behavior agent to communicate.

$$Component(A()) \stackrel{\text{def}}{=} (\lambda\ in\ out) \cdot A() \cdot (v\ out') [out\ out'] \qquad (12.6)$$

12.4.4 The Composition Operation

Now we define the *composition pseudo-application* $\otimes$ from an abstraction to a concretion with an equal arity. Let A_1 and A_2 be two behavior agents. We define two corresponding *Component*'s in (12.7a) and (12.7b).

$$Component(A_1()) \equiv (\lambda\ in_1\ out_1) \cdot A_1() \cdot (v\ out_1') [out_1\ out_1'] \quad (12.7a)$$

$$Component(A_2()) \equiv (\lambda\ in_2\ out_2) \cdot A_2() \cdot (v\ out_2') [out_2\ out_2'] \quad (12.7b)$$

The composition of the two components is defined in (12.8) as the substitution, in the sense of the lambda-calculus [14], of the input streams of the second *Component* with the output of the first *Component*. In this way that the channels of production, management, and consumption will be shared by the two components.

$$Component(A_1()) \otimes Component(A_2()) \stackrel{\text{def}}{=}$$
$$(v\ out_1') (\{out_1\ out_1'/in_2\ out_2\} A_2() \cdot (v\ out_2') [out_2\ out_2'] | (\lambda\ in_1\ out_1) \cdot A_1())$$
$$(12.8)$$

The last part of our definition is there to enable the loop between the first and the last term on our composition chain. For that, we use the term *Composite* to allow the input output substitution to end with a communication loop as defined in (12.9). This definition creates a fresh output channel *out″* that is used as to communicate the outgoing information from the first component. In addition, this term uses the output of the last component *out′* transmitted by the concretion as an input for the first component.

$$Composite(Components())$$
$$\times \stackrel{\text{def}}{=} (v\ out'')\{out'\ out''/in\ out\} Components() [in'\ out'] \qquad (12.9)$$

To have a more *user-friendly* definition of the smart grid design, we propose the definition of the composition operator $\otimes$ to include natively the input and the output channels without an explicit use of the term *Grid Component*. This syntactic sugar did not affect the behavior of the composition operator as illustrated in (12.10).

$$A_1() \otimes A_2() \stackrel{\text{def}}{=} (v\ out_1') (\{out_1\ out_1'/in_2\ out_2\} A_2() \cdot (v\ out_2')$$
$$\times [out_2\ out_2'] (\lambda\ in_1\ out_1) \cdot A_1())$$
$$(12.10)$$

12.5 Illustration

To illustrate our approach, let consider a composition based on the terms defined in (12.3), (12.4), and (12.5). We can define a grid as in (12.11). Please note that here that we are using the syntactic sugar defined in (12.10).

$$Grid3E() \stackrel{\text{def}}{=} Composite(Smart\ Home()\otimes Smart\ Meter() \\ \times \otimes Smart\ Generation()) \qquad (12.11)$$

The reduction of this system ends as a structural congruence with a composition of null processes. That means that this system is stable as illustrated in (12.12a and 12.12b). With $GridE3'$ we denote the system $Grid3E$, obtained after sending and receiving using all the channels.

$$Grid3E() \xrightarrow{\overline{p}\langle unit\rangle,\ \overline{m}\langle unit\rangle,...} GridE3'() \qquad (12.12a)$$

$$GridE3'() \equiv Grid\ Composite(\emptyset \otimes \emptyset) \qquad (12.12b)$$

The case illustrated in (12.12a) and (12.12b) is a simple case where the system ends. Another interesting case is where the system is acting as a loop. In this case the reduction of the system leads to a structural congruence with the original definition as illustrated in (12.13a) and (12.13b).

$$Grid3E() \xrightarrow{\overline{p}\langle unit\rangle,\ \overline{m}\langle unit\rangle,...} GridE3'(), \qquad (12.13a)$$

$$GridE3'() \equiv Grid3E() \qquad (12.13b)$$

So how we can identify a design issue in the system? To answer this question, we redefine the consumption term *Smart Home* for an infinite consumption as in (12.13a and 12.13b). The reduction will highlight the fact that the system *Grid3E* has load balancing to support the demand in terms of energy by the *rtHome*.

$$Smart\ Home() \stackrel{\text{def}}{=} in(c,m,p)\cdot !(c(unit)\cdot\overline{m}\langle unit\rangle.\overline{p}\langle 0\rangle)\cdot(\nu\ p')\overline{out}\langle p,m,p'\rangle \qquad (12.14)$$

In (12.15) we illustrate the result of the reduction of the newly defined *Grid3E*. The two terms *Smart Meter* and *Smart Generation* have been reduced, but the *Smart Home* is still in the definition due to its new replicate definition. This is one of the most interesting contributions of this framework so far: we are able to identify, using the framework, the cause of the issue. As a result the designer can rethink his/her design and determine solutions.

$$Grid3E() \xrightarrow{\overline{p}\langle unit \rangle,\, \overline{m}\langle unit \rangle,...} GridE3'() \qquad (12.15)$$

$$GridE3'() \equiv Grid\ Composite(\emptyset \otimes \emptyset)|Smart\ Home()$$

12.6 Conclusion

Defining appropriate concepts, methods, and tools both for the design and test of CPSs, in the case of the example here for is a huge challenge and research in this area is of critical importance. Since *smart grid* began as an idea of an overlay, on top of existing infrastructure, the languages and tools to help us design such systems are not mature enough to help us meet the significant economic, technical, and strategic challenges brought by the smart grid concept. The challenge of doing the same for CPS is the more general case.

Our efforts here are intended to help the designer and tester think about their activities and to study the critical metrics for CPS success in a conceptual and disciplined way. To this end we offer an algebraic domain-specific language called CPS-DSL and abstract notion of composition.

Our future work will focus on the extension of this language to support a more precise definition of system elements, including the definition of the behavior agents and extension to address other CPS application domains. Moreover, we are designing a tool to help the designer to *reduce* the CPS-DSL definition in order to be able to identify design issues. This tool will provide, e.g., automatic design suggestions based on issues or concerns identified for a system design or for an actual system.

References

[1] J. Zhu, Optimization of Power System Operation, John Wiley & Sons, New York, NY, 2009.
[2] D. Kalyanmoy, Multi-Objective Optimization Using Evolutionary Algorithms, vol. 16, John Wiley & Sons, New York, NY, 2001.
[3] D. Neves, C.A. Silva, S. Connors, Design and implementation of hybrid renewable energy systems on micro-communities: a review on case studies, Renew. Sustain. Energy Rev. 31 (2014) 935–946.
[4] M. Abdullah, A. Agalgaonkar, K. Muttaqi, Climate change mitigation with integration of renewable energy resources in the electricity grid of New South Wales, Australia, Renew. Energy 66 (2014) 305–313.

[5] K. Schaber, F. Steinke, T. Hamacher, Transmission grid extensions for the integration of variable renewable energies in Europe: who benefits where? Energy Policy 43 (2012) 123–135.

[6] S.C. Trümper, S. Gerhard, S. Saatmann, O. Weinmann, Qualitative analysis of strategies for the integration of renewable energies in the electricity grid, Energy Proc. 46 (2014) 161–170.

[7] P. Denholm, R. Margolis, T. Mai, G. Brinkman, E. Drury, M. Hand, et al., Bright future: Solar power as a major contributor to the U.S. grid, IEEE Power Energy Magazine 11 (2) (2013) 22–32.

[8] D. Sangiorgi, D. Walker, The Pi-Calculus: A Theory of Mobile Processes, Cambridge University Press, Cambridge, MA, 2003.

[9] R. Milner, The Polyadic π-Calculus: A Tutorial, Springer Berlin Heidelberg, Berlin, 1993.

[10] W. Saad, Z. Han, H. Vincent Poor. Coalitional game theory for cooperative micro-grid distribution networks, in: Communications Workshops (ICC), 2011 IEEE International Conference on, IEEE, 2011, pp. 1–5.

[11] C. Wang, P. Li, Development and challenges of distributed generation, the micro-grid and smart distribution system, Autom. Electr. Power Syst. 2 (2010) 004.

[12] M. Malawski, M. Bubak, F. Baude, D. Caromel, L. Henrio, M. Morel, Interoperability of grid component models: GCM and CCA case study, Towards Next Generation Grids, Springer, US, 2007.

[13] H.I. Joshi, H.R. Choksi, Development of infrastructue for residential load to reduce peak demand and cost of energy in smart grid, Development 3 (3) (2015).

[14] R. Rojas, A Tutorial Introduction to the Lambda Calculus, arXiv preprint arXiv:1503.09060, 2015.

INDEX

Note: Page numbers followed by "*f*" and "*t*" refer to figures and tables, respectively.

A

Access control for multiuser
    systems, 76–77
Advanced Metering
    Infrastructure (AMI), 261
Adversary strategies, 73–78
  adaptive offline adversary, 73
  adaptive online adversary,
    73–74
  oblivious or stateless
    adversary, 73
Amazon AWS, 204–205
Amazon Elastic Map Reduce
    (EMR), 204–205
Amazon Glacier, 204–205
Amazon Web Services, 204–205
AppEngine, 207
AppFog, 205
Application programming
    interfaces (APIs),
    219
Architectural description
    languages, 134
Attack-countermeasure trees
    (ACTs), 145–147, 147*f*
  for an attack of the border
    gateway protocol,
    146–147, 147*f*
  as an SMT tool, 149
  benefits of using, 149–150
  in computation of risk
    metrics and analysis,
    147–148
  limitations, 150
Attack entry points,
    71, 75*f*, 76
  likelihood of penetration of,
    79
  resource access, 77–78
  vector for, 76

Attack surfaces, 71, 74, 75*f*
  exterior, 75
  of internal component,
    75
Attack vector paths, 71–72
Automatic transmission system
    of a hybrid-electric
    vehicle, software for, 45
Automotive software safety, 8
Autonomic Service Manager
    (ASM), 182–184, 182*f*
  Controller module, 182
  Observer module, 182
AVM component model, 21–24,
    22*f*
  construction of, 23–24
  dynamic interface, 29–32
  physical interactions, 27–28
  reason for, 22–23
  types of interfaces, 27

B

Basicmath (Automotive and
    Industrial category), 193,
    194*f*
Bayesian Belief Networks,
    150
Big data, 168–169
Bitcoin, 155–156
  consensus and
    pseudoanonymity,
    157–158
  design risks, 158–160
  financial loss using, 168
  mixing service threats,
    162–163
  Proof-of-Work, 156–157
  risk engineering in, 163*f*
  security risks, 160–163
  system parameters, 159

Block-chain technology,
    155–164
  consensus and
    pseudoanonymity,
    157–158
  design risks, 158–160
  Proof-of-Work, 156–157
  security risks, 160–163
BO algorithm, 181–182
Bond Graph Language, 32
Bring Your Own Device (BYOD),
    216
Byzantine failures, 71–72
Byzantine Generals,, 156

C

Π-calculus, 258–259
Caspio, 205
Central safety organization, 94
Chief Information Security
    Officers (CISOs), 99–100,
    104, 108
Cloud and mobile cloud
    architecture, security and
    safety, 10–11
Cloud bursting, 202–203
Cloud caching, 203
Cloud computing, 177, 199
  advantages, 199–201
  building applications,
    209–210
  concepts and uses of
    measurement within,
    210–212
  defined, 199
  IBM HS22 Bladecenter,
    experimental results and
    evaluation, 188–194
  important issues with,
    203–204

Cloud computing (*Continued*)
  integration of technologies,
    177—178
  problems solved using,
    201—203
  safety concerns, 212—216
    cloud data storage,
      215—216
    data centers, 213—214
  services' layers, 204—205, 204*f*
  types of clouds, 205—206,
    207*f*
Cloud data storage, 215—216
Cloudlet, 207—208
Cloud security, 178, 216—222
  best practices, 221—222
    encryption, 221
  threat profile and, 218—220
Cloud Service Editor (CSE),
    180—181
Cluster GPU instances, 204—205
Coinbase, 158—159
Common Vulnerabilities and
    Exposures (CVE), 185
Common Vulnerability Scoring
    System (CVSS), 185
Compiler Portable Check-
    Pointing (CPPC),
    183—184, 184*f*
Component interfaces and
    composition semantics
    in OpenMETA, 27
  dynamic interactions of
    component model M,
    27—32
  physical interactions, 27—28
  types of interfaces, 27
Component Models (CMs),
    18—20
  generic requirements, 21
  main elements of, 23
Computer-aided design (CAD),
    17
Computing paradigms, evolution
    of, 199—201, 200*f*
Configuration Engine (CE), 182
"Connected" system security
    modeling, 78—80
  mathematically of, 80

Constraint logic programming
    (CLP)-based semantics,
    27
Consumer retention rate KPI,
    211
Coveted resources, 78
Cryptocurrencies, 156
CVEChecker tool, 184—185, 187
Cyber-physical systems (CPS),
    5, 8, 67—68, 68*f*, 204,
    208—209
  attack surfaces, 71
  capability *vs* system
    complexity, 69*f*
  component models, 24
  defining, 22
  design, 17
    component-based, 18
  design problems, 34—35
  establishment of
    composability and
    compositionality, 17
  heterogeneity in, 16—17, 16*f*
  horizontal integration
    platforms for, 16—17
  interconnected composable
    perspective, 79*f*
  key challenges in the
    engineering of, 15
  model-integrated
    development approach
    for, 15—16
  risks *vs* assets perspective,
    70—72
  "separation of concerns"
    principle, 16—17
Cybersecurity, 98, 98*f*
  along value chains,
    99—104
  commercial advantage,
    104—111
  consumers, managing
    relationships with,
    106—107
    applying design thinking,
      107
    consumer preferences,
      106—107
    user customization, 107

contracting processes,
    101—102
    authentication and
      authorization, 103—104
    reducing vendor leverage
      and reshape markets,
      102—103
  enterprise customers,
    managing relationships
    with, 107—109
    product security, 109
    role of CISO and team, 108
    vendor security
      assessments, 108—109
  implications, 98*f*
  need for, 97
    as a "backoffice" or
      "control" functional, 99
    as a commercial and
      contractual issue, 98
  suppliers, managing
    relationships with,
    109—111
    collaborative relationship
      between security and
      procurement teams, 110
    commercial interactions,
      111
    vendor security and vendor
      rationalization programs,
      109—111
Cybersecurity insurance
    research, 154—155
CyPhyML Model Integration
    Language, 26—27, 32
  semantics of, 33
  specification of, 34

D
DARPA's AVM program, 17.
    See also AVM component
    model
Decentralized safety
    organization, 94—95
Denial-of-service (DDoS),
    218—219, 245
Design failure modes and
    effects analysis (dFMEA),
    89—90

Designing software, 49−56.
    See also Software
        development and
        maintenance
    conventions and guidelines,
        53−54
    design *vs* requirements, 49−51
    important principles, 51−52
        calibrations, 51−52
        change and anticipation of
            change principles, 51−52
        information hiding, 52
        powertrain configurations,
            51−52
    Stateflow truth table designs,
        50−51, 50*t*, 51*t*
Design Models (DMs), 18
Design Space Models (DSM), 18
Desktop computing, 199−201
Development Interface
        Agreement (DIA)
        documents, 115, 116*f*
DevOps-related KPIs, 211−212
Diagnostic coverage, 88
Differential Algebraic Equations
        (DAE), 23
Digital Resilience, 105
Dijkstra, Edsger, 39
    algorithm (Network category),
        193, 194*f*
Directional threat assessment,
        80−81
Distributed Denial of Service
        (DDoS), 178
Doctrine of Public
        Cybersecurity, 154−155
Domain-specific modeling
        languages, 32, 146−147,
        149−151, 260
DSPACE TargetLink, 56−57

E
Early design-space exploration
        process, 23
Economic espionage, 71
ElastiCache, 204−205
Elastic Block Storage (EBS),
        204−205
Electronic CAD (E-CAD), 17

Energiewende, 256−257
Engine Yard, 205
Entry point risk, 76−77
ESMoL, 32
Event Tree Analysis (ETA), 88

F
Fail-safe modes, 71−72
Fault Tree Analysis (FTA), 88
Feature *vs* Bug (FVB) KPI, 212
Fiat Powertrain Engineering,
        116−117
Finite element analysis (FEA), 17
Flawfinder, 184−185
FORMULA's algebraic data
        types (ADT), 27, 29−32,
        34−35
Functional safety, 91−95
    audit and assessment, 92
    implementation of safety
        process, 93
    organizational policy, 92
    purpose, 91
    safety process, 91−93

G
Goal Structuring Notation
        (GSN), 117
    terminology, 114−115, 115*f*
Google, 207
    App Engine, 205
    Compute Engine, 204−205
Grawrock, David, 154

H
Hacker capability, 69
Hacker tools, 68−69
Hadoop, 189
Hazard Analysis and Risk
        Assessment (HARA), 121,
        235−236, 252
    controllability classifications,
        239
    exposure classifications,
        238−239
    major steps in, 237
    "Safety Integrity Level D"
        function, 239−240
    sample hazard list, 238

scenarios associated with
        hazards, 238
    severity levels, 238−239
    use case, 237−240
Hazard and Operability Study
        (HAZOP), 114
Heroku, 205
Human error, 71
Hybrid Clouds, 205−208, 207*f*
Hybrid DAEs, 23

I
IBM HS22 Bladecenter,
        experimental results and
        evaluation, 188−194
    Jacobi's Iterative Linear
        Equation Solver,
        191−193
        overhead in terms of the
            execution time, 192, 193*t*
    MapReduce, 188−191
        resilience against denial of
            service attacks, 190, 191*f*
        resilience against insider
            attacks, 191
        result summary, 192*t*
    MiBench Benchmarks,
        193−194, 193*f*
    test setup, 188
IBM SmartCloud Enterprise,
        204−205
Information and
        communications
        technology (ICT), 8−9,
        132−140, 212−213
    cyber and physical
        environments, 135
    impact on the global
        economy, 142
    interaction of safety and
        security in, 144−145
    intrinsic complexity and
        dynamism, 133−134, 133*f*
    regulatory environment,
        136−138, 139*f*
    technology and policy
        frameworks, 139−140
    ubiquitous connectivity and
        interoperability, 132

Infrastructure as a Service (IaaS), 177, 204–205, 204*f*
Intent of the system, 127
Interconnected risk measurement, 79*f*
Internet computing, 199–201
Internet of Things (IoT), 5
Intuitionistic Type Theory, 117
ISO 26262, 8, 41–42, 114, 116–118, 125, 127
ISO 26262:2011 Road vehicles, 114
ISO/IEC/IEEE Standard 24765, 39

K
Key Performance Indicators (KPIs), 210–211
consumer retention rate KPI, 211
DevOps-related KPIs, 211–212
Feature *vs* Bug (FVB) KPI, 212
Monthly Recurring Revenue (MRR) KPI, 211
Project Burndown (PBD) KPI, 212
Knowledge Representation (KR), 152, 166
declarative form, 152

L
Load balancing, 228–229
Lumped parameter dynamics, 18, 20–21, 23–25
semantic integration concept for, 25*f*
consequences of model integration language concepts, 26–27
distributed cosimulations, 25–26
HLA, 25–26
modeling languages, 24–25
OpenMETA Semantic Backplane, 27, 34–35
target integration domains, 25–26

M
Mainframe computing, 199–201
Maintaining safety of the system, 90–91
Malfunctioning behavior, 85–86
Manufacturing, safety in, 89–90
MapReduce, 188–191
resilience against denial of service attacks, 190, 191*f*
resilience against insider attacks, 191
result summary, 192*t*
Wordcount program, 189
Master Virtual Machines (MVMs), 182
MathWorks, 56–57
Embedded Coder, 56–57
MiBench Benchmarks, 193–194, 193*f*
Microgrids, 234, 254–256
Microsoft Attack Surface Analyzer, 184–185
Miners, 157–158
Mixed Non-Linear Integer Programming (MINLP) solvers, 148–151
Mobile Cloud Computing (MCC), 203–204, 206, 208*f*
communication challenges, 207
for CPS, 208–209
as emergency response systems, 208–209
feedback loops, 208–209
Model-based development (MBD), 6, 40, 43
automatic code generation in, 56–57
benefit of, 43–44
different testing strategies in, 43–44
Hardware-in-the-Loop (HiL), 44
Model-in-the-Loop (MiL), 44
Processor-in-the-Loop (PiL), 44
Software-in-the-Loop (SiL), 44
documentation, 55
software design, 49
verification and validation activities, 58–61
formal, 61
V-Model development process for, 42*f*
Model-based risk engineering, 150–151
Modelica, 32
component-based development using, 33
connectors, 33
in CyPhyML, 33
semantics of, 33
Monthly Recurring Revenue (MRR) KPI, 211
Moving target defense (MTD), 10, 178–179

N
Natural failures, 71
Nessus, 184–185
Network as a Service, 177
Network computing, 199–201
NIST Cyber-Physical Systems (CPS) Framework, 113, 134
N-tier computing, 206–207
N-version programming, 183

O
Ontologies, 152–153
in area of information security, 153
ontological languages, 152
reasoning about complex fields using, 165–166, 166*f*
Open MDAO (Multidisciplinary Design Analysis and Optimization) optimization tool, 19–20
OpenMETA, 17

fundamental model-
    integration challenge for,
    19–20
horizontal integration
    platforms in, 18–21
    execution integration
    platform, 21
    integration platform, 20
    model integration platform,
    20
    modeling functions of design,
    18–19
    Semantic Backplane, 27
Oracle Virtualbox, 189
Original Equipment
    Manufacturers (OEMs),
    40

P

Parametric Exploration Models
    (PEM), 19
Phasor measurement units
    (PMUs), 234
Platform as a Service (PaaS),
    177–178, 204f, 205
Power balancing, 257
Power grid, 225–226. *See also*
    Smart grid
    problems with conventional,
    227–229, 229f
    traditional, 226–227, 228f
    consumption, 227
    distribution, 227
    generation, 227
    transmission, 227
Power systems laws, 257
Private Clouds,
    205–206, 207f
Process failure modes and
    effects analysis (pFMEA),
    89–90
Project Burndown (PBD) KPI,
    212
Proof-of-Work concept,
    156–157, 159–160
Proof-of-Work cryptocurrencies,
    162–163
Public Clouds, 205–206, 207f

Q

Quantitative inference engines,
    152–153

R

Rackspace Open Cloud,
    204–205
Reasoning engines, 150–151,
    151f
Red Hat OpenShift, 205
Renewable energy integration,
    254–257
Resilient Cloud Middleware
    (RCM), 181–182
Resilient cloud services (RCS),
    9–10, 179–180. *See also*
    Cloud computing
    architecture, 180–188, 181f
    Autonomic Service
    Manager (ASM),
    182–184, 182f
    Cloud Service Editor (CSE),
    180–181
    Configuration Engine (CE),
    182
    Resilient Cloud Middleware
    (RCM), 181–182
    Virtual Machines (VMs),
    182
    design methodology
    approach, 179–180
    autonomic management
    (AM), 180
    diversity, 180
    redundancy, 179–180
    shuffling, 180
    determining attack surface,
    185, 187f
    probability of a successful
    attack, 187–188, 187f
    successful attack scenario,
    179, 179f
    unsuccessful attack scenario,
    179, 179f
Retina, 184–185
Risk
    approaches and models for
    security, 140–142

password, 140
    PKI-based authentication,
    140
    risk assessments, 140–141
    shared global infrastructure
    and, 141–142
    calculus, 154
    evaluation, 85–86
    exposure, 86–87
    reducing, 87
Risk engineering, 142–155
    adaptations and integration
    of model-based and
    language-based
    methodologies, 165–169
    case study for security risk
    quantification, 145–150
    challenges in, 143–145
    development of tools and
    methodologies,
    153–155
    of cryptocurrencies, 163–164
    model-based, 150–151
    obstacles to integration of
    risk aspects, 145
    ontology and, 152–153, 166f
    risk composition, risk
    language, and metrics,
    167–169

S

SAE Avionics Architecture
    Description Language
    (AADL), 135
Safety assessors, 94
Safety auditor, 94
Safety critical system, 117–122
    challenges in, 125–126
    decomposing functions,
    117–120, 118f
    hazard argumentation,
    120–122, 121f
    hazard identification, 121,
    122f
    process argumentation,
    120, 120f
    requirements elicitation,
    121, 123f

Safety critical system
(*Continued*)
system design, 121
verification measures, 122,
124*f*
Safety culture, 93
Safety Integrity Level (SIL),
235–236, 239–240
Safety managers and engineers,
94
Safety of a system
concept of, 87–88
definition, 84–85
design requirements for, 89
in disposal, 91
in maintenance, 90–91
in manufacturing, 89–90
safety life cycle of the
product, 85
successful safety
organization, 93–95
Safety (or Security) Case, 113
construction of framework,
114–117, 116*f*
GSN tree of, 124–125
need for, 113–114
primary goal of a, 115
properties associated with,
119, 119*f*
implementation of a
system, 120
two-dimensional
decomposition, 119
rules, 125
UK Defense Standard 00-55,
114
Safety properties, 119–120, 119*f*
formal reasoning for,
122–125
Satisfiability Modulo Theories
(SMT) solvers, 148–151
Security as a Service, 177
Security enhancements to
systems, 70
Security evolution, 71
Semantic integration concept,
24–27
Semantic interface for modeling
languages, 32–34

"Separation of concerns"
principle, 16–17
Service Behavior Obfuscation
(SBO) algorithm,
183–185, 183*f*
Simulink Design Verifier (SDV),
61
Simulink model, 46, 55–57, 60
Data Store Memory, 52–53
information hiding in, 52–53
modeling guidelines for,
53–54
software engineering
principles and, 52–53
subsystems, 52–53
Simulink/Stateflow model, 32,
60
Smart cars, 207–208
Smart grid, 11–12, 233*f*, 255*f*
algebra, 12–13, 257–263,
262*f*
π-calculus, 258–259
composition pseudo-
application ⊗, 263
domain-specific language,
260
illustration, 264–265
basic definition, 231
demand response, 232
design, 253
difference between the
traditional and, 233–234,
235*t*
drivers and motivations,
230
energy production, 231
infrastructure of the, 231–232
laws considered, 257
modernized grid, 231
National Institute of
Standards and
Technology (NIST)
requirements, 230, 232*f*,
246
overview, 225–226
phasor measurement units
(PMUs), 234
renewable energy integration,
254–257

safety analysis, 235–249
background and
terminology, 241–242
main issues, 244–245
need for, 235–236
principles and
requirements, 243
proposed solutions,
246–248
threats, 245–246
vulnerabilities, 243–245
smart power management of,
234
standards and guidelines for,
248–249
EU countries, 248–249
NISTIR and NIST SP1108,
248
Smart Grid Domain-Specific
Language (SG-DSL), 258,
260
Asset Management Systems,
261
Building Automation and
Control System, 261
Decision Support Systems,
261
Distribution Automation, 261
Distribution Management
System, 261
Energy Management System,
261
Grid Component and Grid
Composite, 260
Power Monitoring Systems,
261
Smart Consumption, 261
Smart Generation, 261–263
Smart Homes, 261–262
Smart Meter, 261–262
Software as a Service (SaaS),
177–178, 204*f*, 205
Software design document
(SDD), 54–55
elements, 54–55
present times, 56
template for, 56
Software development and
maintenance, 39–40.

See also Designing software; Model-based development (MBD); Software design document (SDD)
automatic transmission system of a hybrid-electric vehicle, case example, 45
collaboration between software engineers and domain experts, need for, 40
development process, 41–45
    acceptance testing, 43–44
    architectural design, 43
    integration testing, 43–44
    involvement of domain experts, 42–44
    phases, 42–44
    tool support, 44–45
    unit testing, 43–44
future work, 61–62
implementation, 56–58
    code generation, 56–57
    limitations in code generation, 57–58
"requirements" and "requirements specification (SRS)", 45–49
    for driver request arbitration, 47t
    model, 46
    purpose, 46
    role of domain experts, 48
    separating from design, 47–48
    structure and content of, 48–49
    verification and validation, 58–61
    need for, 58–59
    software testing, 59
Software testing, 59
    choosing a, 59–60
Storage as a Service (StaaS), 177
Stuxnet attack, 135
Subgrid, 254–256
System, notion of, 3
Systematic analyses, 87–88
System behaviors, 3–4
System complexity, 69
System resilience, defined, 186
    expected value of the impact of a vulnerability v, 186
    impact i_v (t) of a vulnerability v, 186
    impact of a system with N vulnerabilities, 186
    probability of an attack, 186

T
Test Bench Models (TBM), 19–20
Threat assessment, 71
Threat capability and vulnerabilities, 68–69
Tools in software development and maintenance, 44–45
Toronto i* goal modeling language, 153
TrueTime, 24–25

V
Vendor security assessments, 108–111
Virtual Machines (VMs), 182, 192
Vulnerabilities, 68–70

W
"What we make, makes us", 3
Windows Azure, 204–205
Windows Azure Cloud Services, 205
Worker Virtual Machines (WVMs), 182
Worst case accidents, 237–238